FOREWORD BY
David and Yvonne Freeman

ENGLISH LEARNERS AND THE SECRET LANGUAGE OF SCHOOL

UNLOCKING THE MYSTERIES
OF CONTENT-AREA TEXTS

JANICE L. PILGREEN

HEINEMANN
Portsmouth, NH

Heinemann

361 Hanover Street

Portsmouth, NH 03801–3912

www.heinemann.com

Offices and agents throughout the world

The author and publisher wish to thank those who have generously given permission to reprint borrowed material:

Excerpt from *America: Pathways to the Present* by Andrew R. L. Cayton, Elisabeth Israels Perry, Linda Reed, and Allan M. Winkler. Copyright © 2003 by Pearson Education, Inc. or its affiliates. Published by Pearson Education, Inc. Reprinted by permission of the publisher.

Excerpt from *Focus on California Earth Science Teacher Edition, Grade 6* by Martha Cyr, Michael J. Padilla, and Ioannis Miaoulis. Copyright © 2008 by Pearson Education, Inc. or its affiliates. Published by Pearson Education, Inc. Reprinted by permission of the publisher.

Excerpt from *World History, Medieval and Modern Times*. Copyright © 2006 by Holt McDougal, an imprint of Houghton Mifflin Harcourt Publishing Company. Reprinted by permission of the publisher.

Excerpt from *World History, Medieval and Early Modern Times* by Stanley Mayer Burstien and Richard Shek. Copyright © 2006 by Holt McDougal, an imprint of Houghton Mifflin Harcourt Publishing Company. Reprinted by permission of the publisher.

"How Banks Work" from *Creating America: A History of the United States*. Copyright © 2006 by Holt McDougal, an imprint of Houghton Mifflin Harcourt Publishing Company. Reprinted by permission of the publisher.

(Acknowledgments for borrowed material continue on page iv.)

Library of Congress Cataloging-in-Publication Data

Pilgreen, Janice L.

   English learners and the secret language of school : unlocking the mysteries of content-area texts / Janice L. Pilgreen ; foreword by David and Yvonne Freeman.

      p. cm.

   Includes bibliographical references and index.

   ISBN 13: 978-0-325-01127-1

   ISBN 10: 0-325-01127-3

   1. English language—Study and teaching—Foreign speakers.   2. English language—Study and teaching (Elementary)—Foreign speakers.   3. English language—Study and teaching (Secondary)—Foreign speakers.   4. Interdisciplinary approach in education.   I. Title.

   PE1128.A2P517 2010

   428.2'4—dc22   2009052970

Editor: Lisa Luedeke

Production: Sonja S. Chapman

Cover design: Julie Nelson, Creative Ink

Typesetter: Publishers' Design and Production Service, Inc.

Manufacturing: Valerie Cooper

Printed in the United States of America on acid-free paper

14   13   12   11   10   VP   1   2   3   4   5

Dedication

For my husband, Marty, and my daughter, Lindsey, who believed this book should be written and offered ongoing love and support throughout the entire process.

CONTENTS

FOREWORD

David and Yvonne Freeman

Janice Pilgreen's book, *English Learners and the Secret Language of School: Unlocking the Mysteries of Content-Area Texts* provides strategies middle and high school content-area teachers need to meet the dual challenges of teaching reading to adolescents and meeting the needs of English language learners to develop academic language proficiency. Most secondary teachers see their role as content-area experts who teach their subject matter, not as teachers who teach reading skills to secondary students. After all, adolescents are expected to know how to read and write by the time they reach middle school. However, many adolescents lack the reading skills they need to comprehend grade-level content-area texts.

Harvard Education Review devoted a special issue to adolescent literacy. In the Introduction, the editors comment, "If knowledge is power, then literacy is the key to the kingdom" (Ippolito, Steele, and Samson 2008, 1). However, as the articles in this special issue document, the challenge to teach secondary students to read content textbooks and write about what they read has not been adequately met, and many adolescents leave high school without the "key to the kingdom."

The special issue on adolescent literacy followed a report by Biancarosa and Snow (2006) that concluded that too many students leave secondary schools without the literacy skills they need to succeed in higher education or in the workplace. Their report, *Reading Next*, calls for increased attention to developing literacy skills for secondary students. Federal funds have been allocated for innovative programs to improve reading instruction in secondary schools. Despite the attention focused on adolescent literacy, most secondary teachers still lack the knowledge and skills needed to teach content-area literacy.

In addition to the challenge of teaching reading to secondary students, middle and high school teachers also face the challenge of finding effective ways to instruct the increasing number of English language learners (ELLs) in their classes. As Cohen, Deterding, and Clewell (2005) report, one in five students in public schools has at least one parent born outside the U.S., and this number is expected to grow. Many of the ELLs are in middle and high schools. One in three foreign-born immigrants can be found in grades six to twelve. However, the largest group of students at the secondary level classified as Limited English Proficient are the long-term English learners, students who have attended U.S. schools for at least seven years. These are students who can speak conversational English but lack the academic English needed for school success.

Janice Pilgreen's book is designed to help content-area teachers meet the challenge of teaching reading to ELLs and other struggling readers who need to develop academic language proficiency. The strategies Pilgreen describes are all based on current theory in reading and theory in teaching ELLs academic language. As the author states in the Introduction, "I hope to demonstrate that as teachers address the content standards of their curriculum, they can demonstrate effective literacy strategies to help English learners maneuver more confidently and successfully through school."

Pilgreen begins with the ABCs of effective teaching for ELLs. *A* stands for lowering the affective filter. Krashen (1982) developed a theory of second language acquisition. One of his hypotheses is that we acquire a second language by receiving comprehensible input, messages we understand, in the language. However, affective factors such as nervousness or boredom can serve as a filter that blocks the input. Pilgreen points out ways that teachers can create a classroom environment in which ELLs are motivated and confident rather than nervous or bored.

The *B* in effective teaching stands for background knowledge. Especially in the case of ELLs, it is crucial to build or activate the background knowledge they need to make sense of content-area textbooks. The *C* stands for contextualization. When teachers provide linguistic and nonlinguistic context, they scaffold instruction in ways that make academic content comprehensible.

Throughout this book, Pilgreen emphasizes the need to help ELLs build academic language. She explains that teachers should explicitly teach the general academic terms that make up school language, such as *paragraph* or *pie chart*. In addition, teachers should be sure to teach the language that conveys the academic content. They can do this in a number of ways. For example, they can use visuals, realia, and gestures as they explain concepts in the different content areas. In addition, teachers should be sure to use the content-specific terms associated with their subject area. Further, teachers can show students how to gain information from features of text, such as italics or bold print, as well as from charts, graphs, and tables.

In the second chapter, Pilgreen introduces the metaphor of the jigsaw puzzle. She explains that students need the big picture, like the picture on the cover of a jigsaw puzzle, in order to make sense of the parts. Often, ELLs focus on the details of a lesson but miss the main point. As Pilgreen demonstrates, "There are several powerful strategies for teaching content by utilizing big picture strategies that provide English learners opportunities for using academic language and also give them a framework for the content to come and a sense of the order in which it is presented" (20).

In this chapter and the following chapters, she explains these strategies and illustrates them clearly with extended examples of effective classroom practice. For example, Pilgreen shows how a teacher can create an advance organizer by using headings and subheadings from a chapter. Then students can then turn the headings into questions they answer. In this process, ELLs can learn the structure for WH- questions, such as *who, when,* and *where.*

The different chapters deal with various strategies for reading content texts. In Chapter 6, for instance, Pilgreen provides ways to teach signal words, those conjunctions that show relationships among ideas. Pilgreen focuses on signal words to show sequence and cause and effect relationships. Chapter 7 focuses on making inferences. In each of these chapters Pilgreen includes useful tables and charts to illustrate the main points.

In addition to the chapters that discuss reading strategies, one chapter suggests ways to assess students and use that information to plan instruction. The final chapter highlights the importance of silent reading. For ELLs to build the academic language they need to succeed in school, extensive reading is a must.

As Biancarosa and Snow (2006) point out, too many students leave high school without the knowledge and skills they need to succeed in higher education or in the workplace. In order to meet the challenge of equipping ALL students, and especially ELLs, with the skills they need to navigate difficult content-area textbooks, middle school and high school teachers need practical, research-based strategies. *English Learners and the Secret Language of School: Unlocking the Mysteries of Content-Area Texts* provides a set of useful strategies content-area teachers can draw on to meet the challenges they face and promote literacy for all their students.

References

Biancarosa, G., and C. Snow. 2006. *Reading Next—A Vision for Action and Research in Middle and High School Literacy: A Report to the Carnegie Corporation of New York* (2d ed.). Washington, DC: Alliance for Excellent Education.

Cohen, C., N. Deterding, and B. C. Clewell. 2005. *Who's Left Behind? Immigrant Children in High and Low LEP Schools.* Washington, DC: Urban Institute.

Ippolito, J., J. Steele, and J. Samson. 2008. "Introduction: Why Adolescent Literacy Matters Now." *Harvard Education Review* 78(1), 1–5.

Krashen, S. 1982. *Principles and Practice in Second Language Acquisition.* New York: Pergamon Press.

ACKNOWLEDGMENTS

This book has been in the making ever since I began working with teachers who wanted to become reading specialists. As we tried out new comprehension strategies with children and teens in the Literacy Center at the University of La Verne, we learned what worked and what didn't and how to modify good ideas into even better ones. These teachers—my students—have been an inspiration to me, and it is because of them that this book took shape.

Thank you to my editor, Lisa Luedeke, who has more patience than anyone I have ever met and is always sensitively able to pinpoint exactly what needs to be done while understanding implicitly what I hope to achieve. You honor your writers, and I respect you wholeheartedly. Thank you unequivocally for your continuous and gracious support.

Thank you to my production editor, Sonja Chapman, who was unerringly responsive to my questions and concerns and worked diligently to make sure that every detail was correct. I appreciate your commitment to high standards and your flexibility each time I needed "just one more day." You are a true professional.

Thank you to my colleagues in the Literacy Center, Amber Rodriguez and Janie Stahly, who took on extra responsibilities during my writing times and provided endless coffee, chocolate, laughter, and encouragement—exactly when I needed them most. I couldn't have finished this book without your help and your friendship.

Thank you to our student workers in the Literacy Center, Chelsea, Jessica, Kathy, and Madison, who learned that even professors have identifiable stress thresholds and a wide variety of potentially changing moods—and who tirelessly and seamlessly kept the center work under control while I was completing each chapter. You are all wonderful.

Special thanks to Sarah Sigala, who was more my "assistant editor" than a student worker throughout two separate school years and who came to know my every thought and wish, even when I lost the vocabulary to express them. You were my right-hand lady, and I cannot thank you enough.

Thank you to David and Yvonne Freeman, whose work I admire tremendously and who took valuable time and effort to write the Foreword for this book. I couldn't have chosen anyone who more effectively models best practices for teaching English learners than you do—and I am grateful for your input.

INTRODUCTION

As the director of the Literacy Center at the University of La Verne, a private school in Southern California where graduate students in our Reading and Language Arts Specialist Credential Program tutor students from the local community—and a professor of literacy education, whose job it is to teach these candidates—I watch the educational process unfold on a daily basis. I see highly motivated teachers who attend evening courses after working full-time in their own schools during the day, passionately seeking to learn new ways of helping their students learn to read and write more effectively.

It isn't that teachers haven't been well-versed in the realm of instructional effectiveness, but rather that they typically have so many responsibilities that it is difficult to attend to the needs of students who are falling behind in reading and writing. The multifaceted nature of their daily roles are daunting, and most educators do their best just to keep abreast of school, district, state, and national mandates while they act as content experts, mentors, disciplinarians, and oftentimes surrogate parents.

Providing English learners with access to the core curriculum is an additional significant challenge. Not only do these students need to acquire a command of basic interpersonal communicative skills (BICS), often referred to as *playground language* (or *blacktop language* for older students), but they are very quickly catapulted into the world of reading and writing for school, the academic context of CALP (cognitive academic language proficiency). They have to be able to read and respond to long text pieces from various genres, copy lecture notes, write summaries and research papers, outline chapters, answer questions, and take tests of all kinds.

In our literacy center, the teaching is one-on-one, which is, granted, not the way it will ever be in the regular classroom. However, the center experiences show us that when instruction is matched to the needs of students, not just provided automatically as part of a scope and sequence of skills, magic can happen. Students can learn the strategies they need to be successful.

In this book, I hope to demonstrate that as teachers address the content standards of their curriculum, they can demonstrate effective literacy strategies to help English learners maneuver more confidently and successfully through school. Brief assessments can target areas of student need and help teachers set reasonable literacy objectives that logically fit into their content instruction. Even better, the assessments and literacy strategies make the processes of teaching and learning more interactive and enjoyable.

By teaching English learners academic language, the "secret language of school," during the presentation of literacy strategies within the framework of content-area instruction, we can demystify the comprehension process, making what once seemed unattainable—students' genuine understanding of what they read—a tangible reality. Most importantly, we can move these students toward becoming independent readers and writers who no longer have to rely upon us. If this book can provide some measure of guidance for teachers whose goal it is to support English learners, then it will have been a worthwhile effort.

Teaching the "Secret Language of School"

Academic Language and the ABCs

I n an era of No Child Left Behind, Reading First mandates, historically large numbers of published intervention programs on the market, and high-stakes testing practices, it is no wonder that educators and students alike are overwhelmed. Not only is it important for everyone to work diligently to meet subject matter content standards prescribed for each grade level, but it is critical that students' language skills continue to develop at a rapid pace. They have to understand increasingly more difficult texts at more sophisticated reading levels as they progress through the upper grades. Teachers who have English learners in their content area classes such as social studies, science, math, and government have three tasks: (1) to help their students develop language proficiency and literacy skills; (2) to teach the required grade-level content of their fields; and (3) to support students in developing strategies for demonstrating what they know in a wide variety of testing contexts.

Challenges for Older English Learners

A primary goal for English learners is to gain enough English proficiency to carry out school tasks as well as their monolingual peers. Peregoy and Boyle (2008) remind us that for kindergarten and first-grade students, the linguistic performance gap between English learners and their English-speaking contemporaries is relatively small. However, school presents greater challenges with second language proficiency for older immigrant students than for younger ones; older students have more to achieve and less time to do it. Also, they compete with fluent English speakers in the classroom. Cummins and Schecter (2003) point out that "English-as-a-first-language speakers are not standing still waiting for ESL [English as a second language] students to catch up. Every year their literacy skills are expanding and, thus, ESL students must catch up with a moving target" (8).

Simply put, there is a discrepancy between the challenges confronting an English learner who is beginning elementary school and one who is entering middle school or high school. When children are in the early stages of language acquisition, their main objective is to understand their teachers and peers and to make themselves understood. Much of the language they use is for social purposes, such as interacting with friends during lunch and recess (Peregoy and Boyle 2008). However, as they move into the upper grades, English learners are asked to engage in higher-level thinking and problem solving and have to work diligently to acquire the formal language competence they need for more advanced instruction in the content areas. Often, these students are inappropriately placed into intervention programs that target decoding skills, when what students need is support with comprehension and academic language. Gee (2004) points out that "more children fail in school, in the long run, because they cannot cope with academic language than because they cannot decode print" (14). This increasingly difficult academic language is "the secret language of school" that we must help students acquire.

English learners have to wend their way through complex social and cognitive interactions in their second language, not only orally, but also in reading and writing. Cummins (1980) has shown that in order to become fully proficient, students need to progress beyond the level of basic interpersonal communicative skills (BICS), or social language, to achieve ever-deepening levels of cognitive academic language proficiency (CALP), the ability to use literacy skills in school settings. Educators need effective strategies for supporting English learners toward the goal of full English language and literacy development—development that is at the same level of English language proficiency as that of fluent English-speaking peers. It is imperative that teachers are aware of the differences between conversational fluency and academic language proficiency, so they can "continue to provide the academic support that ESL students may need" (Cummins and Schecter 2003, 8).

Another issue is that expectations regarding literacy achievement have changed. Krashen (2004) points out that although there are few people who have been through the educational system who are completely unable to read and write, there are many more who just don't read and write well enough to handle the complex literacy demands of modern society. Deshler, Palincsar, Biancarolsa, and Nair (2007) concur that "today's generation faces greater literacy demands when compared with prior generations," stating that demands for high-level reading and writing ability are greater today in both higher education and the workplace than ever before (18). They maintain that because of these changes in literary demands, the nature of literacy instruction needs to change after fourth grade and should become increasingly discipline-specific. Therefore, literacy instruction becomes "a requirement of content area learning and thus the responsibility of all teachers" (19). Unfortunately, simply giving students reading assignments does not help them engage in the meaning-making process. Content teachers have a responsibility to prepare students for and guide them through texts so that they can learn effectively (Roe, Stoodt, and Burns 2006; Galda and Graves 2007; Harvey and Goudvis 2000).

Content-Area Literacy Instruction

Over the past decade, a strong emphasis has been placed on the concept of content area reading and writing. However, when working with older students, secondary teachers do not typically have the preparation to teach basic word recognition skills, so they are understandably fearful of having to "teach reading." Most classroom contexts are focused on subject matter, and teachers have enough challenges to meet without having to consider what reading skills might be lacking.

It is not unusual when teaching courses to preservice secondary teachers to hear complaints about having to take a required class in reading. Veteran teachers, too, may dislike attending required staff development literacy workshops when they view themselves as subject matter experts and not reading teachers. However, it *is* their job to provide access to the core curriculum for all students—and in many cases, that goal includes teaching literacy techniques to aid students in negotiating and comprehending class texts. Vacca and Vacca (2007) explain that teaching and learning with texts is a particular challenge in today's classrooms where the range of linguistic, cultural, and academic diversity has been increasing steadily since the 1960s.

This is not to say that secondary teachers are expected to teach beginning or emergent literacy skills to older learners. When the gap is in the area of decoding and word recognition, a school intervention program or the services of a reading specialist may be in order. If the disparity relates to comprehension, writing, and study skills, though, it simply makes sense to address these needs within the context of authentic instruction, much of which occurs in content area classes. When teachers do this, they are helping their students to develop content literacy. This is defined as "the ability to use reading and writing for the acquisition of new content in a given discipline" (McKenna and Robinson 1997, 184).

Alvermann, Phelps, and Ridgeway (2007) are quick to point out that it is also important to use oral language, including small- and large-group discussions, in mediating students' ability to learn from reading and writing activities in their subject matter classes. Adding that learners' prior knowledge of a particular subject and their interest in the topic also strengthen their ability to use content literacy skills, Alvermann and colleagues clearly recognize that there is more to the process of content literacy development than at first may meet the eye.

The ABCs of Instruction

Many teachers who work with English learners are familiar with Krashen's (1985) seminal work on "comprehensible input," which promotes the idea that teachers need to make their messages understandable to English learners in order for them to acquire the language. It is logical that students have access to the content that is being taught only when they understand the instruction. As Krashen (1985) emphasizes, it is incumbent upon teachers to make lessons clear and fully comprehensible for nonnative speakers, regardless of students' levels of competence in English. In our Literacy Center at the University of La Verne, where reading specialists complete their fieldwork by tutoring children from the local community, we find that integrating the "basics," or what we call the "ABCs," can go a long way toward making content-area texts comprehensible. These basic elements include lowering the *affective filter*, activating and building *background knowledge*, and providing linguistic and nonlinguistic *contextualization* (see Figure 1–1).

◎ *Affective Filter*

To lower the *affective filter* is to help learners feel comfortable enough to take risks as they acquire a new language (Krashen 1985). Recognizing that *affect* refers to a mood associated with an idea or action, teachers can plan instruction within contexts that put English learners at ease—that is, to lower the barrier or *filter* that separates them from the instructional arena where they may feel intimidated by having to speak or read in front of others, use "correct" semantic and syntactic structures, and demonstrate a specific level of proficiency with the language to others in the classroom. Allowing students to work in groups or pairs, giving them practice time before asking them to participate in a whole-class

What Are the ABCs?

Every lesson designed for English learners should include the ABCs: lowering of the *affective filter*, activation and development of *background knowledge*, and support through *contextualization*.

Lower the *affective filter* by helping learners feel comfortable enough to take risks as they acquire a second language—to be receptive to language acquisition processes. These are some methods for keeping the affective filter low:

- asking learners to work in groups or pairs collaboratively
- allowing students to plan how they will "participate" in class activities (e.g., reviewing content before speaking in front of the class, previewing a reading selection)
- modeling correct grammatical structures for students (rather than error correcting on the spot)
- offering a supportive environment where students feel comfortable making mistakes

Activate and develop *background knowledge* by providing information to students about the reading topic before the reading itself commences. When learners know the topic they will be reading about (and perhaps even learn some new information about it before they begin to read), their comprehension will increase. Methods for increasing background knowledge include:

- reading easier texts first
- watching video segments or using video streaming options
- viewing illustrations related to the topic
- utilizing alternate forms of texts with illustrations, such as graphic novels
- listening to a "minilecture" before reading

Provide both linguistic and nonlinguistic *contextualization* by offering additional help, through clues, to students who are struggling with the language. Linguistic (language-based) clues can be provided in the following ways:

- adopting a slower speech rate
- enunciating clearly
- providing synonyms and antonyms for unknown words
- avoiding unfamiliar idioms
- using cognates when possible

Figure 1–1

(Continues)

Similarly, nonlinguistic (non–language-based) clues can be added during instruction:

- using realia (simulations of real objects, such as stuffed animals or plastic artifacts)
- providing manipulatives (experiments, models, technological support such as SMART Boards)
- including visuals and graphics (maps, charts, diagrams, organizers)
- incorporating gestures and attending to tone of voice during lessons

The following organizer includes space to list ideas for building the ABCs into classroom practices. Think about options that are fun and creative!

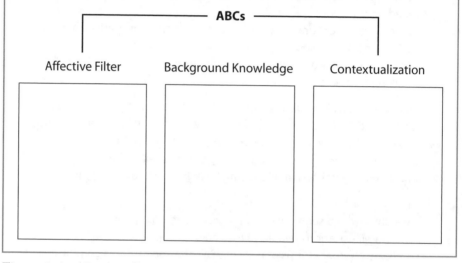

Figure 1–1   *(Continued)*

activity, and modeling back correct grammatical structures instead of using on-the-spot error correction practices are only a few examples of ways to support learners emotionally. The objective is for students to remain psychologically open to the instructional opportunities that are offered. No matter how skillful the teacher may be at presenting content, unless the instructional context also allows for feedback that does not lead to embarrassment and that encourages supportive and structured interactions, barriers will exist between learners and the educational context, limiting the language development that needs to occur. English learners increasingly need to gain confidence in their abilities, rather than being made to feel inadequate while they are struggling to acquire a target language.

© Background Knowledge

The activation and development of *background knowledge*, also known as *schema* or prior knowledge, are also a critical component of the instructional process for English learners, especially as the content becomes more challenging in the upper grades. Vocabulary in content-area texts tends to be subject-specific, for example, in classes such as chemistry, government, and biology. Language terms typically reflect more technical definitions, rather than common ones. For example, the word *revolution* used in a conversation between two high school students about the engine of a car (RPMs, or *revolutions per minute*) would have a different meaning in a history class discussion, perhaps referring to a revolt, or in a science class lesson, representing the Earth's rotation.

Research done by schema theorists (Anderson 1984; Rumelhart 1982) tells us that readers will not comprehend what they read unless they can connect the information they are reading to ideas that they already know from previous experiences. What many students are missing is appropriate background knowledge for the content they read. If they are unable to make meaningful connections, this inability undermines their efforts to make sense of unfamiliar text (Buehl 2007; Marzano 2004). English learners who are asked to read a text piece about a young man who rides in a canoe down the river will have little understanding about what the character is doing if they have no concept of what canoes and rivers are in the first place. It would take a very skilled reader to be able to figure out the gist of such a piece without any prior knowledge about these concepts, but for a learner who is also acquiring the language, identifying the necessary clues to accomplish this task is nearly impossible.

A teacher who knows that most of the class members have background knowledge about a reading topic (e.g., volcanoes) needs to *activate*, or "stir up," what the learners currently know before asking them to read the piece so that they can easily make the connections between what is known and what is offered in the text. This may entail discussion about the topic, looking at illustrations that generate ideas about the topic, or some other type of sharing. On the other hand, if students know very little about the topic, then the teacher needs to help them *develop* background knowledge, to add on to what they already know. The teacher may have them view a video segment, read a simple text piece about the topic that will precede the reading of the more difficult piece, do a short minilecture with props, or bring in an expert to share information about the content. Any preteaching efforts to link prior knowledge, the "building blocks of cognition," with the content to be read will result in higher levels of student understanding and longer retention of the information (Rumelhart 1982, 16). According to Alvermann, Phelps, and Ridgeway (2007), this prior knowledge, or schemata, acts as a kind of mental filing system from which the individual can retrieve relevant existing knowledge and into which new information can be filed.

One motivational way to help learners develop background knowledge about a topic is to read an easier text to them about the subject matter. Publishing companies have recently been creating popular, innovative expository texts that are beautifully illustrated and do not seem childish, yet they are written at fairly low readability levels. The Rosen Publishing Group, National Geographic, and Capstone Press are only a few groups that have been successful at publishing content-area material that matches upper-grade content standards but is more accessible in terms of difficulty level than typical textbooks.

A particularly engaging form of these texts is the graphic novel, which adopts a comic book format but covers historical and scientific events accurately. Though some teachers may view the comic genre as nonacademic, it is popular with young people and provides content knowledge that they may not access elsewhere. In our Literacy Center, the tutors appreciate the fact that young people need to "make meaning" as they read these texts. If readers do not understand what is going on and who is talking in any given frame or dialogue bubble, they cannot continue because they don't comprehend enough to move on; therefore, they work hard to make sense of the illustrations, commentary, and dialogue. As a way of having students learn a bit of content knowledge before they turn to their "real" textbook chapters, the use of graphic novels can be both entertaining and effective.

In any case, as educators, we should be open to new and different ways of presenting content information to our learners before they read difficult texts. Galda and Graves (2007) comment, "Given the vital importance of prior knowledge to comprehension and memory, it is critical to recognize that different students bring different stores of prior knowledge into the classroom and are thus differentially prepared to read some selections" (85). They emphasize that recognizing and accommodating these differences in today's culturally and linguistically diverse classrooms are major challenges any teacher faces. Yet they are challenges that we have to meet in order to help all students reach their potential as readers. Marzano (2004) suggests that "given the relationship between academic background knowledge and academic achievement, one can make the case that it should be at the top of any list of interventions intended to enhance student achievement" (4). He highlights the disparity that may exist between students who have more academic background knowledge than others. Certainly English learners may face disadvantages. Apart from encountering language differences, they may have had different curricula or even interrupted school experiences in other countries, putting them several steps behind native speakers in terms of content knowledge (Hadaway and Young 2006).

◎ Linguistic and Nonlinguistic Contextualization

Providing linguistic and nonlinguistic *contextualization* is another basic component that should be part of any instruction for English learners. *Linguistic contextualization* refers to the use of language clues that support students who are struggling with the content. For example, teachers can use slower speech rates; enunciate clearly; make certain that the vocabulary they use is appropriate for the level of their learners' proficiency; allow extended pause times for processing new terms; provide synonyms, antonyms, and cognates whenever possible; and limit the use of idiomatic expressions since they cannot be translated literally.

Idiomatic expressions pose a specific problem for English learners during class conversations when teachers do not devote any special attention to their figurative meanings. I recall commenting during a tenth-grade English class that it was "raining cats and dogs outside" and shouldn't have been surprised when several of the English learners in my class ran to the window to see this phenomenon.

In addition, since the target language represents the major difficulty for English learners, teachers should also provide *nonlinguistic contextualization* for students so that other opportunities for representing content are available. Nonlinguistic clues include the use of realia (simulated "real" objects such as a papier-mâché volcano, a stuffed grizzly bear, or a clay model of a helmet, etc.), illustrations, manipulatives, visuals, graphics, and any other information-bearing sources not entirely dependent upon the use of language. Remarking that the "nonlinguistic aspect of information processing is most observable as the mental images associated with one's experience," Marzano (2007) recommends including activities such as graphic representations that will help students to visualize the content (35). Cary (2000) suggests including such collaborative nonlinguistic elements as storyboarding (physically illustrating events in sequence on butcher paper or a timeline), role-plays, and readers' theatre (developing scripts from text to practice and read aloud) so that learners have multiple pathways for understanding, including eye contact, gestures, and body movements. Any task in which there is no other

Figure 1–2

source of help other than the language itself is considered to be "context reduced," referring to the lowest level of support (Finders and Hynds 2007, 91).

Taken together, the ABCs are powerful basics that belong in any instructional plan for English learners, and especially within the context of content-area instruction, which represents technical vocabulary and domain-specific academic concepts. When teachers are careful to integrate these elements into their lessons, their students have a much higher chance of comprehending and retaining the content they need to know. Another way to say this is that they have a higher probability of having access to the core curriculum.

Academic Language for Classroom Conversations

Although the ABCs are critical components in instruction for English learners, there is another influence related to school success that merits strong consideration: the development of academic language. Academic language is not particular to any content area, but rather, it represents the *vocabulary of school*. An overwhelming obstacle that English learners face when sitting in classrooms is that a "secret" language is used. They proficiently use common, everyday language, but outside of social or real-life situations, specifically in school contexts, they are challenged by the unique language that is inherent in lectures, discussions, tests, and textbooks. This language includes terms such as *title*, *subtitle*, *passage*, *chapter*, *paragraph*, *table*, *caption*, and *excerpt*, as well as *note taking*, *summarizing*, *tracing events*, *outlining*, and *comparing and contrasting*, to name only a few.

Although we need to focus on the ABCs of instruction, we should also teach English learners the academic terms that accompany the concepts they are learning. Otherwise, they will not make the transition from merely possessing BICS to achieving proficiency in CALP. Fortunately, teachers can use an explicit approach to teach academic concepts and their related terms that is as beneficial for fluent English-speaking students as it is for English learners (Pilgreen 2007). Academic language is required for managing a wide variety of reading tasks such as previewing text, skimming and scanning, understanding organizational structures such as cause-effect and compare/contrast, and highlighting the main points and details related to specific chunks of text. For example, when talking about the "little title" under the "big title," it is important to use the term *subtitle*. Teachers should introduce the "slanted letters" of a text as *italicized print* and "dark letters" as *boldface print*, demonstrating how they are used to highlight or emphasize important vocabulary terms or phrases. Similarly, pictures, photographs, comic strips, and drawings should also be referred to as *illustrations*. The explicit teaching of academic language is crucial; students will not just "pick it up" along the way (Alvermann, Phelps, and Ridgeway 2007, 9).

The words in Figure 1–3 represent the kind of school talk that educators engage in regularly. Three of the most commonly confused terms are *paragraph*, *passage*, and *excerpt*. Many fluent English-speaking students have problems differentiating among the three definitions, so logically English learners have an even greater struggle dealing with such technical language. Unless these terms are taught as part of each lesson focus and with planned repetition, students are not likely to retain and use them correctly.

For example, *paragraph* means a collection of sentences that revolve around one central, or main, idea (in expository text, in particular). The main idea is contained in the paragraph's topic sentence, assuming of course that the text is well written. The topic sentence is supported by details (reasons, examples, or incidents).

How is *paragraph* different from *passage*? A *passage* is a set of sentences, divided into paragraphs (or contained in only one long paragraph). Each paragraph

---

Text Terms

chapter	font/print	conclusion
title/heading	boldface type	transition
subheading/subtitle	italicized type	quotation
paragraph	font size	indentation
paraphrase	graph: pie, line, bar	title page
passage	chart	table of contents
excerpt	table	preface
column	figure	handbook
section	map	glossary
page	summarize	index
illustration/picture	diagram	bibliography
caption	introduction	author index

Figure 1–3

has its own main idea. If a passage has three paragraphs, then each paragraph has its own main idea, and the passage itself, as a whole, has a large main idea: four main ideas in all. If the passage has a title, the title most likely reflects the main idea of all three of the paragraphs put together, and sometimes this "title" is actually a subtitle within a text chapter.

Students must also consider how *excerpt* is different from *paragraph* and *passage*. An excerpt is a section of text, which can be taken from the beginning, the middle, or the end of a larger text. An excerpt may be confusing because much of the context may be missing. Readers have to use critical reading skills to make sense of an excerpt, to fill in the missing information around the edges.

We might conceivably ask ourselves why such specificity of language is important. The fact is, in order to read, comprehend, analyze, and talk about text, readers have to be able to use these terms and see how they function. These terms help students and teachers talk about how text is organized and see how the ideas relate to one another. Good readers, according to Alvermann and Phelps (2005), are able to see the macrostructure of the text, which includes the relative importance and interrelation of the various ideas presented.

The student in the cartoon in Figure 1–4 certainly recognizes the efficacy of engaging in school talk with his teacher; however, it is probable that she is not impressed with his facility for using academic language in this case, as he apparently has not followed the required guidelines for his reading assignment.

"I didn't read that scene, but I did highlight several passages."

Figure 1–4

Directions such as "Please read the following passage and identify the main idea of paragraph two" are common in classrooms of all grade levels, usually starting as early as third grade. They are also common on standardized, norm-referenced tests. Such directions reflect the academic language used in school. If teachers spend time with students analyzing paragraphs and looking at *passages* that are made up of one, two, four, six or more *paragraphs*, students will better understand these terms. They will be able to read pieces of text for the big ideas, for the details, or for both. They will notice when a text contains cause-effect or compare-contrast structures and be able to follow the patterns set forth by the authors. We know that "explicit instruction with regard to the structure of a text facilitates the development of important comprehension strategies" (Droop and Verhoevan 2003, 101).

Appendix A includes basic definitions for the academic terms listed in Figure 1–3. These terms should become part of every teacher's classroom vocabulary. We should all remember, though, that just giving students definitions is not enough. Teachers should use the terms authentically and as routinely as possible in class, modeling their use and highlighting text features in print so that students can follow suit. Harvey and Goudvis (2000) assert, "For too many years we have been telling students what to do without showing them how" (12).

It is effective to show examples of captions and illustrations systematically and demonstrate how to find important information embedded in them; choose excerpts from texts, magazine articles, diary entries, and so on and talk about what can be learned from them, both in and out of context; and use the information in pie, bar, and line graphs to quantify the general information given in a chapter. Most importantly, teachers must repeat academic terms over and over, bringing them up explicitly in different situations, using a "think-aloud process" (Daniels and Zemelman 2004). First, we need to provide comprehensible input (e.g., "the *slanted letters* you see here")—and then add the academic terms (e.g., "which we call *italicized*") that match the concepts. Even though English learners might know something about a content-area topic, they may be unfamiliar with the academic language of teaching and instruction, getting lost in the verbiage and thereby feeling frustrated (Abedi 2004).

◎ *Integrating Academic Language into the Curriculum*

One of the easiest ways to begin introducing academic language in the classroom is to present it along with the subject matter content that is being taught. Instead of manufacturing activities that students can do to practice using the language, teachers can weave the terminology into the fabric of their content lessons so that it becomes part of authentic—but academic—classroom conversation.

Suppose that I want to introduce a text section called "Rocks and the Rock Cycle" to my students, with the intention of focusing on the content of approximately three pages (Figure 1–5).

Before asking students to read even one word of the text, we would look at the first page of the section, where we see the subtitle "Rocks and the Rock Cycle," and we would flip back to the beginning of the chapter to note that it is part of the overall chapter entitled "Minerals and Rocks." We would then read all of the other subtitles in the section, starting with "Forming Igneous Rock," "Forming Sedimentary Rock," "Forming Metamorphic Rock," and "Pathways of the Rock

Minerals and Rocks

Rocks and the Rock Cycle

Minerals are one of the main building blocks of rock. Rock is the solid material made up of one or more minerals or other substances. Rock makes up Earth's hard crust. How do the different kinds of rocks form? Forces deep inside Earth and at the surface produce a slow cycle that builds, destroys, and changes rocks. The **rock cycle** is a series of processes on and beneath Earth's surface that slowly change rocks from one kind to another. Geologists classify rocks into three major groups: igneous rock, sedimentary rock, and metamorphic rock. The rocks in each group form through different steps in the rock cycle.

Forming Igneous Rock

The rock cycle begins when molten material forms inside Earth. Then, this material slowly cools and hardens at or beneath the surface. The result is **igneous rock** (IG nee us). The granite formed when molten material cooled slowly beneath the surface. Because it cools slowly, granite is made up of large crystals.

Other igneous rocks form when molten material erupts onto Earth's surface. Basalt forms when molten material cools and hardens on the surface. Because it cools quickly, basalt is made up of very small crystals.

Forming Sedimentary Rock

The rock cycle continues as **sedimentary rock** (sed uh MEN tur ree) forms. Water and weather cause rocks on Earth's surface to break down, forming sediment. **Sediment** is small, solid pieces of material that come from rocks or living things.

Water and wind carry sediment and deposit it in layers. Layers of sediment build up and are squeezed together by their own weight. At the same time, minerals in the rock slowly dissolve in water. These minerals harden and glue the sediment together. Over millions of years, the sediment slowly changes to sedimentary rock.

Some sedimentary rocks, such as sandstone, are made up of particles of other rocks. The remains of plants and animals can also form sedimentary rock. For example, limestone forms in oceans from shells and skeletons of coral and other animals. Another type of sedimentary rock forms when minerals dissolve in water and form crystals. That's how rock salt, made of the mineral halite, is formed.

Forming Metamorphic Rock

As the rock cycle continues, any rock can change into **metamorphic rock** (met uh MAWR fik). Forces inside Earth can push rocks down toward the heat of

Figure 1–5

Earth's interior. The deeper the rock is buried, the greater the pressure on that rock. Under great heat and pressure, the minerals in a rock can be changed into other minerals. The rock has become metamorphic rock. For example, heat and pressure can change granite into gneiss.

Pathways of the Rock Cycle

There are many pathways through the rock cycle. Here is one possible pathway: The igneous rock granite formed beneath the surface millions of years ago. Then, the forces of mountain building slowly pushed the granite upward, forming a mountain. Slowly, water and weather wore away the granite, forming sand. Streams carried the sand into the ocean.

Over millions of years, layers of sandy sediment piled up on the ocean floor. Slowly the sediments were pressed together and cemented to form sandstone, a sedimentary rock. Over time, the sandstone became deeply buried. Heat and pressure changed the rock's texture from gritty to smooth. Over millions of years, the sandstone changed into the metamorphic rock quartzite.

Metamorphic rock does not end the rock cycle. For example, the heat of Earth's interior could melt the rock. This molten material could then form new igneous rock.

Figure 1–5   (*Continued*)

Cycle." We would see that the font size of these subtitles (called level 2 subtitles) is smaller than the section subtitle (called a level 1 subtitle), and the section subtitle font size is smaller than the chapter title font size. All of the level 2 subtitles relate to one another because they represent three types of rock formations and end with a description of the rock cycle, which is exactly the content we would predict from the level 1 section subtitle—and each of these subtitles is connected to the title of the chapter, "Minerals and Rocks." We recognize that the section we will be focusing on deals with the "rocks" part of the chapter and can infer that other parts of the chapter will deal with minerals. Clear titles and subtitles show the organization of sections or chapters, overall content emphases, and the smaller pieces of content that relate to the larger ones.

Looking at the titles and subtitles is also an ideal way for teachers to frontload important vocabulary before students begin to read. (Four specific strategies that utilize this technique, the advance organizer, the PLAN procedure, skimming, and the anticipation guide are described later in this book.) In Figure 1–6, we see concepts that teachers would need to present prior to the reading experience; we can also understand the way in which the text sections are organized,

Minerals and Rocks

Rocks and the Rock Cycle

Forming Igneous Rock

Forming Sedimentary Rock

Forming Metamorphic Rock

Pathways of the Rock Cycle

Figure 1–6

from the larger category of "Minerals and Rocks" to the smaller category of "Rocks and the Rock Cycle," followed by types of rock formations and the pathways of the rock cycle.

Finally, as part of previewing any chapter or chapter section, we would look at the full array of text *illustrations* in the form of *maps*, *photographs*, *cartoons*, and *reproduced paintings and artifacts*, making certain not to label them as simply *pictures*, the easier, more common "default" word that English learners would be certain to understand. Instead, the teacher can start with the term *pictures* and then add the academic language used in school, starting with *illustrations* and then analyzing that category into *photographs*, *maps*, *charts*, *drawings*, and so forth. Focusing on the academic language takes some thought as teachers use it automatically all the time, but students need to hear us use the language in class, over and over again. According to Wilhelm, Baker, and Dube (2001), one problem that keeps teachers from providing the necessary help to students is that the teachers are "expert readers," unaware of the things they do automatically. Therefore, it is difficult for teachers to consciously explain literacy concepts to learners who do not yet have this "seamless" facility with language strategies (69).

When we analyze an excerpt of text, we may look at how many paragraphs are on the pages, based on the text *indentations* (or publishers' practices where the first paragraph of each section is actually not indented, but put into *block style* next to the subtitles). In this way, we begin to use the "secret language," to demystify it, so that everyone can talk about text features and literacy processes with a higher degree of understanding.

As Nicholas, one of the students in our Literacy Center program, put it, "I sometimes feel like a nerd when I use these words, but it's really kind of fun." It *is* fun and gratifying when we all begin to use the special vocabulary that is the stuff of academic conversations. Such language use opens doors to a deeper understanding of the reading and writing processes that are continuously being developed in the classroom. In short, "Students need to become increasingly comfortable with the insider language of academic texts; they have to develop the facility to 'talk the talk' of an academic discipline" (Buehl 2007, 203). Freeman and Freeman (2009) emphasize that a challenge for teachers of English learners is to help students learn the appropriate "registers" to use in their classes—that is to say, the oral and written language used in school settings as contrasted with that used with their friends or parents (50).

◎ *Text Play*

Although I have never heard anyone label it as such, the kind of discussion that occurs when students and teachers start to use their new vocabulary is what I see as "text play." Just as young children love to experiment with letter sounds and rhyming, alliterative and repetitive language, and specific rhythms of the language, older students enjoy being able to participate in the more sophisticated world of academic language. When I speak to groups of teachers about ways to introduce this language, I try to model procedures that offer opportunities to "play" with the terminology.

For example, looking again at the text selection in Figure 1–5, we note that the targeted *section* from the larger *chapter* on minerals and rocks begins with the subtitle "Rocks and the Rock Cycle," it is *not* written in a *column* format, and there are four level 2 *subtitles*. If I ask students to add to this information by using more examples of academic language, they will point out that important vocabulary is written in *boldface type* and that that there are ten *paragraphs* in the section as shown by the *indentations*. If the full text were provided (which we do not see here), they might also say that there is a *process diagram* of how sedimentary rocks form, which is a type of *illustration*. Each time I say, "What else do you see?" there is a scramble to find even more examples of academic language, and we all revel in our success when we sound so scholarly!

Text play can be utilized in any classroom, not just English as a second language or specially designed academic instruction in English courses, as a way of developing academic language continuously and creating opportunities for classroom conversations about reading topics, different types of texts, and strategy choices. As long as this kind of talk is occurring throughout the year across multiple contexts, students at all levels will become more successful in their classrooms, but English learners will benefit doubly. Fisher and Frey (2008) note that adolescents who are English learners face two challenges: learning the content while simultaneously learning a new language. We know that "language and learning are inexorably bound; thus, their ability to understand and produce the academic language needed is essential if they are to learn the content standards of the course" (19).

Commentary

In this chapter, we have looked at ways that teachers can incorporate the ABCs into content-area instruction in order to help English learners feel more comfortable as they interact in their classrooms, to provide pathways for them to connect what they already know with new content knowledge, and to support them through linguistic and nonlinguistic contextualization so that they are not completely dependent upon the language of texts. We have seen how students can begin to learn the "secret" language of school, developing the vocabulary needed to discuss text organization, levels of content, important concepts, meanings of illustrations, and much more that will lead to higher levels of comprehension, as well as to advantages in the test-taking arena. In the next chapter, we turn to "big picture" strategies that will prepare learners to interact with text effectively, leading to deeper understandings and longer retention of the content. We will see that by "preparing students for the texts they will encounter, they are helped to recall and organize what they already know about the topic and to anticipate the content and the focus of the materials" (Lewis 2007, 150–51).

The Jigsaw Puzzle Big Picture
Preparing Students for Reading

As students progress through the upper-grade levels, many seem to be quite proficient at reading. We can ask them to stand up and read a section from a text, and they will do it seemingly with no glitches at all. Yet, if we ask them questions about what they have read, a large number cannot actually answer the questions or tell us anything about the subject matter. It is an "erroneous assumption that if a student can read the words that appear in a text accurately and quickly, comprehension will be the natural end product" (Deshler et al. 2007, 14).

Unfortunately, students often believe that sounding out words is reading. After all, when they hear their peers make few or no oral miscues (mistakes) and maintain a steady pace that sounds fluent, students consider them to be "good readers." Yet, if these same students were in first or second grade, teachers might refer to them as "word callers," readers who can decode the print but do not understand the text. Decoding print is not reading; it is only one part of the process that leads readers toward making sense of what is read. Gunning (2008) asserts that comprehension is, in fact, the main purpose of reading. Without it, there is no reading, because reading is the process of constructing meaning from print.

Remembering the *B* in the ABCs, we have already touched upon the idea that readers vary extensively in the amount and type of background knowledge they possess. In addition, they also utilize different strategies for reading and writing and possess disparate attitudes toward reading, in general. The type of text being read and the purposes for reading play a large role in how well comprehension is achieved. There is a "wide range of text types that middle and high school students are expected to read and write, including literature, which contains multiple genres from poetry to novels to essay—but also scientific and technical writing, mathematical notation and equations, historical documents, Internet sources, encyclopedias and other reference materials" (Deshler et al. 2007, 19). Further, comprehension instruction does not always receive much attention in secondary classrooms; text comprehension often takes second place to content coverage.

Jigsaw Puzzle Process

One of the most important vestiges of the whole language teaching philosophy of the 1970s and 1980s is the concept that readers need to look at the "big picture" before they analyze the parts. Teachers who help students gain this overview before reading usually find that the resulting comprehension is higher and retention is greater. There are several powerful strategies for teaching content by utilizing big picture strategies that provide English learners opportunities for using academic language and also give them a framework for the content to come and a sense of the order in which it is presented.

When I first introduce the idea of the big picture to reading specialist candidates in our Literacy Center or teachers at staff development workshops, I relate the concept of the advance organizer to the illustration on the top of a jigsaw puzzle box. (See Figure 2–1.)

I ask participants to put themselves into a hypothetical situation. If they were asked to put together a thousand-piece jigsaw puzzle on a rainy afternoon, would they choose the puzzle with the clearly drawn illustration on the top of the box, or the puzzle with a scratched surface, perhaps peeling in different places, and without any recognizable picture? Given that we have only one afternoon to complete the task in this scenario, most people say that they would choose the puzzle that had the most specific features on top. That's because it is easier to put together the smaller pieces when we know what the "whole" looks like.

So it is with reading: If a reader knows something ahead of time about the content and its organizational structure, the details of the text make more sense and are easier to slot into their respective places during the process of reading. This means that the content is organized logically and will be therefore be memorable. There are a number of big picture strategies that work especially well for

Figure 2–1

use within a variety of content areas. Four particularly effective ones are the advance organizer, the PLAN technique, skimming, and the anticipation guide.

◎ *Advance Organizer*

Ausubel (1963), a psychologist, first proposed the notion of using an *advance organizer* as a way for students to link their ideas with new materials or concepts. Based upon the idea that students must relate new knowledge to what they already know, the basis upon which schema research is founded, advance organizers can technically be verbal phrases or graphics. However, to support English learners, the nonlinguistic features of graphic structures offer more potential scaffolding, at least in the beginning. They represent what Walker (2008) terms *idea frameworks*, which support learners in determining how the content is organized and related (243).

Advance organizers are outlines created from the titles and subtitles of a text piece that are constructed *before* students read. Advance organizers can be used with any kind of expository text that includes a title and separate subtitles. For example, if we were to look at the full chapter titled "Colonial America" in a history text, we would immediately notice that the chapter spans twenty-six pages. It contains four separate sections, with the following titles: (1) "Early English Settlements," (2) "New England Colonies," (3) "Middle Colonies," and (4) "Southern Colonies." The first section, "Early English Settlements," is comprised of four pages, as seen in Figure 2–2.

We should also recognize that this chapter is written in what we call a "column format." There are two columns of print, as we would see in various magazine or newspaper articles, meaning that students need to know to read down one column

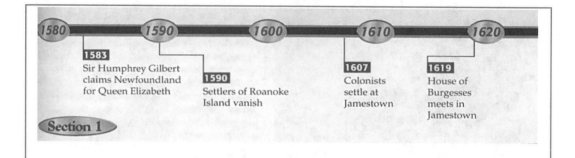

1580 — **1590** — **1600** — **1610** — **1620**

1583
Sir Humphrey Gilbert
claims Newfoundland
for Queen Elizabeth

1590
Settlers of Roanoke
Island vanish

1607
Colonists
settle at
Jamestown

1619
House of
Burgesses
meets in
Jamestown

Early English Settlements

READ TO DISCOVER . . .
- why England's first two attempts to start a colony failed.
- what crop saved the Jamestown colony.
- how the colonists received political rights.

TERMS TO LEARN
charter   burgesses
joint-stock company

The Storyteller

In the summer of 1588, Spanish warships sailed toward the coast of England. King Philip of Spain had sent the armada, or war fleet, of 132 ships to invade England. With 30,000 troops and 2,400 guns, the Spanish Armada was the mightiest naval force the world had ever seen. Yet the smaller, swifter English ships quickly gained the upper hand. The Spanish Armada fled north to Scotland, where violent storms destroyed and scattered the fleet. Only about one half of the Spanish ships straggled home.

England and Spain had been heading toward war for years. Trading rivalry and religious differences divided the two countries. Philip II, Spain's Catholic king, wanted to put a Catholic ruler on the throne of England and bring the country back to the Catholic Church. He did not consider Queen Elizabeth, a Protestant, the rightful ruler of England.

Attacks on Spanish ships and ports by such English adventurers as **Sir Francis Drake** infuriated Philip. He thought that Queen Elizabeth should punish Drake for his raids. Instead, she honored Drake with knighthood. Philip sent the Spanish Armada to conquer England-but failed.

The English victory had far-reaching consequences. Although war between England and Spain continued until 1604, the defeat of the armada marked the end of Spanish control of the seas. Now the way was clear for England and other European nations to start colonies in North America.

The Lost Colony of Roanoke

The English had made several attempts to establish a base on the other side of the Atlantic before their victory

Figure 2–2

over Spain. In 1583 **Sir Humphrey Gilbert** claimed Newfoundland for Queen Elizabeth. Then he sailed south along the coast looking for a place to establish a colony. Before finding a suitable site, he died at sea.

The following year Queen Elizabeth gave **Sir Walter Raleigh** the right to claim any land in North America not already owned by a Christian monarch. Raleigh sent an expedition to look for a good place to settle. His scouts returned with an enthusiastic report of **Roanoke Island**, off the coast of present-day North Carolina. The land was good for farming, they said, and the local people were "most gentle, loving and faithful."

Roanoke Settlements

In 1585 Raleigh sent about 100 men to settle on Roanoke Island. After a difficult winter on the island, the unhappy colonists returned to England.

Two years later Raleigh tried again, sending 91 men, 17 women, and 9 children to Roanoke. **John White**, a mapmaker and artists, led the group. The new settlers began building a permanent colony. They needed many supplies, however, and White sailed to England for the supplies and to recruit more settlers. Although he had hoped to be back within a few months, the war with Spain delayed his returning for three years.

When White finally returned to Roanoke, he found it deserted. The only clue to the fate of the settlers was the word *Croatoan* carved on a gatepost. White thought the colonists must have gone to Croatoan Island, about 100 miles to the south. Bad weather kept White

from investigating. The Roanoke settlers were never seen again.

Jamestown Settlement

Roanoke was Sir Walter Raleigh's last attempt to establish a colony. For a time his failure discouraged others from planning English colonies in North America. However, the idea emerged again in 1606. Several groups of merchants sought **charters**, the right to organize settlements in an area, from King James I.

The Virginia Company

One group of merchants, the Virginia Company of London, received a charter to "make habitation... into that part of America, commonly called Virginia." The Virginia Company was a **joint-stock company**. Investors bought stock, or part ownership, in the company in return for a share of its future profits.

The company acted quickly. In December 1606, it sent 144 settlers in 3 ships-the *Godspeed*, the *Discovery*, and the *Susan Constant*-to build a new colony in North America. The settlers were to look for gold and attempt to establish trade in fish and furs. Forty of them died during the voyage.

In April 1607, the ships entered **Chesapeake Bay** and then sailed up a river flowing into the bay. The colonists named the river the James and their new settlement Jamestown to honor their king.

The settlers built Jamestown on a peninsula so they could defend it from attack. The site had major drawbacks, however. The swampy land teemed with mosquitoes that carried malaria, a

Figure 2–2 (*Continued*)

disease found in warm, humid climates. Jamestown also lacked good farmland and was surrounded by Native American settlements.

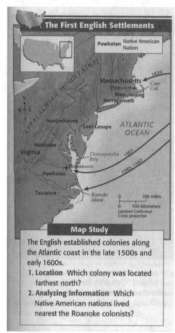

The First English Settlements

Powhatan — Native American Nation

Massachusetts
Plymouth
Wampanoag
Narragansett
Cape Cod
1620

Susquehanna
Leni-Lenape
ATLANTIC OCEAN

Nanticoke
Virginia
Chesapeake Bay
1607

Powhatan
Jamestown
1585, 1587

Tuscarora
Roanoke Island

APPALACHIAN MOUNTAINS

0   100 miles
0   100 kilometers
Lambert Conformal Conic projection

Map Study

The English established colonies along the Atlantic coast in the late 1500s and early 1600s.
1. **Location** Which colony was located farthest north?
2. **Analyzing Information** Which Native American nations lived nearest the Roanoke colonists?

The colonists faced mounting difficulties over the next several months. Many of them were unaccustomed to hard labor. Because the London investors expected a quick profit from their colony, the settlers searched for gold and silver when they should have been growing food. In addition, disease and hunger devastated the colonists. By January 1608, when ships arrived with additional men and supplies, only 38 of the Jamestown colonists remained alive.

Captain John Smith

Governing Jamestown was perhaps the biggest obstacle the colonists faced. The colony survived its second year under the leadership of 27-year–old **Captain John Smith**, a soldier and explorer who arrived in 1608. Smith forced the settlers to work and managed to get corn from the Powhatan people. "It pleased God," he wrote, "to move the Indians to bring us corn…when we have rather expected they would destroy us."

The Virginia Company replaced Smith with a governor, Lord De La Warr, and a period of strict rule began. The colonists barely survived the winter of 1609-1610, called the "starving time." One settler reported, "Having fed upon horses and other beasts as long as they lasted, we were glad to make shift with [such] vermin as dogs, cats, rats and mice." Trouble also broke out with the Native Americans, and the 300 desperately hungry colonists had to barricade themselves inside their walls. When new settlers arrived in May, they found only 60 survivors.

Tobacco Saves the Colony

Although the Virginia colonists found no gold or silver, they did discover another way to make money for the investors. They began to grow tobacco.

Tobacco had become popular in Europe, though some people found smoking unhealthy and disgusting. King James I, for example, called it a "vile and stinking" custom.

One colonist, **John Rolfe**, learned to grow a type of tobacco that was less bitter. The first crop was sold in England in 1614. Soon planters all along

Figure 2–2 *(Continued)*

the James River were raising tobacco, and the colony of Virginia began to prosper and grow. Relations with the Powhatan also improved after Rolfe married **Pocahontas**, the daughter of Chief Powhatan.

Representative Government

In early years of the Jamestown colony, nearly all of the settlers were men. They worked for the Virginia Company and lived under strict military rules. The governors imposed rigid discipline and organized the settlers into work gangs.

As the colony grew, the settlers complained about taking orders from the Virginia Company in London. In 1619 the company agreed to let the colonists have some say in their government. It sent a new governor, Sir George Yeardley, to the colony with orders to end military rule.

Yeardley allowed the men of the colony to elect representatives called **burgesses** to an assembly. The assembly had the right to male local laws for the colony. On July 30, 1619, the **House of Burgesses** met for the first time in a church in Jamestown.

New Arrivals in Jamestown

In 1619 the Virginia Company sent 100 women to Jamestown. As a company report noted: "The plantation can never flourish till families be planted, and the respect of wives and children fix the people on the soil." Colonists who wanted to marry one of the women had to pay a fee of 120 pounds of tobacco. Men still outnumbered women in the colony, but marriage and children began to be part of life in Virginia.

The First Africans in America

A Dutch ship brought another group of newcomers to Jamestown in 1619-20 Africans who were sold to Virginia planters to labor in the tobacco fields. These first Africans may have come as servants-engaged to work for a set period of time-rather than as slaves.

Until about 1640 some African laborers in Jamestown were free and even owned property. William Tucker, the first African American born in the American colonies, was a free man. In the years to follow, however, many more shiploads of Africans would arrive in North America, and those unwilling passengers would be sold as slaves. Slavery was first recognized in Virginia law in 1661.

In the early 1620's, the Virginia Company faced financial troubles. The company had poured all its money into Jamestown, with little return. The colony also suffered a disastrous attack by the Native Americans. In 1624 King James canceled the company's charter and took control of the colony, making it England's first royal colony in America.

Figure 2–2 (*Continued*)

and then move their eyes back to the top of the second column before they read down again. When I tell teachers that once I had a tenth-grade English learner in my class who tried to read across the columns when given an article, they are amazed. Yet, this young man didn't know about column reading, not having been exposed to it before, even in his textbooks. When I asked him if he understood what he was reading, he said, "No, but then I hardly ever understand what I'm reading, Dr. P."

Because his teachers assumed that he would know about column reading, nobody ever explicitly pointed it out to him. He had also just failed the "exit exam" from his English as a Second Language (ESL) Level 3 (intermediate) class in the school's English Language Development program and had to retake the course during the following summer. It is no surprise that though the reading selections on the test were written in column format, he passed it the next time he took it and moved on to ESL Level 4 (early advanced). Our own lesson as teachers is that we can't assume what students know about text layout or conventions.

Suppose that the classroom teacher wants to focus only on the first section, "Early English Settlements." We know that when students—in advance (hence the name of the strategy)—have the big picture of the content that will be presented, along with an idea of how this content is organized, their comprehension will be higher when they read. Therefore, the teacher can give them this overview by providing them with a predeveloped advance organizer (see Figure 2–3).

The next step is to have the students identify the section title and subtitles.

First, the section title, signaled by the largest font size (approximately twenty-two-point font) and placed at the top of the first page of the section, is placed onto the advance organizer. In Figure 2–4, the section title "Early English Settlers" is chosen because it is the focus of the lesson at this time. (If we wanted to analyze multiple sections within the chapter, we would place the chapter title at the top of the organizer.)

Next, students scan for the level 1 subtitles identified by the next largest font size (about eighteen-point font) and place them within the organizer.

Third, the level 2 subtitles, indicated by the smallest font size (fourteen-point font), are placed onto the structure.

Stepping back and viewing the complete organizer, we can now see the major chunks of content that are emphasized in this section.

Students may ask how to determine the actual font sizes of the print, but this is not a critical issue. What is important is that they are leveled so that the font size for the title is the largest, and the font sizes for the next levels of subtitles are increasingly smaller, with detailed information becoming embedded in the larger pieces of the organizer. I encourage them to label the subtitles as level 1, level 2, level 3, or even level 4 subtitles, depending upon the text piece, with

Advance Organizer
Chapter 3: Colonial America
Section 1: Early English Settlements

Title	_____	**(twenty-two-point font)**
Subtitle	_____	***(eighteen-point font)***
Subtitle	_____	*(fourteen-point font)*
Subtitle	_____	***(eighteen-point font)***
Subtitle	_____	*(fourteen-point font)*
Subtitle	_____	*(fourteen-point font)*
Subtitle	_____	*(fourteen-point font)*
Subtitle	_____	***(eighteen-point font)***
Subtitle	_____	***(eighteen-point font)***
Subtitle	_____	*(fourteen-point font)*

Figure 2–3

Advance Organizer
Chapter 3: Colonial America
Section 1: Early English Settlements

Title	**Early English Settlements** (twenty-two-point font)
Subtitle	***The Lost Colony of Roanoke*** *(eighteen-point font)*
Subtitle	*Roanoke Settlements* (fourteen-point font)
Subtitle	***Jamestown Settlement*** *(eighteen-point font)*
Subtitle	*The Virginia Company* (fourteen-point font)
Subtitle	*Captain John Smith* (fourteen-point font)
Subtitle	*Tobacco Saves the Colony* (fourteen-point font)
Subtitle	***Representative Government*** *(eighteen-point font)*
Subtitle	***New Arrivals in Jamestown*** *(eighteen-point font)*
Subtitle	*The First Africans in America* (fourteen-point font)

Figure 2–4

level 1 representing the largest subtitle under the title. That way, exact font size is not a subject for endless debate.

At this point, the teacher can offer multiple opportunities to help students build background knowledge about the concepts and related vocabulary that will appear in this selection as the students read it. Recognizing that *activating* (what may be referred to as "stirring up") and *developing* (adding onto what is already known) schemata for the content will increase reading comprehension, the teacher can then choose effective methods for presenting important terms such as *settlements*, *colony*, *company*, *representative*, and *arrivals*.

Linguistic support from the organizer might consist of synonyms or antonyms (e.g., *departures* for *arrivals*), slower than normal speech rates in discussing the vocabulary, and any of the other elements described in Chapter 1.

Nonlinguistic support, such as maps, laminated pictures, graphs, simulations, and video segments, could also be selected to help English learners visualize these ideas.

Dictionary definitions are not usually sufficient when learners are unfamiliar with content concepts, so teachers should strive to find alternative ways to help students make memorable connections. Teaching new concepts, unfortunately, "demands more work and more time than does teaching new labels for existing concepts" (Galda and Graves 2007, 86).

Previewing the text illustrations and reading the captions is another effective way to emphasize important concepts and make them more tangible. If students can work in pairs or small groups to learn the vocabulary concepts being presented, so much the better, as they will feel free to take risks with personal comments, perceptions, and questions that they might not feel relaxed enough to contribute in a whole-class setting.

Aside from helping teachers and students focus on content, an advance organizer also highlights how the information will be organized. In this case, the order is chronological, detailing the development of each of the following: first, the Roanoke Colony, then the Jamestown settlement, followed by the governmental system, and ending with the new arrivals in Jamestown. This information readies the reader to predict the content during reading, supporting the meaning-making process. In many ways, familiarity with text organization is as important a part of schema as content knowledge in facilitating comprehension (Walker 2008; Freeman and Freeman 2009).

Of course, as the teacher models the advance organizer technique for the students, not just *telling* them how to do it, but *showing* them, learners will become more independent in their use of the strategy and begin to do increasingly more of it on their own. The teacher can consider providing the title and level 1 subtitles in subsequent organizers, leaving the level 2 subtitles blank for the students to figure out, until they can do it completely on their own when given a new section or chapter of text. Eventually, learners should be able to analyze any text piece and create their own advance organizers independently, illustrating how "instructional scaffolds can support text learners by helping them achieve literacy tasks that would otherwise have been out of reach" (Vacca and Vacca 2007, 28).

Advance Organizer with Q and A

A second step that can be added to the advance organizer strategy is to have students create their own questions for the titles and subtitles. This is reminiscent of the SQ3R technique, originated by Robinson (1946) and used extensively in the 1950s and 1960s. SQ3R, composed of five steps (survey, question, read, recite, review), introduced the idea of getting the big picture and asking questions to set purposes before reading. However, the advance organizer does not include the "recite" and "review" components (reading their own written questions and answers aloud from the text), primarily because it is difficult to get students to do it. They are, frankly, embarrassed to make the act of reading and writing so public. Yet, the act of writing personal questions and searching for the answers in the text is highly motivational as long as it is done without too much risk-taking.

In our Literacy Center, we recognized that some of our English learners were having difficulty with question writing, as well as matching the appropriate answers to the question words provided in Figure 2–5. Therefore, we developed an illustration that would help them to review detail questions (using *WH* words— words that begin with *w* or *h*) and highlight the kinds of responses that would answer them appropriately. See Appendix B for a list of ten detail question key words and their corresponding illustrations (a flag representing a thing—*what*; pyramids representing a place—*where*; a stop watch representing time—*when*; eight eggs representing a number—*how many*, etc.).

Teachers can make multiple copies of this chart and distribute them to students so they can refer to them as they write their questions for advance organizers. We have actually seen a few of our students in the Literacy Center "mouthing" the question words and linking them with the visuals: *Who* should be a *person*; *how* should be a *way* to do something; *how much* should be an *amount*. In this way, the chart works as a metacognitive prompt for English learners who are checking themselves on *WH* words as they use them. Conversely, as they read to locate answers to questions, they should then be predicting what the answers will look like in text.

Admittedly, these are words that represent questions at the lowest level of Bloom's taxonomy, but teachers can begin with them and, over the course of the

Detail Question Key (*WH*) Words

Who	Which
What	How
When	How long
Where	How much
Why	How many

Figure 2–5

school year, raise the level of questioning by modeling examples that represent higher levels of critical thinking.

It is important to note that questioning is most powerful when it is planned in advance. Alvermann and Phelps (2005) explain that it is easier to plan and ask effective questions if a teacher has some way to conceptualize or categorize questions. By developing a "core" of questions, teachers can "target specific information or concepts and encourage different kinds of thinking" (218). Beginning with detail questions is a comfortable starting point for English learners when approaching the advance organizer because they lead to what our students call "findable" answers in the text, ensuring a higher level of success than starting with questions that can only be answered using clues, such as inference questions.

Looking again at the advance organizer from the section on "Early English Settlements," we can see that different questions might be posed for the title and subtitles. At first, the teacher should model the questioning process on a whole-class basis, with the intention of helping the students become more adept at it on their own over time. Teachers should ask students to use as many of the different *WH* words as possible so that they put thought into their creation, rather than repeatedly defaulting to the easier question words. (One of my students once wrote ten questions for an advance organizer starting with the word *What*. Though he turned the assignment into an easy task, he did not get much practice in using different kinds of question words. I now require students to use all of the question words before utilizing a second one twice unless they can justify why they should not have to, based on the content.) Figure 2–6 shows detail questions that the class members might generate for this section.

Advance Organizer with Q and A
Chapter 3: Colonial America
Section 1: Early English Settlements

Title   **Early English Settlements** (twenty-two-point font)
Q. Where were the early English settlements?
A.

Subtitle   ***The Lost Colony of Roanoke*** *(eighteen-point font)*
Q. Why was this colony "lost"?
A.

Subtitle   *Roanoke Settlements (fourteen-point font)*
Q. How many Roanoke settlements were there?
A.

Subtitle   ***Jamestown Settlement*** *(eighteen-point font)*
Q. Why was this settlement famous?
A.

Subtitle   *The Virginia Company (fourteen-point font)*
Q. What did the Virginia Company make or sell?
A.

Subtitle   *Captain John Smith (fourteen-point font)*
Q. Who was Captain John Smith?
A.

Subtitle   *Tobacco Saves the Colony (fourteen-point font)*
Q. How did tobacco save the colony?
A.

Subtitle   ***Representative Government*** *(eighteen-point font)*
Q. Which people were the representatives of this government?
A.

Subtitle   ***New Arrivals in Jamestown*** *(eighteen-point font)*
Q. How many new arrivals came to Jamestown?
A.

Subtitle   *The First Africans in America (fourteen-point font)*
Q. When did the first Africans come to America?
A.

Figure 2–6

Asking questions is important because readers, in order to be engaged, need to set purposes for reading. When students answer teachers' questions, they are not setting their own purposes for reading. It is human nature for us to want to find the answers to the questions we have posed, not the questions others would like to have us answer. Once students have written down the questions they hope the text will answer for them based on the key words from the title and subtitles, they begin to read, concentrating on finding reasonable answers to their questions. Of course, this does not mean that they pay no attention to the rest of the content; what it does mean is that their reading is focused and that they are attending to the print, not daydreaming.

Finally, I suggest having students write the question for the title of the selection after doing all the other questions for the subtitles. By the time they return to the title, which is very general, they have a much better idea of the text content and what they might want to ask about the overall topic, based on what they have learned from the rest of the subtitles. In this way, their eventual answer for the title question becomes more of a synthesis of the whole selection and begins to approximate a main idea.

A benefit of having students read chunks of text at a time, which is what they are doing when they read to answer their own questions, is that it is easier for them to concentrate piece by piece, rather than trying to follow multiple pages of content. This is actually a "stop and respond" process. Once readers have gotten through the text material by stopping and responding along the way, they generally have gathered enough information to comprehend what the selection is about. If teachers want to go back later to emphasize other, more specific content information, then it is easy to do so because students have gained a general knowledge of the text piece beforehand.

Minskoff (2005) cautions educators to consider the amount of reading students are required to do relative to answering literal comprehension questions. If teachers wait to ask questions until learners have read lengthy passages, "they may not be able to recall all the information or integrate it with other information" (179). The chunking technique, followed by stopping and answering one question for each subtitle during the reading process, ensures that students will be able to recall the content of each passage.

◎ PLAN Procedure: A Study-Reading Strategy

The PLAN procedure, created by Caverly, Mandeville, and Nicholson (1995), provides a way to introduce multiple modalities into the advance organizer procedure. According to the authors of this version, struggling readers in the fourth grade and above have problems with "metacomprehension"; they read informational text as if it is unrelated to what they already know or to their purposes for reading. They also approach reading as if all texts were structured in the same way. In short, "these ineffective readers need to learn to read strategically...to develop control over their reading processes—from thinking about what they are going to read and why, through monitoring their understanding as they read, to using and applying the information after they've read" (Caverly, Mandeville, and Nicholson 1995, 190).

The technique these authors developed is a study-reading strategy that helps students develop strategic approaches to reading. PLAN, of course, is an acronym, as most teachers would predict from the capitalization of the four letters and their own schema for "educationalese." It stands for *predict, locate, add,* and *note*.

With the PLAN strategy, students analyze the titles and subtitles, focusing on the different levels as indicated by the font sizes. Instead of putting together a horizontal outline, however, they create a map that represents these levels and that includes the technical vocabulary of the subtitles. This map lends itself to spatial rather than linear organization, offering options for students to arrange and color-code the titles and subtitles in a way that makes the most sense to them. Such maps are particularly helpful when students need to "study-read" a large amount of textual information, which is the purpose of the PLAN technique.

The concept of study-reading is slightly different from the idea of reading itself. Study-reading involves an in-depth "study" perspective, which means that students may read and then reread parts that are confusing or difficult. In the PLAN procedure, the text reading is done within a stop and respond format. Students move from part to part, stopping to take notes as they read, enabling them to focus on specific concepts for a short period of time before going on to the next set. They can take time to concentrate and to make meaning. For English learners, especially, chunking the reading into manageable parts is particularly helpful. Some note taking is usually included, along with the use of graphic organizers or maps, and the emphasis is upon assimilation and recall of information.

"'How To Do Well In School Without Studying' is over there in the fiction section."

Figure 2–7

When I speak with students about their study habits in content-area classes, I frequently hear that they are frustrated because they do not know how to select important information and organize it; there is just too much information! Their comments emphasize the need for teachers to demonstrate practical approaches to handling significant content information. Most of these students are not trying to take the easy way out by not studying; they simply need help in knowing how to do it effectively.

The PLAN procedure is a study-reading strategy that not only supports students in culling out important textual information but also leads to long-term retention, as well. It includes the following steps.

Step One: Predict

First, students analyze the text piece and *predict* the content and structure of the text by creating a "prediction map" of the author's ideas with the chapter title at the center and the subtitles as major and minor branches. This content can be color-coded on the map, with the title highlighted in one color, level 2 subtitles in another, level 3 subtitles in a third, and so on, in order to differentiate among levels. Some teachers even ask their students to add boldface words from the text to the map and highlight them in an additional color.

It is also possible to use sections of chapters as the focus of this procedure, asking students to put the section title at the center and the lower-level subtitles as major and minor branches. See Figure 2–8 for a "prediction map" that illustrates the chapter section "Early English Settlements" that we looked at previously.

Step Two: Locate

Next, students *locate* known and unknown information on the map by placing checkmarks next to familiar concepts and question marks by unfamiliar topics. This way they can decide what they already know about the topics in the section and determine what they need to find out when they read, thereby setting purposes for reading. Actually, by doing this activity, they evaluate their own background knowledge (schema) for the topics contained in the title and subtitles. Even better, as students place check marks next to these topics, teachers can see what prior knowledge their learners possess and provide extra help in areas that need more activation or development prior to reading. The *locate* activity in PLAN provides teachers with this opportunity to see what schema students possess for a particular reading assignment.

If extra support is required, teachers can provide the necessary contextualization or front-loading of concepts and vocabulary terms before the reading is done. Buehl (2007) explains that when readers are missing appropriate back-

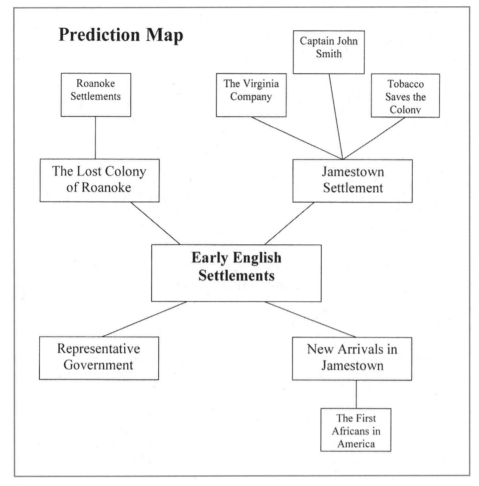

Figure 2–8

ground knowledge, they are unable to make meaningful connections, which in turn undermines their efforts to make sense of an unfamiliar text. Recognizing that prior knowledge for any given subject will differ from assignment to assignment, Buehl (2007) notes, "Teachers need to recognize that comprehension is contextual; sometimes even proficient readers assume the guise of struggling readers" (202).

Another benefit of the *locate* step is that learners can deal with one box or two as a first reading assignment (see Figure 2–9) and others during subsequent reading assignments; they do not have to do everything at once. This makes it easier for students to pace themselves and keeps them from feeling overwhelmed by the hefty amount of text in a chapter or section.

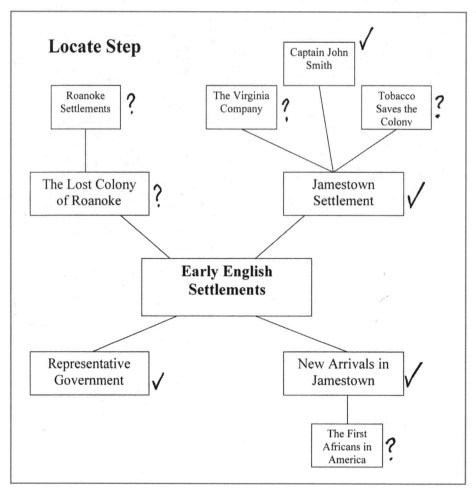

Figure 2–9

Step Three: Add

Step three of PLAN, *add*, represents the "real reading" portion of this procedure. As students read, they add words or short phrases to their predication maps:

1. to explain the concepts marked with question marks

2. to confirm and extend what they already know beside the check marks

In this way, their maps essentially become prompts for short notes that are taken on the reading. Figure 2–10 is an example of a prediction map that contains student notes made during the *add* step.

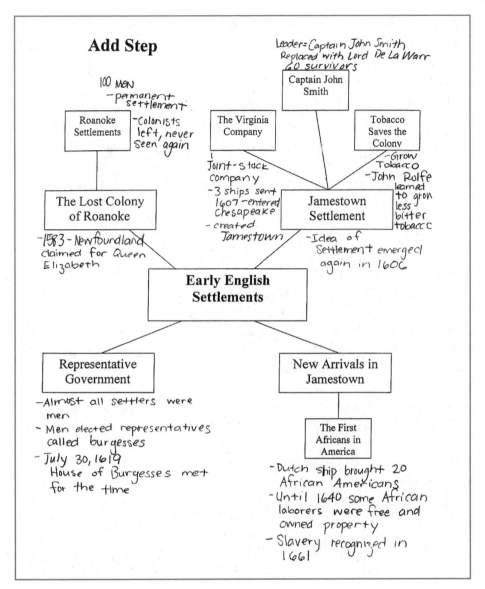

Add Step

100 MEN
- permanent settlement

Roanoke Settlements
- Colonists left, never seen again

The Lost Colony of Roanoke
- 1583 - Newfoundland claimed for Queen Elizabeth

The Virginia Company
Joint-stock company
- 3 ships sent
1607 - entered Chesapeake
- created Jamestown

Leader = Captain John Smith
Replaced with Lord De La Warr
60 survivors

Captain John Smith

Tobacco Saves the Colony
- Grow Tobacco
- John Rolfe learned to grow less bitter tobacco

Jamestown Settlement
- Idea of settlement emerged again in 1606

Early English Settlements

Representative Government
- Almost all settlers were men
- Men elected representatives called burgesses
- July 30, 1619 House of Burgesses met for the time

New Arrivals in Jamestown

The First Africans in America
- Dutch ship brought 20 African Americans
- Until 1640 some African laborers were free and owned property
- Slavery recognized in 1661

Figure 2–10

Though students can read and add notes on their own, it is perhaps even more effective if two students engage in a "paired reading" process where they take turns reading a paragraph or short text piece at a time and then alternate; in this way, they can clarify or elaborate for each other in order to identify or explain the most important concepts. (For more on paired reading, see page 194.) This collaborative process ensures greater understanding of the text as the partners move from one part of the map to another. Such an approach to the *add* step of this procedure also lowers the affective filter for English learners who may need the comfortable support of a peer who is more proficient with the language.

Step Four: Note

Note, the last step of PLAN, offers students opportunities to synthesize their content learning from the text. They can be asked to summarize the text piece, to reconstruct their maps, or to make them into other types of graphics. The information can also be illustrated, become the subject of a class role-play, be developed into dialogue for a readers' theatre presentation, or be converted into questions for a quiz game such as *Jeopardy*. What students do with the information depends upon how they will need to use it. The *note* step may look different if they have to write a paper instead of taking a test—or if they simply need to understand the content for the next lesson to come.

One of my favorite activities for the *note* step of this procedure is to ask groups of students to combine their individual notes on specific parts of the map that I assign. For example, if a group were given "Jamestown Settlement" (one of the four sections of the chapter on early English settlements), they would draw their part of the map on larger butcher paper or poster board, contributing all of the notes that they had already written in pairs or individually. Then, their papers would be hung on the classroom wall to be used for the next step, a type of gallery walk, where all students move from poster to poster (as in a museum), adding new ideas on their own papers drawn from their classmates' notes on the other sections of the text.

If each group does the same, then the notes on the wall represent a compilation of all the class notes that were taken by the students, so there is a kind of "class schema" represented. Letting students walk around the classroom as a gallery walk procedure to look at all the posters and add any notes that they missed gives them an opportunity to revisit and extend the content. They can get clarification from peers on ideas they may not understand while filling in the gaps in their own notes. When everyone has all the notes, the teacher can share with students which ideas or terms may be more important than others for the next step of the planned instructional sequence (e.g., a test, a quiz, a paper, a project, etc.). Therefore, as students study or prepare for the next part of the unit, they have a new purpose in mind. An example of four group posters used for a gallery walk with "Early English Settlements" is illustrated in Figure 2–11.

An Embedded Into-Through-Beyond Process

The authors of PLAN indicate that the philosophy underlying the procedure reflects comprehension research, which tells us that true understanding is an

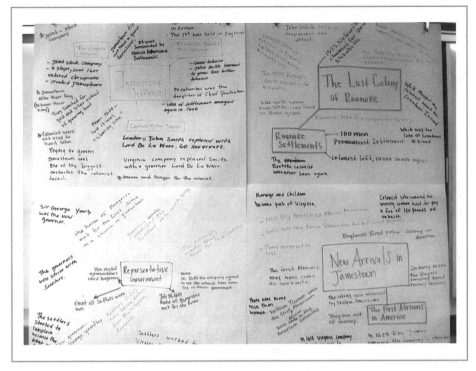

Figure 2–11 *PLAN Student Posters for "Early English Settlements"*

"active process beginning before the reader engages the text, proceeding as the reader interacts with the text, and continuing after the reader has left the page" (Caverly, Mandeville, and Nicholson 1995, 190). They emphasize that comprehension is a multistage, formative, constructive process rather than a summative product identified at the conclusion of the reading event.

If we look at the first two steps of the procedure as the *into* portion of the lesson, we can see that *predicting* the titles and subtitles and *locating* information that is known and unknown are part of setting the stage to read: Students see the most important concepts and terms from the text piece; identify the order in which the content will be presented; recognize what prior knowledge they have for the content and what knowledge is missing; and by virtue of their "taste" of the content and what they know and do not know, set purposes for reading.

The second step, *add*, is the reading part. After having gotten the big picture from the predicting and activation of background knowledge, students are ready to read the text for the main points and the supporting details. They do this in a stop-and-respond process, adding notes as they move from subtitle to subtitle. Teachers can oversee the note-taking process and provide immediate feedback if students are noting information that may be incorrect or insufficient, allowing learners to made revisions. This kind of support during the reading process is typically what we think of as a "through" activity.

Finally, the *note* step of PLAN invites students to use what they've learned and take the content further—perhaps even beyond the text itself. The result may be a more comprehensive view of the content as shown in the group note taking, gallery walk, or other activities including discussions, reading of new texts that are related, projects, video segments, computer streaming excerpts, or any opportunity to synthesize the information they've learned and expand it. In this way, the "beyond" portion is built into PLAN, and from this point, teachers can take students into the next phase of their class units. It is important that new content is actually applied in some way. "Once completed, a graphic organizer should lead to something else: a discussion with a peer, a presentation, an essay, a project display. Students must transform information in their mind or on paper before the information becomes their own" (Fisher and Frey 2008, 132).

Figure 2–12 represents one such transformation of information, a type of quiz game (similar to *Jeopardy*) that utilizes all of the notes from students' posters on early English settlements. After learners have added notes so that the entire class has the same information, students collaborate with peers in studying to

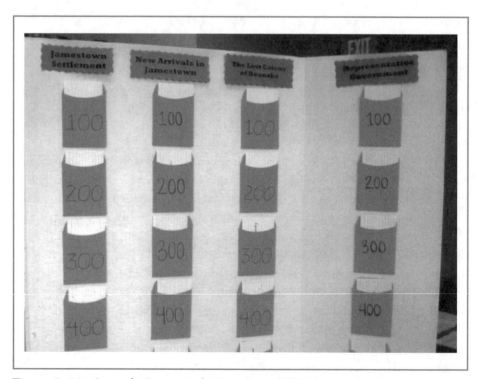

Figure 2–12 Jeopardy *Categories for Note Step of PLAN*

Jeopardy Questions and Answers for "Early English Settlements"

The Lost Colony of Roanoke

$100	How many men did Raleigh send to settle on Roanoke Island?	100
$200	For whom was Newfoundland claimed?	Queen Elizabeth
$300	Who was John White?	map maker/artist
$400	How many years did it take for White to come back to Roanoke Island?	3 years
$500	Why did White take so long to return to Roanoke Island?	war with Spain

Jamestown Settlement

$100	What saved the colony?	tobacco
$200	Who grew less bitter tobacco than others?	John Rolfe
$300	After whom is Jamestown named?	King James
$400	Who replaced John Smith?	Lord De La Warr
$500	What did the colonists search for instead of growing food?	gold and silver

Representative Government

$100	What date did the House of Burgesses meet for the first time?	July 30, 1619
$200	What were the elected representatives called?	burgesses
$300	Who organized settlers into work gangs?	governors
$400	Who lived under strict military rule?	settlers
$500	Which group made local laws for the colony?	The Assembly

New Arrivals in Jamestown

$100	When was slavery recognized?	1661
$200	Who attacked the colonists?	Native Americans
$300	When were some African laborers freed and allowed to own property?	1640
$400	How many African Americans did the Dutch ship bring?	20
$500	Who took control of the colony in 1624?	King James

Figure 2–12 *(Continued)*

answer the quiz questions. Using a generic poster with columns of pockets for holding question cards, the teacher categorizes the content of the cards under each level 1 subtitle in the chapter or chapter section. Students select pockets based on question difficulty, with $100 questions being easier than $400 questions. This ensures success for students, especially if they are concerned about not being able to answer some of the harder questions. In that case, they simply choose less expensive categories! Participation in the game allows learners to synthesize and review the content information and have a fun, interactive experience at the same time.

◎ *Skimming Technique*

Another big picture strategy is *skimming*, which has a technical and specific definition that many people do not know. If we were to ask most adults what skimming entails, they would probably say that it means running the eyes very quickly over a page of information. This response is common because the idea of skimming implies speed. However, it is not that skimming has a faster pace than reading, but rather that information is skipped during the process. The definition of skimming is reading only the main ideas of a text piece, which are typically contained in topic sentences—and avoiding the details in the body of each paragraph, as described in the steps listed in Figure 2–13.

If we were to skim the chapter section "Early English Settlements," we would read the title and look at the illustrations and captions first of all. Next, we would read the entire introduction, which gives us important information before we read the rest of the section. If there were a section conclusion (although in this case, there is not), we would also read it. Then, we would read the subtitles to give us the beginning of the big picture.

The next step is to read the topic sentences of each paragraph. This is an interesting process because it is difficult to find topic sentences quickly with the intention of not stopping the process in the middle. The idea is to get a quick overview of the main ideas of the text before going back and reading it thoroughly. By doing this, we add to the big picture that we developed when we previewed the text, as described previously.

Figure 2–14 (pages 44–47) shows the results of the skimming process with the first two parts of the "Early English Settlements" section indicated by the two level 1 subtitles, "The Lost Colony of Roanoke" and "Jamestown Settlement." In this case, the teacher has read aloud the first three paragraphs of "Early English Settlements" as an introduction (underlining all of the sentences to indicate that they should be read) and then put a copy of the text on an overhead transparency.

Skimming

Skimming is a method of *locating the main ideas in paragraphs, utilizing topic sentences*. (Therefore, materials that do not contain topic sentences are not good sources for skimming.) When you skim, you want to get the "big picture," or main ideas—and leave the details behind.

The skimming procedure includes:

- reading the title
- looking at the illustrations and captions
- reading the *first* (introductory) and *last* (conclusion) paragraphs completely
- reading the subtitles
- reading the topic sentences of each paragraph only (usually they are placed first, second, or last; if implied, skimming won't work!)
- thinking about the "big picture" represented by the topic sentences

Figure 2–13

Next, the class advised the teacher which sentences to underline with an overhead transparency pen, one by one: the first statements in each paragraph, representing topic sentences. (Of course, if a school is lucky enough to own a document camera, then it is easy enough to demonstrate this procedure using technology.) Later, once the teacher has modeled the process for the group, students can place blank overhead transparencies or heavy-duty sheet protectors directly upon the pages of their texts and do the skimming page by page with pens in groups or with partners.

After students have highlighted the topic sentences in a selected text piece, they should take a moment to read each of them again in order. The process can be done silently or orally. The point is to see just how much information is actually contained in the topic sentences and to use it to frame the content in preparation for a second reading. Most learners are amazed at how much content knowledge they can derive from skimming. They become aware of the ideas of the text and the order in which they are presented by the author. Eventually, the skimming process becomes automatic, and students will no longer have to rely upon highlighting as a means of support; they will simply be able to skim the text without visual scaffolds of any sort. Combining content vocabulary and concepts with knowledge of text organization is a powerful way to enhance students' comprehension when they read the text completely.

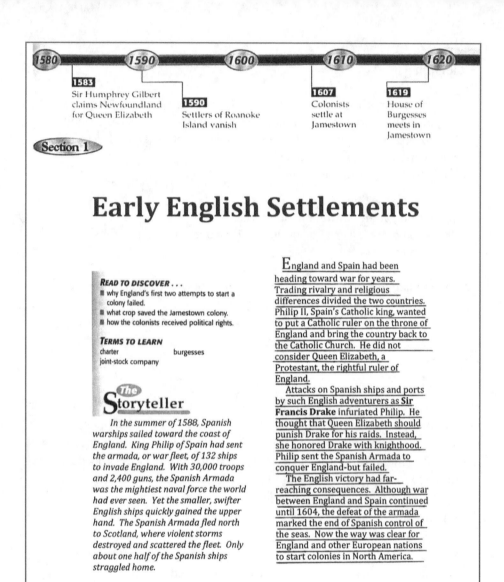

1580 **1590** **1600** **1610** **1620**

1583
Sir Humphrey Gilbert claims Newfoundland for Queen Elizabeth

1590
Settlers of Roanoke Island vanish

1607
Colonists settle at Jamestown

1619
House of Burgesses meets in Jamestown

Section 1

Early English Settlements

READ TO DISCOVER . . .
■ why England's first two attempts to start a colony failed.
■ what crop saved the Jamestown colony.
■ how the colonists received political rights.

TERMS TO LEARN
charter   burgesses
joint-stock company

The Storyteller

In the summer of 1588, Spanish warships sailed toward the coast of England. King Philip of Spain had sent the armada, or war fleet, of 132 ships to invade England. With 30,000 troops and 2,400 guns, the Spanish Armada was the mightiest naval force the world had ever seen. Yet the smaller, swifter English ships quickly gained the upper hand. The Spanish Armada fled north to Scotland, where violent storms destroyed and scattered the fleet. Only about one half of the Spanish ships straggled home.

England and Spain had been heading toward war for years. Trading rivalry and religious differences divided the two countries. Philip II, Spain's Catholic king, wanted to put a Catholic ruler on the throne of England and bring the country back to the Catholic Church. He did not consider Queen Elizabeth, a Protestant, the rightful ruler of England.

Attacks on Spanish ships and ports by such English adventurers as **Sir Francis Drake** infuriated Philip. He thought that Queen Elizabeth should punish Drake for his raids. Instead, she honored Drake with knighthood. Philip sent the Spanish Armada to conquer England-but failed.

The English victory had far-reaching consequences. Although war between England and Spain continued until 1604, the defeat of the armada marked the end of Spanish control of the seas. Now the way was clear for England and other European nations to start colonies in North America.

Figure 2–14

The Lost Colony of Roanoke

The English had made several attempts to establish a base on the other side of the Atlantic before their victory over Spain. In 1583 **Sir Humphrey Gilbert** claimed Newfoundland for Queen Elizabeth. Then he sailed south along the coast looking for a place to establish a colony. Before finding a suitable site, he died at sea.

The following year Queen Elizabeth gave **Sir Walter Raleigh** the right to claim any land in North America not already owned by a Christian monarch. Raleigh sent an expedition to look for a good place to settle. His scouts returned with an enthusiastic report of **Roanoke Island**, off the coast of present-day North Carolina. The land was good for farming, they said, and the local people were "most gentle, loving and faithful."

Roanoke Settlements

In 1585 Raleigh sent about 100 men to settle on Roanoke Island. After a difficult winter on the island, the unhappy colonists returned to England.

Two years later Raleigh tried again, sending 91 men, 17 women, and 9 children to Roanoke. **John White**, a mapmaker and artists, led the group. The new settlers began building a permanent colony. They needed many supplies, however, and White sailed to England for the supplies and to recruit more settlers. Although he had hoped to be back within a few months, the war with Spain delayed his returning for three years.

When White finally returned to Roanoke, he found it deserted. The only clue to the fate of the settlers was the word *Croatoan* carved on a gatepost. White thought the colonists must have gone to Croatoan Island, about 100 miles to the south. Bad weather kept White from investigating. The Roanoke settlers were never seen again.

Jamestown Settlement

Roanoke was Sir Walter Raleigh's last attempt to establish a colony. For a time his failure discouraged others from planning English colonies in North America. However, the idea emerged again in 1606. Several groups of merchants sought **charters**, the right to organize settlements in an area, from King James I.

The Virginia Company

One group of merchants, the Virginia Company of London, received a charter to "make habitation... into that part of America, commonly called Virginia." The Virginia Company was a **joint-stock company**. Investors bought stock, or part ownership, in the company in return for a share of its future profits.

The company acted quickly. In December 1606, it sent 144 settlers in 3 ships-the *Godspeed*, the *Discovery*, and the *Susan Constant*-to build a new colony in North America. The settlers were to look for gold and attempt to establish trade in fish and furs. Forty of them died during the voyage.

In April 1607, the ships entered **Chesapeake Bay** and then sailed up a river flowing into the bay. The colonists named the river the James and their new settlement Jamestown to honor their king.

Figure 2–14 (*Continued*)

The settlers built Jamestown on a peninsula so they could defend it from attack. The site had major drawbacks, however. The swampy land teemed with mosquitoes that carried malaria, a disease found in warm, humid climates. Jamestown also lacked good farmland and was surrounded by Native American settlements.

The First English Settlements

Powhatan — Native American Nation

Massachusetts
Plymouth
Wampanoag
Narragansett

APPALACHIAN MOUNTAINS

ATLANTIC OCEAN

Susquehanna
Lenni Lenape
Virginia
Chesapeake Bay
Jamestown
Powhatan
Tuscarora
Roanoke Island

0 ____ 100 miles
0 ____ 100 kilometers
Lambert Conformal Conic projection

Map Study

The English established colonies along the Atlantic coast in the late 1500s and early 1600s.
1. **Location** Which colony was located farthest north?
2. **Analyzing Information** Which Native American nations lived nearest the Roanoke colonists?

The colonists faced mounting difficulties over the next several months. Many of them were unaccustomed to hard labor. Because the London investors expected a quick profit from their colony, the settlers searched for gold and silver when they should have been growing food. In addition, disease and hunger devastated the colonists. By January 1608, when ships arrived with additional men and supplies, only 38 of the Jamestown colonists remained alive.

Captain John Smith

Governing Jamestown was perhaps the biggest obstacle the colonists faced. The colony survived its second year under the leadership of 27-year–old **Captain John Smith**, a soldier and explorer who arrived in 1608. Smith forced the settlers to work and managed to get corn from the Powhatan people. "It pleased God," he wrote, "to move the Indians to bring us corn...when we have rather expected they would destroy us."

The Virginia Company replaced Smith with a governor, Lord De La Warr, and a period of strict rule began. The colonists barely survived the winter of 1609-1610, called the "starving time." One settler reported, "Having fed upon horses and other beasts as long as they lasted, we were glad to make shift with [such] vermin as dogs, cats, rats and mice." Trouble also broke out with the Native Americans, and the 300 desperately hungry colonists had to barricade themselves inside their walls. When new settlers arrived in May, they found only 60 survivors.

Tobacco Saves the Colony

Although the Virginia colonists found no gold or silver, they did discover another way to make money for the investors. They began to grow tobacco.

Tobacco had become popular in Europe, though some people found smoking unhealthy and disgusting.

Figure 2–14 *(Continued)*

King James I, for example, called it a "vile and stinking" custom.

One colonist, **John Rolfe**, learned to grow a type of tobacco that was less bitter. The first crop was sold in England in 1614. Soon planters all along the James River were raising tobacco, and the colony of Virginia began to prosper and grow. Relations with the Powhatan also improved after Rolfe married **Pocahontas**, the daughter of Chief Powhatan.

Representative Government

In early years of the Jamestown colony, nearly all of the settlers were men. They worked for the Virginia Company and lived under strict military rules. The governors imposed rigid discipline and organized the settlers into work gangs.

As the colony grew, the settlers complained about taking orders from the Virginia Company in London. In 1619 the company agreed to let the colonists have some say in their government. It sent a new governor, Sir George Yeardley, to the colony with orders to end military rule.

Yeardley allowed the men of the colony to elect representatives called **burgesses** to an assembly. The assembly had the right to make local laws for the colony. On July 30, 1619, the **House of Burgesses** met for the first time in a church in Jamestown.

New Arrivals in Jamestown

In 1619 the Virginia Company sent 100 women to Jamestown. As a company report noted: "The plantation can never flourish till families be planted, and the respect of wives and children fix the people on the soil." Colonists who wanted to marry one of the women had to pay a fee of 120 pounds of tobacco. Men still outnumbered women in the colony, but marriage and children began to be part of life in Virginia.

The First Africans in America

A Dutch ship brought another group of newcomers to Jamestown in 1619-20 Africans who were sold to Virginia planters to labor in the tobacco fields. These first Africans may have come as servants-engaged to work for a set period of time-rather than as slaves.

Until about 1640 some African laborers in Jamestown were free and even owned property. William Tucker, the first African American born in the American colonies, was a free man. In the years to follow, however, many more shiploads of Africans would arrive in North America, and those unwilling passengers would be sold as slaves. Slavery was first recognized in Virginia law in 1661.

In the early 1620's, the Virginia Company faced financial troubles. The company had poured all its money into Jamestown, with little return. The colony also suffered a disastrous attack by the Native Americans. In 1624 King James canceled the company's charter and took control of the colony, making it England's first royal colony in America.

Figure 2–14 (*Continued*)

Reflections on Skimming

When teachers begin to teach students how to skim, sometimes there is a bit of resistance because it feels like such a loose technique. That is to say, in looking only at the first sentence of each paragraph, it is likely that we may miss the actual topic sentence. After all, topic sentences can be located first, second, or last in a paragraph. They may even be implied (but if this is the case, we should not choose such a text as a model for skimming).

However, as students become more comfortable with the idea of searching for the main ideas located in topic sentences, they will also start to identify where the comprehensive idea really is in a paragraph. For example, in the second topic sentence under "The Virginia Company" in Figure 2–14, there are two sentences, rather than one. As a group of students from the Literacy Center skimmed this text section, they decided that the first sentence was only an entrée into the "real" topic sentence, which they felt was the second sentence in the paragraph. They could see that sometimes first sentences are only introductory, leading into the main idea of the paragraph in the second sentence, so they highlighted both the first and second sentence. Such ability to identify topic sentences accurately becomes more ingrained as students utilize the skimming process more frequently and as they begin to use other strategies such as "triple read" (described in Chapter 5).

It is important that teachers recognize the flexible nature of the skimming process and allow students time to discover how to find the comprehensive ideas early in the paragraph. If learners miss the actual topic sentence in a paragraph, it is not a serious issue; as time goes by, they will get better at recognizing topic sentences. Also, missing one or two topic sentences does not change the overall big picture that is achieved by skimming before reading.

Finally, though skimming is used to provide the big picture before reading, it can also be used for other purposes, which students will eventually come to understand. It can serve as a way to review information before taking a test, for choosing articles to use in research papers, and for summarizing text pieces. Knowing that a summary consists primarily of main ideas with only a few details, skimming is the natural approach to take before writing one. Again we see that the strategies readers choose to use depend upon their purposes for reading.

◎ *Anticipation Guide*

The final big picture strategy in this chapter is valuable for introducing students to and immersing them in metacognitive processes, such as prediction and confirmation/disconfirmation of those predictions. The anticipation guide, sometimes called a "reaction guide" or "prediction guide" guide (Richardson, Morgan, and Fleener 2006, 180) is exactly that: a method for teaching learners to anticipate possible content and to think about the connections among ideas. It also serves to "motivate and stimulate curiosity about the topic being studied," enhancing the learning and retention of students (Fisher and Frey 2008, 51).

For example, Figure 2–15 reflects an anticipation guide for a passage contained in "Early English Settlements," under "Tobacco Saves the Colony" (representing a

---

Applebee et al., *The American Journey*
Chapter Title—"Colonial America"
Section—"Early English Settlements"
Glencoe-McGraw Hill, 2000
Page 73

Tobacco Saves the Colony

Although the Virginia colonists found no gold or silver, they did discover another way to make money for the investors. They began to grow tobacco.

Tobacco had become popular in Europe, though some people found smoking unhealthy and disgusting. King James I, for example, called it a "vile and stinking" custom.

One colonist, John Rolfe, learned to grow a type of tobacco that was less bitter. The first crop was sold in England in 1614. Soon planters all along the James River were raising tobacco, and the colony of Virginia began to prosper and grow. Relations with the Powhatan also improved after Rolfe married Pocahontas, the daughter of Chief Powhatan.

Anticipation Guide

1. The Virginia colonists did not find any gold or silver in Jamestown.   T F
2. The colonists discovered a way to make money for their investors.   T F
3. King James I thought that smoking was a highly entertaining pastime.   T F
4. The first crop of tobacco was sold in English in 1600.   T F
5. John Rolfe grew an extremely bitter tobacco that was popular because it was cheap to purchase.   T F
6. John Rolfe improved the relationship between the colonists and Powhatan Indians by marrying Pocahontas.   T F

Figure 2–15

level 2 subtitle). The guide is done *before the students actually see the passage*, but the text piece is included here to show how the statements may be written.

First, the teacher hands out the anticipation guide to the students, knowing that there may be some vocabulary terms that need to be front-loaded, or presented and developed before the guide is completed. Once the teacher introduces the terms and students feel that the vocabulary is comprehensible, they are asked to commit to a position for each statement that represents whether they believe it to be true or false, right or wrong. They can do this individually, in pairs, or in groups, depending upon their language proficiency and the level of support, or scaffolding, needed for the activity. Remembering that even one part of a statement that is false makes the entire statement false, students mark what they believe (or guess) to be true.

The point of the activity, aside from introducing vocabulary and concepts, is to set a purpose for reading. Once students have taken a position, they want to see if they are correct. When they read the text that accompanies the anticipation guide (Figure 2–2), they "chunk" their reading into manageable parts, stopping when a statement that they have marked can be confirmed (proved) or disconfirmed (disproved). If it is confirmed, they place a check mark next to it, and if it is disconfirmed, they write the correct information under the statement that is wrong.

This technique is reminiscent of the reading that is done in chunks for the advance organizer and the PLAN procedure, in which a stop-and-respond approach is adopted. Students move through the text, part by part, enabling them to make meaning more easily, to concentrate fully on each part, and therefore to stay engaged with the text for a longer period of time. In addition, such anticipatory activities "can enhance the learning and retention of students by serving to motivate and stimulate curiosity about the topics being studied" (Fisher and Frey 2008, 51).

An enjoyable twist to the development of this guide is to use terms other than true/false, right/wrong, or yes/no. Our older students in the Literacy Center especially like it when we add slang to the guides. For example, instead of yes and no, we might write "For Sure" and "No Way." Somehow the use of their informal conversational language lends another layer of appeal to what is already an interesting activity. Teachers can also experiment with using statements in the guides that are outrageous, partially wrong, or just fun, in general.

It is important that we consider what our students can do in determining the number of statements to write, the difficulty level of the language, and the length of the text pieces they reflect. Figure 2–16 contains a summary of the purposes and guidelines for writing anticipation guides. Not only do teachers become better at

The Anticipation Guide

Purposes

Activate interest
Set purpose(s) for reading
Introduce key vocabulary terms
Engage students
Provide stop-and-respond opportunities
Allow for confirming/disconfirming predictions

How to Write the Statements

Use some factual information from the text.
Add some incorrect information to some of the statements.
Write a few interesting, funny, or even outrageous statements.
Be sure the statements correspond with the order in which they appear in the text.
Let students practice doing this, using more difficult statements over time.
Use longer text pieces for the guides as students become proficient.
Eventually ask students to write anticipation guides for new texts.
Enjoy the process!

Figure 2–16

developing good ones, but eventually, with practice and feedback, students are able to write anticipation guides for their peers also!

Commentary

This chapter has been devoted to showing how big picture strategies can scaffold the comprehension process for learners by offering an overview of the major content ideas and their organizational structures as the context for reading. The smaller pieces of text make sense when embedded within this larger context, and the text selection, as a whole, makes more sense to readers when they get the "jigsaw puzzle picture on the top of the box" first. Alternatively, the cartoon in Figure 2–17 represents the kind of approach students may take in getting the big picture if they are not supplied with the academic strategies they need.

"I'm in the den mom, reading the newspaper for my social studies class."

Figure 2–17

In the next chapter, other literacy strategies will be introduced that link with a variety of purposes for reading. As we will see, readers who are "flexible" are better readers than those who tend to read everything the same way. The reasons people read are diverse, depending upon the demands of the moment and the types of personal, academic, or professional contexts they are in. "It is important for teachers to recognize that every text has a certain meaning potential, but different readers construct different meanings depending on their background knowledge and their purpose for reading" (Freeman and Freeman 2004, 26). Helping students learn how to develop a repertoire of strategies from which to choose in order to match these purposes is an important goal if students are to become truly proficient readers and writers.

Reasons for Reading

Teaching Students to Match Their Purposes to Their Practices

This chapter contains a discussion of how readers approach text, depending upon their purposes for reading it. Personal, academic, and professional purposes change constantly, calling upon readers to choose their strategies carefully in order to reach specific goals. When we first see children in our Literacy Center, it quickly becomes clear who the more proficient readers are. They are the ones who vary their reading approaches to match their reasons for reading. For example, when asked to predict what a chapter might be about based upon the title, one seventh grader based her answer not only on the information in the chapter title, but also on the content contained in the subtitles of the text piece and the illustrations, explaining that her teacher at school had taught the class how to "preview" text. Fjeldstad (2006) clarifies that previewing is "a very helpful strategy to 'turn on' your brain, help you remember what you already know about the subject, and get ready to absorb new information" (400).

Knowing how to preview text is unusual behavior for children in our center because most of them come to us precisely because they are not proficient readers and lack such strategies as these. When learners are able to think about what should be done to meet specific goals, they employ metacognitive behaviors that guide them in their reading processes. Essentially, by consciously identifying their intentions as they read and coming to rely upon a repertoire of different kinds of strategies to choose from that will meet their needs, they represent what we call "flexible" readers.

Struggling Reader Perspective

The more typical readers in the Literacy Center are the children who read everything exactly the same way. In other words, whether they are reading a short story, a selection from a science chapter, a magazine or newspaper article, a set of pool rules posted at the community park, a DMV manual, a restaurant or television menu, or even an Internet source, they start at the top with the first word and continue reading until they come to the end. Usually, when asked what a selection is about, they are unable to tell us because their goal is to get through the piece, not to assimilate the information in any particular way. In short, they have no strategic plan for understanding what they read.

For many readers, especially those who struggle, reading is seen primarily as a school task. In fact, some people, children and adults alike, avoid reading whenever they can because they do not feel accomplished at it. Reading is like any other skill that we acquire in life; if we aren't good at it, we won't want to do it. In order to support learners in the reading process, we have to offer them instructional support that helps them to become better at it. Otherwise, they may develop avoidance strategies. Giving up on or withdrawing from situations that involve learning from text is a tactic students may use when the material they are assigned to read seems too difficult or uninteresting (Gunning 2008, 33).

One of the first steps in this process is to inform students that readers do actually read for different reasons. A second step is to teach them how to "read" appropriately to match their purposes, recognizing that sometimes we do not read a text in the usual way at all: We may scan for information, skim for the main points, or preview it, depending on what we wish to get out of it. A third step is to encourage students to become avid readers, those who read frequently and regularly—and this is such an important issue that it is a primary subject of Chapter 9 in this book.

Personal Purposes for Reading

When I work with teachers at schools or in conference settings, the idea of *why* we read comes up naturally because we typically read on our own for different reasons than we read in school. For example, the young man in Figure 3–1 has a personal agenda that guides his choice of reading materials. He clearly has the need for a specific type of information that will help him be successful in his classes—though perhaps not in the way we would ideally like him to be!

We read differently depending upon what we want to get out of our reading. For example, we tend to "read" recreational books however we like. As an English major, I have analyzed *setting* in novels so many times that when I read for pleasure, I often omit the longer descriptions of setting, just because I can. I recognize that setting contributes to the mood, tone, and theme of the literary work, but sometimes I simply want to get to the plot; it is my choice to do that because I am reading for my own pleasure.

Though it is somewhat embarrassing to share, another practice that I engage in is skimming for social purposes. In my daily work, I talk mostly about literacy practices, discussing research theories with colleagues and listening to others in my

"Do you have any books on managing disruptive students? I want to know what the opposition is up to."

Figure 3–1

department who tell me about their academic projects and teaching experiences, so I have less-than-adequate time to keep abreast of what is going on in the media. Every once in awhile, I do a blitz; I find several copies of magazines (news, entertainment, health) and choose a few articles from each. I then use the skimming strategy (described in Chapter 2) to get an overview of this information, using the highlighter technique to mark topic sentences and systematically skipping the details. Believe it or not, I learn so much information from this approach that I can hold a conversation with the best of them at social gatherings about any subject that I select. This is an authentic example of how readers set goals and then choose literacy strategies that are most efficient in reaching those goals.

When I ask secondary students in our Literacy Center how they choose their materials for independent reading, they almost always have very specific reasons. Such motivations include the following: They have graphics that are "cool" and help explain the text (comics, graphic novels), they are easy to read because I already know a lot about the character (series books), they teach me things that I want to know (expository pieces about volcanoes, planets, dinosaurs, global warming), they help me learn to do something better (skateboard, snowboard, paint, draw, make things out of wood, put together model planes, develop relation-ships, cook, meditate), they help me solve real-life problems (school challenges, problems with parents or siblings, health issues, friendship conflicts, addictions, peer pressure).

Initially we can certainly see that these students' choices reflect their inter-ests and personal needs, but it takes a moment to dig deeper and determine that each "text" would probably be approached differently, depending upon the genre and the reader. For example, a student who is reading a novel or short story would probably deal with it sequentially, starting at the beginning and having few illus-trations or chapter titles (if any) to rely upon for content support. With narrative text, it is not possible to skip around and maintain any sense of cohesion, especially if part of the lure is suspense or a surprise ending. Engaged devotees of series books might find that pacing goes faster when they get into the reading, as they rely upon past history of the characters and their relationships, the author's general style and vocabulary, and even plot structures that are familiar. Gunning (2008) points out that in general, stories are easier to read than science articles, how-to features, and descriptions of historical events, noting that because of its structure and linear quality, narrative text is generally more predictable than expository text.

However, readers of expository texts, knowing that they can read simply for personal pleasure, might look first at the illustrations and captions; read specific sections first, some next, and others perhaps not at all; and find the content that they want to know, based on their own preferences and level of schema for the topic. Recognizing (and probably reveling in the fact) that they do not have to take a quiz, answer questions, or do a project after reading frees these readers to select what they want to read and to pursue the reading in ways that suit their needs for the moment.

◎ No Rules for Pleasure Reading

It's enlightening to talk to students about pleasure reading because, no matter how much we define "pleasure reading," what they view as the rules for in-school assigned reading are so ingrained in some of them that they can't be easily released. One young man who had asked for a book on bats was looking a bit for-lorn during independent reading time, so I asked him why he did not seem inter-ested. He replied that he loved to read about bats but that the book in hand was kind of easy for him and contained a lot of information that he already knew, so his attention was wandering. When I told him that he could choose another more sophisticated book that would match his needs better, he looked surprised and said, "Shouldn't I finish this one first? I already started it." Committed to finish-ing a book he had begun, he was willing to have an unsatisfactory reading experience in order to do what he thought was "correct": read it all before choosing another one. Being given the freedom to abandon his choice and to find another book was an eye-opening experience for him—and taught me a lot about how important it is to let students know explicitly and adamantly that pleasure reading does not come with the restrictiveness that in-class reading assignments do.

Along the same lines, I had a high school student once who came from a household in which there was much conflict and stress. She loved to read novels to escape her real life, but she had a habit that I suspect most teachers would try to break her of if given the chance: she read the endings first. I admit that when she told me this, I gave her "the book would be so much better if you didn't know what would happen, don't you think?" talk. She silenced me by saying that she simply couldn't bear to read a book that might end sadly since she read to make herself feel better. Knowing that the book would have a positive ending made the reading of the book a soothing experience for her, she said. Reflecting upon her home life and hearing her words, I realized that she was right. I decided immediately that she should be able to read her book any way she wanted—and that the same reasoning should apply to all students during pleasure reading.

Classroom Purposes for Reading

If we contrast this purposeful kind of personal reading with what students are asked to do in classes, we see a difference because, for the most part, teachers set the purposes for reading for their students. Purposes are determined by a number of factors, according to Galda and Graves (2007), including the students who are reading the selection, the selection itself, and what students need to know. If a health and guidance teacher asks his students to read Chapter 9, then students are responsible for everything in Chapter 9 unless the teacher narrows down the objectives. How does one read a long chapter and get everything out of it? For students who are overwhelmed by large amounts of text, especially English learners who have to acquire the target language as they are learning content at the same time, narrowing down these purposes is essential. Purpose is "what motivates us, helps focus out attention, and gives us a goal, something tangible to work towards . . . without it, there is no way to measure success (Galda and Graves 2007, 79).

Starting with big picture strategies and then moving on to other strategies that focus on the smaller pieces (details/factual information) or the relationships among ideas (cause/effect connections, inferences, sequence of events, main ideas with supporting evidence) is most practical. If a content-area teacher asks his students to skim the chapter, to do an advance organizer with it, or to use the

PLAN technique as a way of getting the main ideas and subject content, then students will have the foundation for doing a closer analysis of the text as a next step, which means, of course, setting other purposes for reading.

Though these purposes may primarily be teacher-set, it is possible to help students have some choices about how they read, which portions they read, and what they will focus on, depending upon the nature of the classroom instruction (Guthrie 2008). When students have some involvement in the reading plan, their motivation to read increases and their engagement with the content deepens. Descriptions of such methods for ways to help students do this are included throughout this book in the many discussions on strategy implementation.

So how is it that teachers can support students with in-class reading assignments, keeping in mind that readers should read with specific purposes in mind? Providing students with guidance on what information is most important is the starting point. For example, if the events leading up to a battle in a social studies chapter are what the students need to focus on most, then the teacher can ask the students to "chunk" their reading into parts (perhaps relying upon subtitles as stopping points), finding major events and listing them on a timeline as they read. The simple act of building in a stop-and-respond activity with an emphasis upon the events will help readers target the main information; it also "slices the task" for them, reducing the amount of text that students must read and comprehend at a given time (Wood 1986). If the dates of these events are critical for students to recall, students can "scan" back for them later as a second step after listing the events on a timeline so that they are certain to validate their correctness—and help emphasize the dates at the same time.

Suppose that there are several events that require discussion. After having students do the timeline, a teacher can ask them to get into groups and choose one event for each group to discuss and report on to the class. They can then go back to the description and context of the event they have chosen and orally discuss it with their peers. Their goal is to become group experts on the events and then to share that information with their classmates as a jigsaw type of activity. When the students go back into the text to find out everything they can about their selected "event," they have set a new purpose for reading. However, because of the added element of choice in this activity, their purpose is not solely the teacher's.

At one middle school, a science teacher asked his class, composed mainly of English learners, to read what he considered to be an easy, two-page piece of text on volcanic eruptions. He was disappointed when, after giving his students a quiz, he determined that they hadn't even recognized what the selection was mostly about. Yet, if we analyze the text piece (Figure 3–2), we can see why students may have felt challenged by the content. The subtitle of the piece (a level 1 subtitle, because it is positioned under the title of the entire chapter), "Benefits of

From Chapter 8 ("Volcanoes")
Section 3 ("Effects of Volcanic Eruptions")
"Benefits of Volcanic Eruptions"
Pages 280–281
Holt *California Earth Science*, 2007
Holt, Rinehart, and Winston

Benefits of Volcanic Eruptions

Volcanic eruptions present various dangers to humans and to wildlife habitats. But volcanoes also provide benefits to humans and to the environment. These benefits include fertile soils, a renewable energy source, and construction materials.

Volcanic Soils

Volcanic soils are some of the most fertile soils on Earth. Volcanic rocks are made of minerals that contain a wide variety of elements that are important to plant growth. When volcanic rocks break down to form soils, these soils contain nutrients that plants can use. Volcanic soils are heavily farmed in many parts of the world.

Geothermal Energy

Magma heats the rocks that surround it. These rocks often hold water that also becomes heated. This heated water, called *geothermal water*, may reach temperatures of hundreds of degrees Celsius. As a result, the water contains large amounts of heat energy. This energy can be tapped by drilling wells to reach the hot water or by pumping water through the heated rocks. The water can be used to drive turbines that generate electricity, to heat homes, to grow crops, and to keep roads free of ice.

The world's largest producer of geothermal energy is currently the Geysers geothermal power plant, near Santa Rosa, California. The city of San Francisco gets some of its electricity from the Geysers power plant. The world's greatest consumers of geothermal energy are the residents of Reykjavik, Iceland. In Reykjavik, 85% of the homes are heated by geothermal power.

Other Benefits of Volcanic Eruptions

Volcanic rocks are often used in construction. In about 300 BCE, the Romans began to mix volcanic ash from Mount Vesuvius with wet lime to make concrete. This material was used to build the Colosseum in Rome. As recently as the 20th century, volcanic ash was used to make concrete for dams in the United States. Today, basalt and pumice are often used in the construction of roads and bridges and in the production of concrete.

Figure 3–2

(Continues)

Volcanic rocks have many other uses. Volcanic ash absorbs moisture, so it is used in cat litter. Because pumice is abrasive, it is used in small facial scrubs, soaps, cleaners, and polishes. Pumice is also added to soil to allow air and water to circulate more easily through the soil. And because metals in pumice are not water soluble, pumice is used alone or with silica sand to filter drinking water.

Figure 3–2 *(Continued)*

Volcanic Eruptions," contains words that are central to the main point of the selection: *benefits*, *volcanic*, and *eruptions*.

If the teacher does not front-load these concepts, the level 2 subtitles underneath "Benefits of Volcanic Eruptions" will have virtually no meaning for readers. They need to understand that "Volcanic Soils" and "Geothermal Energy" are benefits, or advantages, of volcanic eruptions and that the information under the third subtitle, "Other Benefits of Volcanic Eruptions," will continue to add to this list of positive results. They must also understand *soils* and *geothermal energy* in order to see how the piece is organized logically. "Preteaching some of the most challenging and crucial words in an upcoming selection will foster both vocabulary development and comprehension. Like many sorts of instruction, preteaching vocabulary is important for all students but particularly important for English-language learners" (Galda and Graves 2007, 85).

Certainly, a one-minute video segment of an erupting volcano would help learners internalize the concept of the explosion—and an intensive look at the first introductory paragraph with attention paid to the technical vocabulary would have contributed to higher levels of understanding. Perhaps, then, neither the teacher nor the students would have been so disappointed after the quiz was given.

For the students, the purpose was to get through all of the reading. Maybe some even honestly read the words—but did not actually comprehend them. It is impossible to know what the science teacher's purpose for having them read was because he didn't help them navigate the text or engage them in any type of activity that would emphasize a particular focus or set of major ideas to be taken away from it. When people read to gain information—or "carry away information"—we say that they are reading "efferently" (as contrasted with reading "aesthetically" where the reader is "carried away by feelings evoked by the text" [Gunning 2008, 435]), but no reader can recall everything that he reads, especially on the first attempt.

A growing problem in secondary classrooms is that some teachers, understandably agitated about students' difficulties with texts and the task of covering content standards, are beginning to drop the expectation that learners will read texts at all. It is true that English learners, especially, have a particularly difficult struggle with academic information that is written at grade level in English. Therefore, teachers may decide to read much of the information aloud to the class or to summarize it for them. Vacca and Vacca (2007) point out that students often give up on reading, expecting that teachers will impart information through lecture and recitation. Unfortunately, when they become dependent on teachers as their primary source of information, they do not learn to think and learn with text. So, although teachers may feel better about covering the content, students are not being given support in discovering how texts work and in developing strategies for reading different kinds of texts (Wilhelm, Dube, and Baker 2001, xvii). In addition, they need this guidance in order to succeed in other classes and future endeavors. "We do not help students gain proficiency with academic texts if we avoid using them because we think students won't or can't read them. We need to scaffold with explicit instruction that guides students through comprehension of the text and construction of meaning" (Lewis 2007, 149).

Assessment Purposes for Reading

Perhaps the biggest challenge of all for both students and teachers is the issue of testing. Students, for the most part, simply hunker down and get through them the best they can, taking all kinds of different approaches: doing their absolute best, working hard for a portion of the testing time until they are bored, choosing multiple choice answers that make interesting formations on their response sheets (referred to in our Literacy Center as "drawing Christmas trees"), or simply being absent on the day the testing is scheduled. For their part, teachers bemoan the time taken out of the curriculum for required assessments and worry that their students will not do well, despite their most earnest efforts to teach the required content.

In fact, one of our goals as educators should also be to help students show what they know in testing contexts, at least to the degree that this is possible. Assessment is characterized as "high stakes" because so much depends upon the results: placement of students in different classes or levels, retention decisions, redesignation of English as a second language students from limited English proficient to fluent English proficient, assessment of yearly progress numbers that drive school curricula and influence teacher and student morale, and a myriad of other consequences that occur when assessment data is published. There is no doubt that we are in an era of accountability in which such testing practices are promoted.

To say that we will ignore the assessment process is irresponsible. Tests exist, affecting teachers, schools, our students, and their families in many ways, and we need to face them head on. I am certainly not an advocate of standardized, norm-referenced testing—in fact, I agree with Kohn (2000) who states, "The only thing at which standardized tests are uniquely efficient is ranking one school, or state, against another" (41). In fact, I shudder when our Literacy Center tutors have to explain to parents that Johanna or Ramir is testing at the 17th percentile in reading comprehension, vocabulary, or phonics; all we are doing when using such numbers is indicating that the child is doing worse than 83 percent of the rest of the students at his grade level nationally. What help does this provide parents, the students, or even ourselves in supporting learners to become more proficient? We have to move further with analyzing data, looking to see what skills and strategies students need to develop as they move toward proficiency. Stanines and percentiles on standardized, norm-referenced tests do not tell us this; they are simply used for ranking purposes. Instead, gaining information from informal assessment instruments will help us serve students better because we can more specifically identify areas of strength (which need to be built upon), as well as weaknesses (target areas of instruction). In Chapter 8, we will discuss options for carrying out a variety of these kinds of assessment practices within classroom settings.

However, I also want students to do as well as they can when it is time to demonstrate what they know. When they put forth effort throughout the school year and then feel confused by test questions that presumably measure what they know, morale drops when the test is, as Irina—a center eighth grader—put it, "still too hard." If we think about what "reading" looks like in a testing context, we realize that once again, students' strategies for reading are different from personal or professional reading and perhaps even from class reading behaviors. Test takers are given selections to read, followed by questions that represent many different purposes for reading—not just one or two. If I am asked to read a passage and find the main idea of paragraph two (one purpose for reading), then I need to look for the topic sentence of paragraph two. Hopefully, if the topic sentence makes sense to me and the details that support it are well written, then I may also recall an important detail that is also embedded in that paragraph at the end of the piece. If I can't remember it, then I need to *scan* back to find the answer, using another reading strategy that matches a second purpose for reading.

Perhaps I will also be instructed to determine the meaning of a new word as it is used in the selection (as in Figure 3–3). Chances are that as I read that word, I bring to bear what I know about its possible meaning, but the meanings of words change as their contexts do, which is an especially difficult obstacle to overcome

---

Typical question on a norm-referenced, standardized test:

Directions: Choose the meaning of the italicized word as it is used in the sentence below:

Because pumice is abrasive, it is used in facial scrubs, soaps, *cleaners*, and polishes.
- a. a person employed to clean the interior of a building
- b. a commercial establishment for cleaning clothes
- c. a device or substance for cleaning
- d. a candidate who wins an election

Figure 3–3

for an English learner. Even though I may think that *cleaner* means "someone who cleans" when I first see the word (Figure 3–2, last paragraph), I realize that I may need to go back to see how it is being used in its specific context in case the meaning is different from my expectation. This is a third purpose for reading that I need to set for one passage, in one test, on possibly even just one page, in just a few minutes.

Such bombardment of information (for which many of our English learners do not have sufficient background knowledge), coupled with multiple purposes for reading, which are determined by the test makers (not the test takers), poses a severe challenge to our students. It is no wonder that they are frustrated with the assessment process. As teachers, remembering what it felt like to take state-mandated norm-referenced standardized tests for the teaching profession, we may recall that it was more than likely exasperating because we were trying to second-guess the question askers. We were not reading for information to meet personal objectives but rather reading to get the answers right so that we would be told that we could move on to the next step in our lives. This is not an authentic behavior, to be sure. Unfortunately, due to time and budget constraints (and much political maneuvering), standardized norm-referenced tests have become the instruments of choice for assessments that are supposed to "show what we know."

A major difficulty arises with the assumption that test questions can even accurately reflect the constructs of reading (Miller, Linn, and Gronlund 2009). It is not probable that they can even begin to approximate the complex processes a reader engages in during reading because the questions, by virtue of being multiple choice, can only represent "known answers" (Afflerbach 2007, 52). That is to say, they must follow the initiate-respond-evaluate discourse form. This model was set up to describe classroom processes in which the teacher *initiates* classroom talk by asking questions, students *respond* to the questions, and the teacher *evaluates* students' responses. Of course, the teacher already has in mind what the array of possible correct answers might be, so students are trying to figure out how to match their responses to the teacher's expectation. This practice occurs frequently, but as Afflerbach (2007) points out, the questions focus primarily on literal comprehension of text. He notes, "It is not that such comprehension is not important—it is critical. It is that failure to move beyond such understanding with our questions is a missed opportunity, to both promote and evaluate students' more complex thinking" (52). Certainly standardized tests adhere to the initiate-respond-evaluate principle, not allowing for short responses or elaborated answers of any kind and severely limiting the possibility of capturing the meaning-making process that occurs when one reads.

Once we acknowledge that norm-referenced, standardized tests in their present form cannot sufficiently measure complex thinking, we need to move on to what we need to do to help our students become proficient readers and complex thinkers within the classroom. We should keep in mind, though, that as students develop more flexible reading approaches and stronger metacognitive abilities through the demonstration and application of explicit comprehension strategies, students will be more likely to do better on test questions that measure many, but certainly not all, of the skills good readers possess. "We should advocate an emphasis on test wisdom, where students receive integrated practice throughout the school year" (Fisher and Frey 2008, 208). This will occur as teachers focus on students' development of academic language and reading strategy instruction within content-area classes. Teaching literacy strategies for access to the core curriculum is the primary goal, as opposed to "teaching to the test"; however, there are substantial connections between these kinds of effective instructional approaches and higher levels of student success in the testing arena.

Snapshots

This test doesn't understand me.

Figure 3–4

Professional Purposes for Reading

When working with secondary students, it is not unusual to find that many of them have part-time jobs that call for some level of literacy. They are employed at such places as McDonald's, Cold Stone Creamery, Chili's, T.J. Maxx, movie theaters, grocery stores, and various offices and businesses in the community. If we were to ask them what reading and writing skills they need for their jobs, we would probably be surprised by the quizzical looks they might give us. What do jobs have to do with reading and writing? After all, those are school tasks.

However, Elsie, a student from our center who now works at PETCO, tells me that new employees there are required to take what they call "animal tests." That is, hirees are given books on dogs, cats, and small animals (such as hamsters, guinea pigs, chinchillas, and rabbits) and then tested on the information within a month of their employee start dates. The test contains about eighty multiple choice items. Personnel who do not pass it are given one more opportunity to do so prior to completing six months of employment with the company. The books also contain guidelines for customer assistance, to which employees are expected to adhere in their everyday interactions at the store, so their knowledge of the content is authentically assessed on a daily basis by their supervisors.

In addition, if employees are interested in becoming "specialists" at the store (which allows them to attain a higher status in the company and earn financial bonuses), they are given six books on a category of their choice (aquatics, birds, small animals, or reptiles) and have to pass another exam in their chosen area of specialization. Even I was surprised to hear how much reading is entailed in this job! Some students find the idea of working at such a store enticing because of their love of animals, but I'm sure that most of them would be truly amazed at the high level of literacy that is actually required for the job.

Greg, another student from our Literacy Center who just recently graduated from high school, has secured a job at Trader Joe's. He tells me that Trader Joe employees have to read the bulletin that is printed once a week by the company, which contains information about new and old products, discontinued items, and descriptive facts about specific foods. If a customer asks for additional information, staff members also need to be able to go online on the computer to check the status of items, including times and dates of product arrivals, as well as prices. If an employee is on the "demo team," the group that cooks food items for customers as in-store taste samples, he has to read the ingredients on the packages, follow the cooking instructions, and help customers with ideas for substitutions of ingredients if they are lactose intolerant, have high blood pressure, are vegan, or simply are not fond of a particular food substance.

Employees at Trader Joe's are also asked to read pamphlets on the history, mottos, and credo of Trader Joe's and be able to discuss the company's philosophy in depth. Every employee is reviewed orally on a six-month basis, at which time their reactions to Trader Joe perspectives are monitored. A written review is then provided, and Greg says that employees "had better be able to read their reviews. Otherwise, they won't know if they still have jobs!"

All of these positions require employees to be able to read and comprehend information in order to be successful at their jobs. Yet, what they are asked to do is different from one task to another. Therefore, they use the strategies that best suit their needs. For example, Elsie said that she read the introductory paragraphs on each type of animal before choosing to read the rest. Later, when she had a better idea of the scope of the information, she went back and read it all. Eventually, she used a highlighter to mark important details that she thought would be on the multiple-choice test, based on the information her more seasoned coworkers had given her. Greg indicated that he didn't read anything "all the way through" when he was looking for customer information (he was *scanning*), but that he was sure to read all the subtitles on the weekly bulletin first before going back and reading it more thoroughly so that he could identify the specials for the week. It is interesting that these adolescents were able to figure out the best way to meet the demands of their jobs, but they both said that when they were in high school, they defaulted to the position of reading everything the same way, from beginning to end. They didn't realize that there was more than one way to approach reading. It seems that we would be doing students an enormous service if we began teaching them how to match purposes to strategies before they got out of school.

Commentary

This chapter has focused on different kinds of general purposes for reading—personal, academic, and professional—and the need for instructors to help students learn literacy strategies that match selected purposes for reading so that students will be prepared to read and write in many different contexts.

The primary goal is for students to become flexible readers, learners who know how to meet the literacy demands of any given situation, drawing from a repertoire of strategy choices to reach those objectives. Clearly, it is ideal if secondary teachers can demonstrate a wide scope of methods within their content areas. In the next chapter, we will look at explicit instructional strategies for the identification and recall of basic details, along with suggestions for concept development prior to reading. As Minskoff (2005) remarks, "A knowledgeable, competent, relentless teacher is key to success for teaching reading" (26).

4

The Devil Is in the Details

Teaching Students to Recognize and Recall What Matters Most

There are numerous explicit literacy strategies that can easily be implemented in content-area, language arts, and English as a second language (ESL) classrooms. The key to effective instruction is to help students set purposes for reading and then to model and demonstrate strategies for meeting those purposes that students can apply as they develop over time into independent readers. Teachers need to have a clear idea of the strategy components and how to demonstrate them to learners in a scaffolded manner, using longer and more difficult selections over time with gradually less teacher support.

Scaffolding not only means guiding students' learning but also "helping them to become comfortable with a wide variety of content text and organizational structures" (Irvin, Buehl, and Klemp 2007, 91). When learners experience how teacher support with specific strategies can boost their comprehension of challenging text materials, they begin to see themselves as capable of interacting with text—as being readers. "Effective instruction contributes to the development of students' reading skills and strategies, motivation, commitment to reading, and to students' broadening conceptualization of reading as contributing to success in life" (Afflerbach 2007, 7).

The comprehension process is a transaction between reader and text, in which readers construct mental representations of the text by using their existing knowledge, along with the application of flexible strategies with that purpose in mind (Rupley and Willson 1997). Therefore, if a reader is interested in getting the overview, or the big picture, of a magazine article, she may choose to read the title, the subtitles, and perhaps even the first sentence of each paragraph—before she decides whether to read the whole article (or she may just read the topic sentences, as I do, to identify the key points!). In the same way, teaching strategies should focus on reading as an authentic process, keeping in mind that readers highlight different information for themselves as they read, based on their individual purposes for reading.

The objective is to teach students to access many different kinds of information, by becoming good at such comprehension processes as (but not limited to) *recall of details, identification of main ideas, understanding of chronological order* of events as opposed to sequential order (order of the telling, or presentation, in the text), *analysis of cause-effect* relationships, ability to *make inferences* based on textual clues, and *use of context clues* to determine the meaning of unknown or difficult vocabulary.

Such processes are often put into place when questions are raised. Sometimes teachers pose these questions; sometimes they are presented at the ends of chapters or on quizzes and tests; but ideally, learners who are reading actively ask them (Pilgreen 2006). Fortunately, texts typically contain identifiable key words, labels that come from the pool of academic language, which direct readers to the metacognitive use of an appropriate strategy (or strategies) that can used to answer them. A beginning step for content areas is to help students answer detail questions correctly. Not only is the process for answering questions an authentic one that we all use in our everyday lives, but it is also one that students need to use in school in order to find many answers to questions quickly and accurately.

Starting with Detail Questions

When asking students the most basic questions about stories and texts, teachers take for granted that students know how to answer the "easy" questions. Detail questions, which begin with *WH* words (words that start with *w* or *h*, such as *who, what, when, where, why,* and *how*), are frequently asked during class and listed at the ends of chapters. In teacher preparation courses, educators learn that these kinds of questions are at the bottom of Bloom's taxonomy at the level of recall. Teachers may consciously attempt to avoid using too many detail questions so that they can aspire to asking questions that represent a higher level of critical thinking, therefore not modeling for students how to answer the easier ones. However,

English learners need these demonstrations, because they often confuse the *WH* words and have not had as much time to acquire their structures and meaning as their fluent English-speaking counterparts. Also, detail questions still abound in academic contexts, as well as in real life (e.g., When did the Revolutionary War begin? How much does my favorite dessert on this menu cost? How long will it take for this Internet company to ship me the item?), so it is important that these questions are not left out of the instructional agenda.

◎ *Visual Support*

As we saw in Chapter 2, it is important to provide students with the *WH* words that are contained in detail questions (Figure 2–5). The practice of using the illustrations to match the *WH* words has been effective for us in the Literacy Center. By linking icons that match the detail questions (provided in Appendix B), we have found that our English learners are doing better at answering detail questions correctly. They are able to visualize what the answer should look like, as soon as they see the question. The link between the exact *WH* word and an appropriate answer is made much faster and with a higher degree of accuracy when students first practice answering questions using the *WH* words with such support.

In our Literacy Center, we have reproduced multiple copies of the graphic in Appendix B and laminated them. Whenever students participate in questioning activities—or use the scanning strategy (explained next)—they have these illustrations beside them to help remind them of what the *WH* words are asking and the form the answers should take. This is our way of avoiding the confusion that comes from our often mistaken assumption that students can already differentiate among the *WH* word meanings. (See Figure 4–1.)

◎ *Scanning*

Along with using a pictorial aid, teachers can model how to *scan* effectively. Scanning is not really reading, in the true sense of the word; it is searching quickly (running

Figure 4–1

one's eyes over the page) to locate target information. For example, if a person wants to know someone's telephone number, he must first recognize that he will be looking for a set of numbers and then think about how the information is organized—in this case, alphabetically by name. So, he focuses on the person's last name and searches until he can finally zero in on the exact name and number. The procedure for scanning is listed in Figure 4–2.

After the teacher models these steps a number of times, students do the procedure in groups, then in pairs, and finally individually, Vygotskian-style (1978). The teacher works with the students until they have internalized the task and can carry it out on their own. Once they feel comfortable, the teacher raises the bar and, as Valencia and Riddle Buly (2004) recommend, asks students to apply the procedure often, using different types and levels of materials throughout the school year. Students might utilize the scanning strategy with the "Decline and Fall of the Empire" passage in Figure 4–3.

To answer the first question, students look at the *WH* word (*when*), visualize what the answer looks like (*a time*), find key words in the question (*empire, stop, expanding*), notice that the writing is organized in a *narrative format* (story-like), and scan for the answer (*second century* AD). In the same way, to answer the second question, students look at the *WH* word (*who*), visualize what the answer looks like (*person, group of people*), find key words in the question (*desperate, growing expenses*), recall that the writing is organized in a *narrative format*, and scan

---

The Scanning Procedure

Scanning is *locating target information quickly*, such as when you need to find a date in a TV guide or a name in a phone directory. It is also frequently used to identify dates, statistics, and short pieces of information in textbooks, reference materials, charts/graphs, and other numerous kinds of sources.

The scanning procedure includes these steps:

- selection of the *target information* you need
- identification of specific *question words* (who, what, when, where, etc.)
- visualization of the *answer format* (person, thing, time, place, etc.)
- identification of *key words in the question* you are asking
- determination of where the answer will probably be located in the reading
- a quick search to *find* the target information

Figure 4–2

World History, 2006
McDougal Littell
"Medieval and Early Modern Times"
Chapter 2, Lesson 2, pp. 53–54
"Decline and Fall of the Empire"

Decline and Fall of the Empire

Internal Weaknesses Threaten Rome

Late in the second century AD, Rome began to decline. The empire still appeared as strong as ever to most who lived under its control. Yet a series of internal problems had begun that would put mighty Rome on the road to ruin.

Economic and Social Difficulties

During the second century AD, the empire stopped expanding. The end of new conquests meant an end to new sources of wealth. Officials grew desperate to pay the empire's growing expenses, including the rising cost of maintaining its army. As a result, the government raised taxes. This caused a hardship for many citizens.

Other aspects of Roman society suffered as well. For example, many poor Romans found it harder to become educated—as the cost of education grew out of reach. In addition, distributing news across the large empire became more difficult. As a result, people grew less informed about civic matters.

Decline in Agriculture

A decline in agriculture also weakened the empire. Throughout Italy and western Europe the soil had become difficult to farm due to constant warfare and overuse. As a result, harvests grew increasingly weak.

The use of slave labor added to the problem. Like other societies throughout history, the Romans practiced slavery. The slaves were mainly war captives who were forced to work in the fields. The use of slave labor discouraged improvements in technology that might have improved farming. As Roman agriculture suffered, disease and hunger spread and the population declined.

Military and Political Problems

Meanwhile, Rome's once powerful military began showing signs of trouble. Over time, Roman soldiers in general became less disciplined and loyal. They pledged their allegiance not to Rome, but to individual military leaders.

Figure 4–3

(Continues)

Feelings of loyalty eventually declined among average citizens as well. In the past, Romans eagerly engaged in civic duties and public affairs. Roman politics, however, grew increasingly corrupt. Politicians became more interested in financial gain than in public service. As a result, many citizens lost their sense of pride in the government. They no longer showed a willingness to sacrifice for the good of Rome.

Scanning Questions for Economic and Social Difficulties *Passage:*
1. *When* did the *empire stop expanding*?
2. *Who* grew *desperate* to pay *growing expenses*?
3. *What* meant an *end* to *new sources* of *wealth*?
4. *Why* did the *Romans* who were *poor* find it *harder* to become *educated*?

Figure 4–3 *(Continued)*

for the answer (*officials*). Students follow the procedure again to answer other similar, detail questions, such as numbers 3 and 4 in the example.

In my experience, the step most frequently missed by students is the fourth one: identification of *key words* in the question. If they understand the kind of response that is needed (a person, a place, a time, etc.), they may still not be able to narrow down the textual area where the answer will most likely be found. Teachers should encourage students to be sure that, in addition to using any available subtitles, they identify other key words in the questions *before* they jump into the text to find the answers they are seeking. After all, there can be many *who*s or *what*s or *why*s in a selection—but only one of them represents the correct answer to a specific question.

One suggestion is that teachers can ask students to underline the *WH* words before they begin the scanning process; then they use a highlighter to mark the possible key words in the rest of the question (italicized in the questions in Figure 4–3). It does not matter how many key words students mark. What is important is that they use those words in the scanning process to determine the correct location of the answer. I usually ask students to read the sentence that the key words are in, plus the ones before it and after it. That way, they can feel fairly certain that that they have found right area to locate the information they are seeking.

Having a handle on how to locate specific information in reading is very important for English learners who are overwhelmed by large pieces of text, especially older students who are faced with long assignments to read. Researchers have found that English learners do not perform very well in the classroom or on state assessments because of their unfamiliarity with academic language (Abedi, Lord,

Hofstetter, and Baker 2000). However, focusing on important details through the use of the scanning procedure gives them a concrete way to learn about detail questions and practice finding target information in any context when they cannot recall the facts they have read. The answers to such questions are "usually located verbatim" (Fisher and Frey 2008, 105) so students have an opportunity to get them right and feel successful right from the start. For English learners, such support is critical, as they are struggling with the language at the same time that they are learning the skill.

◎ *Read and Run*

An interactive and stimulating way for students to practice finding the answers to detail questions is to have them participate in "read and run." This activity, developed by Helgeson (1993), puts a competitive twist on the process of scanning. Students work in pairs, and instead of having the text pieces in front of them, excerpts are placed on the walls by the teacher. Posting copies on all four walls is helpful so that students do not crowd around in one area. Using enlarged, laminated copies of the text selections is recommended, but if that is a financial luxury, smaller copies will do.

If we chose two text passages from the text we used to teach scanning in Figure 4–3, we could not only extend students' content knowledge of the weaknesses that threatened Rome but also give them an interactive opportunity to apply their scanning skills. We can assign the passage under the level 2 subtitle "Decline in Agriculture" to one partner and the passage under the level 2 subtitle "Military and Political Problems" to the other. The idea is for the students to take turns running to the wall after having circled the *WH* words on their response sheets and highlighting other key words to target for scanning.

Partner A looks at the first scanning question on the response sheet (which would relate only to the passage on "Decline in Agriculture") and "runs" to the wall to find the answer, after which she returns and orally shares the answer with her partner. If any explanation is necessary, the partners talk about the answer, and then each of them writes it on their own response sheets. Partner B would do the same for the first question related only to the passage on "Military and Political Problems." With information from partner B, partner A would then answer the second question for her passage, and so on. In this way, partners alternate looking at the questions and then scanning for the answers on the wall. Figure 4–4 shows the kind of response sheet that can be used for read and run with these two passages.

As well as helping students learn to find answers to detail questions, this activity promotes collaboration, lowers the affective filter, emphasizes key vocabulary

Read and Run with Passage from "Decline and Fall of the Empire"

15 Points Possible
2 points per question (12 total)
1, 2, or 3 points for collaboration/respectful interaction

Partner A (Name _____)

Decline in Agriculture
1. *Why* had the soil in Italy and western Europe become difficult to farm?
2. *What* discouraged improvements in technology?
3. Mainly, *who* were the slaves?

Partner B (Name _____)

Military and Political Problems
1. To *whom* did Roman soldiers pledge their allegiance?
2. *Why* did Roman politics become increasingly corrupt?
3. *What* did many citizens lose?

Score

_____/12 (correct answers to questions)

_____/3 (credit for collaboration/respectful interaction—*up to 3 points* given by teacher)

> Total Possible: _____/15
>
> *2–4 OK!*
> *6–8 Good Start!*
> *10–12 Nice Job!*
> *13–14 Great Job!*
> *15 Terrific!*

Figure 4–4

and concepts in the text (building content schemata), and encourages the development of oral language skills. Because answers are completed on both students' papers by the end of the activity, there is a purpose for reading—that is, *scanning*—because each pair typically wants to have a perfect score, and their answers must be exactly the same. One optional component to this activity is to give collaboration points to pairs who work especially well together and with peers in the class. Because the idea of read and run sparks energetic responses from students, it is important to set some ground rules before beginning the activity. There should be polite interactions at all times (without any pushing, shoving, or elbowing aside), and voices should be kept low and controlled. Students who adhere to the guidelines can earn extra points, simply for their classroom courtesy and respect toward one another, as shown at the bottom of Figure 4–4.

In the Literacy Center, we give as many as 3 extra points for how the students interact, so they are typically motivated to follow the guidelines. We feel that positive interactions among students are critical and that when they practice respectful behaviors, they are learning important messages about how people should behave not only within the classroom, but outside of it as well.

Teachers who do "read and run" often note that there is a high level of interaction and also a strong probability of seeing smiles and hearing laughter, as students seem to enjoy this activity for its gamelike quality. Most students find that they are successful at scanning once they understand how to do it effectively— and the knowledge that they can find answers in connected text is validating for them, particularly if they are English learners who are used to being lost in the language.

One way to scaffold this activity is to allow students, especially English learners, to take the scanning questions to the wall with them when they are searching for the target information. As they become better at scanning, the support of having questions directly in front of them as they scan can be withdrawn. Each student can run to the wall with her assigned question in mind, thinking about the key words that she should look for to find the target answer. Another scaffolding method is, at first, to allow all students with correct final answers to become the "winners," but later as students hone their abilities to scan, include a requirement to finish within a prescribed period of time. A last suggestion is to embed the *WH* words into the middle of the questions as students find that scanning is becoming easier. In question number 3 for partner A in Figure 4–4, the *WH* word is not at the very beginning of the question, but rather, is the second word. Questions can also start with a prepositional phrases or clause, in which case the *WH* word is positioned even further away from the beginning of the sentence, which makes the scanning task more difficult—and more authentic as an example of real-world question types. For example, in this sentence, the *WH* word is placed in the middle: As Roman soldiers became less disciplined and loyal, to *whom* did they pledge their allegiance? Teachers would not want to begin teaching scanning by embedding the *WH* words in the middle of the question, but as students become more skilled with the process, it is logical to use questions with more difficult syntax.

Social studies teachers in a summer institute sponsored by the California Subject Matter Project and the National Geographic Alliance participated in this activity, making the observation that it would be more fun for partners to go to the wall together in order to be sure of answering each question correctly. They also noted that the affective filter of English learners would be lowered considerably with such a twist. However, they thoroughly enjoyed the cooperative aspect of having students move around and rely upon each other for support.

During the implementation of the activity, the institute program administrator, Janice Hamner, noted that this activity is technically mislabeled *read and run*: She commented, "It should be called *skip and scan* because students cannot really 'run' in a classroom setting—and besides, they don't really 'read' for the answers—they scan!" She was emphasizing the idea that academic terminology matters. Since then, our staff development participants always hear about the secondary title of *skip and scan*, with all due respect given to the author of the original activity!

◎ *Cloze Procedure*

The cloze procedure is a second technique for helping students identify and recall details. Students are first asked to read a selected passage of text. Next, the full passage is removed, and they must then fill in a new version of the text with deleted words. The task is for them to insert the correct words into the blanks in order for the passage to be accurate and make sense.

Originally developed by Taylor (1953), the cloze procedure was used as a method of testing reading comprehension. If a reader completed a specific percentage of the blanks correctly, it was said that he could "read" the text at a specific reading level. However, more recently cloze has been used by content-area teachers to highlight unfamiliar, confusing, or important technical vocabulary. Although cloze-type materials are available commercially from publishing companies, "teachers often produce the most effective cloze passages because they are in the best position to gear the material to the needs of their students" (Vacca and Vacca 2007, 230).

When we use the cloze procedure in our Literacy Center, each teacher determines what content words should be omitted, depending upon his student's prior knowledge and language proficiency level. For English learners, the selected vocabulary should represent some concepts for which the student has schema and some for which he does not. The job of the tutor is to activate the learner's prior knowledge for the content he does know and to develop it for the new content. Omitted information can include new vocabulary, names, dates, and technical concepts (such as *photosynthesis*). In ESL and English classes, sometimes examples of parts of speech are deleted, such as verbs, prepositions, and articles. As discussed in Chapter 1, there are a variety of linguistic and nonlinguistic ways for teachers to provide contextualization, or support, for new concepts and terms, and this should be done before students do any reading at all.

Fortunately, the steps for creating a cloze activity are fairly easy but not technologically challenging. Here are the steps involved:

1. The teacher determines which words from a text piece to omit.

2. Using a bottle of correction fluid and a ruler, the words are deleted on a copy of the text piece (cloze version), which can be put onto an overhead transparency or photocopied for each student (to be used after the reading has occurred).

3. After activation and development of students' schema for the deleted words, the teacher gives students the full passage to read.

4. The students then fill in the blanks with the correct words using the cloze version of the passage.

When beginning the process with English learners, it is helpful to provide them with a word bank, or list of the deleted words, as they attempt to insert the words into context. Later, when they feel more confident with the procedure, the word bank can be removed.

This procedure is excellent for students who need additional support with specific content details or word forms, and it leads to success if the teacher is careful about the choice and length of the text passage and the number of the terms to be deleted. However, it does not take into consideration reader variables such as schema, interest, and knowledge of content vocabulary, so teachers must take the time to prepare learners for the activity. It is a method that measures how well students can comprehend a selection based on how they interact with the reading materials. "Closure" takes place when the reader is able to supply enough of the deleted words to understand the passage. As Sejnost and Thiese (2006) note, as students move through a cloze passage in which they are reading actively, thinking, and filling in blanks appropriately, they must make use of their prior knowledge and manipulate their knowledge of content-based vocabulary.

If teachers wanted to present the passage in Figure 4–5 to their students, for example, they would need to determine the proficiency levels of their students and the difficulty of the content, in general, before deciding how many blanks and which terms to include in the word bank, or set of target words.

In a classroom with English learners who are not yet at an intermediate or advanced level, this narrative text might be extremely difficult for a number of reasons: first, there are common words (conversational words, as opposed to

Take Me Out to the Ball Game!

Background

A ball game called *pok-a-tok* was played in most Meso-American civilizations. This game seemed to have special significance for the Maya. It was hugely popular, and the Maya treated the best players like heroes. The great players also grew rich from the game. But fame and riches came at a price. Some Mayan inscriptions suggest that members of the losing team were sacrificed. As you read the following story, imagine that you're Mayan ballplayer about to step onto the *pok-a-tok* court.

The crowd goes wild when you and other players step onto the stone court. Only nobles like you can play. You wear your finest jewelry and a headdress made of bright parrot feathers.

Sometimes you play the game as a sport. At other times, like today, you play for religious reasons. In these special games, you and your fellow ballplayers act out an ancient battle between the gods of the day and the night. Today the stakes are high. The losing captain pays with his life. His blood ensures that the gods will continue to let the sun shine. Without the sun, the crops will die. Without food, the Mayan people will die too.

Figure 4–5

content-area technical vocabulary) that are "uncommon" to English learners, such as *crowd*, *religious*, and *ensures*. Second, there are a number of idiomatic expressions that cannot be literally translated, such as and *goes wild* and *pays with his life*. Next, there are words that have multiple meanings that readers must define through context, such as *court* in paragraph 1, meaning *playing area*, and *stakes* in paragraph 2, meaning *risk*. In short, though this passage is part of a story that may be required at a middle school grade level, it is beyond the scope of what many English learners can handle. Therefore, using a cloze procedure might be one way to introduce the story and provide students with background knowledge for some of the language that could cause confusion. Of course, the first step is for the teacher to determine what to focus upon. He can choose a combination of potentially problematic words, or he can highlight a specific category of words, such as those mentioned above (e.g., idioms, multiple meaning words). Then, once the words have been chosen, it is the teacher's responsibility to present them in a way that makes them come alive for the students before they read the text piece.

Let's assume that nouns (including multiple meaning words) are the focus for a lesson using a history selection entitled "Take Me Out to the Ball Game," a piece about the *pok-a-tok* game played by the Maya. In this case, the teacher might choose some or all of the nouns and put them into a word bank such as the one in Figure 4–6.

Terms like those in Figure 4–6 lend themselves well to role-playing or acting out as a way of defining them. After the teacher demonstrates each one through photos or illustrations, perhaps, students could be divided into groups and secretly assigned one term per group. Then, students in each group would determine how they want to act out the term they have received. For example, one group could model putting on "jewelry" and strutting around; another might act out a "battle" with peers. After a bit of practice time (lowering the affective filter), students can act out their term (using nonlinguistic contextualization) while their classmates try to guess which one it is. Of course, as students participate in this activity, they are also building their background knowledge for the reading to come, so all of the ABCs are included at once.

When everyone feels comfortable with the language, the text passage can be distributed. For this selection, it would be logical for the teacher to read the background paragraph in Figure 4–5, or introduction, aloud. Because the students now have some knowledge of the new vocabulary and have been provided with an overview of the content from the introduction, they can read the next chunk of the text piece (paragraphs one and two) quietly in pairs or silently. Upon completion of the reading, the teacher provides learners with a copy of the same passage, this one containing cloze blanks where the terms originally occurred in the story, as illustrated in Figure 4–7. They then try to recreate the terms from memory—or use the word bank for support. If there are additional chunks to complete, students may then continue using the cloze procedure in the same way. To their own amazement, students often find that they are quite successful with the cloze method—and certainly enjoy it (and learn more vocabulary from

Word Bank	
players	crowd
crops	blood
people	jewelry
court	stakes
battle	sport

Figure 4–6

Cloze Passage

The _____ goes wild when you and other _____ step onto the stone _____. Only nobles like you can play. You wear your finest _____ and a headdress made of bright parrot feathers.

   Sometimes you play the game as a _____. At other times, like today, you play for religious reasons. In these special games, you and your fellow ballplayers act out an ancient _____ between the gods of the day and the night. Today the _____ are high. The losing captain pays with his life. His _____ ensures that the gods will continue to let the sun shine. Without the sun, the _____ will die. Without food, the Mayan _____ will die too.

Figure 4–7

it) more than looking up definitions in a dictionary that they will immediately forget.

A word bank for this passage may look similar to Figure 4–6, or it may be much more limited (or expanded). If this is a group's first attempt at the cloze procedure, fewer words should probably be emphasized. For an intermediate-level group that has been practicing the procedure over a period of time, however, it may be appropriate to use a longer set of terms from a bigger chunk of text. The true test is whether students have problems creating closure, or making meaning, by filling in the blanks. If they do, then the teacher knows that more time should be spent on developing vocabulary and concepts before students are asked to read any other parts of the text.

Scaffolding this strategy over time would consist of using longer passages as the year progresses, choosing a greater number of words for each word bank, selecting more difficult words, moving from group or paired work to individual work, and taking away the word bank as a support during the filling in of the cloze blanks. Another technique is to match the length of the cloze blank to the length of each word or expression in the beginning but to make the blanks exactly the same length later, even though they may represent words or expressions that do not fit perfectly in the spaces.

◎ Story Impressions

A prelude to the cloze procedure—or a separate activity entirely—can be students' participation in "story impressions" (McGinley and Denner 1987). Essentially, students put specific content vocabulary words together to "predict" what a real text may include. The focus on concept development is the same as in the cloze procedure where specific terms are targeted, but the activity ends in a writing assignment prior to the reading of the actual text piece.

Figure 4–8 includes another word bank for the last part of the narrative on "Take Me Out to the Ball Game." In order to develop the word bank, the teacher first identified words, including a wide variety of verbs that would help to tell the story plot, and then front-loaded the concepts and terms. Before actually reading the story excerpt, students were asked to use the words from the word bank to put the ideas together as part of a prediction strategy for thinking about what events they thought the biographical sketch might contain. Note that in this case, the terms in the word bank are listed in the exact order in which they occur in the text excerpt. This is so that students have an easier task of putting the words together in a logical story format when they predict the text.

In order to scaffold the activity (because this was a first attempt for the students), the teacher also orally told the class some basic information about the point of the Mayan game prior to giving directions to develop a story from the word bank. One student's story impression activity is illustrated in Figure 4–9.

We can see from her attempt to predict the narrative that she was right about a significant number of the events in the plot. Although she had to think ahead to how it might unfold, given the vocabulary pieces she was given to start with, she did an excellent job of making up a text that made sense. When she finally read the text excerpt, she was surprised by how much information she had correctly predicted—and then focused on the elements that she had not anticipated, emphasizing and reinforcing the actual events in the original text, as indicated in Figure 4–10.

Word Bank

teammates	play	victory
ring	control	death
padding	knee	sun
breath	chest	Maya

Figure 4–8

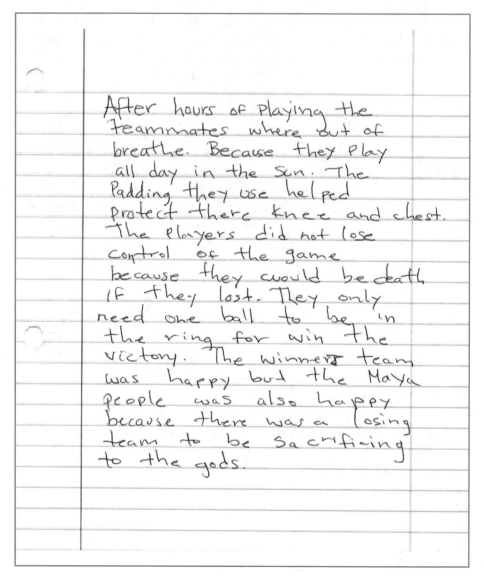

After hours of Playing the teammates where out of breathe. Because they Play all day in the Sun. The Padding they use helped protect there knee and chest. The Players did not lose control of the game because they cwould be death if they lost. They only need one ball to be in the ring for win the victory. The winners team was happy but the Maya people was also happy because there was a losing team to be Sacrificing to the gods.

Figure 4–9   *Student Sample—Story Impressions*

This strategy can be especially powerful if pairs or groups write stories, which are shared orally with the rest of the class. The strength of story impressions comes from the repetition of the target words in context and the focus on meaning making. When the teacher front-loads the terms, the students are exposed to new vocabulary; then they write stories and share them aloud, creating additional opportunities to hear the words used in slightly different—but still meaningful—contexts.

To win, you and your teammates must shoot rubber balls through a stone ring. But this isn't easy. The ring hangs some 20 feet over your head. The solid rubber ball weighs over 5 pounds. And you can't use your hands or your feet. You must hit the ball off padding on your hips, wrists, elbows, chest, or waist.

You take a breath and start to play. After a really long time, your team finally takes control of the ball. As the ball flies your way, you drop to one knee and use your chest to force it through the stone ring. Victory is yours!

Once again the Mayan people have cheated death. The blood of the defeated captain will keep the sun shining. You wonder, will the Maya always be so fortunate?

Figure 4–10

By the time the original text piece is read, there have been multiple opportunities for students to hear the vocabulary used orally, so the words are more recognizable during the reading process. This approach to reading, where writing is done first, reinforces the concept that reading and writing are reciprocal processes. As students read more examples of good writing, their own writing will mirror some of the structures they have experienced, which in turn results in their ability to predict text more accurately.

Sarah, a college junior at the university who is a student worker in the Literacy Center, tried the story impressions activity described here to see how closely her version would match the original story, which she read after she created her own. When I asked her if she thought it was a valuable activity for understanding the events in a story, she said, "Wow, you see what you wrote but then you read what the real events are—and you remember them better because of what you didn't know before. It really makes an impression on you!" I laughed and said that the strategy was properly named, then, since it is called *story impressions*.

Commentary

When students use a combination of academic language and strategy implementation, the probability is substantially higher that they will be able to demonstrate their content-area knowledge and literacy proficiency however it is asked of them, even in testing contexts. Being able to recognize and recall important details is an ability required of all students in every content-area classroom. These details, however, have very specific roles to play, linking up to main (or comprehensive) ideas in reading selections. When students understand how the smaller pieces connect with the larger overriding ideas, they have a solid perspective for comprehending the piece thoroughly and for a longer period of time.

In the next chapter, specific strategies for associating important details with main ideas will be addressed. Through modeling and demonstration during class instruction, teachers can provide learners with the tools they need to access content that is difficult for them. Then "with practice and experience, strategies are likely to become habitual and automatic" (Graves, Juel, and Graves 2007, 273).

5

What's the Big Idea?

Teaching Students to Distinguish Main Ideas from Supporting Details

W hen people read, if they are reading actively, they notice relationships among ideas, not just isolated facts and details. Depending upon why they are reading, they may pay attention to main ideas and supporting details, causes and effects, sequences of events, or any number of combinations of ideas. If readers are seeking answers to questions, whether posed by others or by themselves, then their purposes for reading automatically match the kinds of questions that are asked.

In an academic context, key words within questions frequently tell readers what specific kinds of information are targeted. Often, students are unaware of these key words and do not use the support they offer to help them navigate text for information. English learners, especially, may not see the questions as containing academic instructions to elicit specific reader responses. For example, if a student is asked to identify the *main idea* of a paragraph, the words *main idea* specifically direct the reader to look for the comprehensive idea of the piece. The next step is for students to use an appropriate reading strategy to find this comprehensive idea.

Through effective instruction and demonstration, teachers can help students develop an array of strategies needed to read for the different kinds of information they seek. Galda and Graves (2007) note that when teachers choose activities to focus students' attention on particular aspects of a text as they read it, they provide supported reading opportunities. This chapter focuses on appropriate strategies for the identification of main ideas and their corresponding supporting details, helping students to focus on relationships within the text, to "keep from drowning in a sea of details or having to cull out trivial information" that does not match their purposes for reading (Gunning 2008, 287).

Identifying Main Ideas

As we saw in Chapter 4, students can effectively learn how to use a scanning approach to answer detail questions. These questions typically begin with *WH* words, which indicate what the answer format will be (person, place, thing, amount, time, etc.). Certainly, these are the easiest questions to answer, positioned at the "recall" level of Bloom's taxonomy. They are the questions that English learners find the least intimidating because they can locate a tangible answer directly stated in the text. Many English learners are uncomfortable with other types of questions that they are asked to answer, such as main idea questions, because they have not been explicitly taught how to find the information to answer them. Also, they may not recognize the benefits of comprehending main ideas as they read.

Good readers always have a sense of the main ideas presented within connected text. After all, put together as a whole, main ideas carry the message of a selection. However, it is common for readers' concentration levels to change from one situation or context to another. If students have a date coming up on Friday evening, are hungry for lunchtime to come, didn't get enough sleep, or are irritated with a friend's behavior, their ability to attend to the reading task will be lessened. However, with focus, they know how to get the gist of what they read; they have strategies for identifying the main ideas to ensure higher levels of comprehension as they read.

In class, students are sometimes asked to determine the main ideas of a text selection so that the comprehensive ideas of the content (rather than the smaller details) are emphasized in a lesson. Even though questions may begin with *WH* words (at first appearing to be detail questions, e.g., "How does lava become magma?"), they may contain specific key words that alert the reader that a different type of question is being asked. For example, in a question such as "What is the main idea?" readers may at first think that because the question starts with *What*, it will be a detail question, but when they read the question completely, they can see the words *main idea*, which override the *What*. Therefore, this is a main idea question, which will require the use of a *main idea* strategy, rather than the use of scanning. Figure 5–1 illustrates typical questions that contain specific key words, indicating that main idea strategies are needed in order to answer them. In fact, these key words are additional examples of academic language that students must know in order to obtain information they need when they read.

When we talk about the "big idea" in a paragraph (or, the "gist of it"), we are speaking of the main idea. The main idea can be defined as "a summary statement that includes the other details in a paragraph or longer piece; it is what all the sentences are about" (Gunning 2008, 281). A reader who can identify the main, or comprehensive, idea of each paragraph in a passage or selection will come away with what we referred to in Chapter 2 as the "jigsaw puzzle picture on the top of the box." If students can determine the comprehensive idea of a paragraph or larger text piece, they will automatically have a better idea of how the supporting details in that piece fit together, so their understanding of the entire selection will be higher. As shown in Figure 5–1, key words for main ideas include phrases such as *main idea, mainly about, mostly about, provides information about, primarily, contains information about*, and other phrases that reflect the *title* of a piece (such as *good title, best title, another possible title, alternative title*).

Reading a paragraph to identify the main idea—and then rereading it to assimilate all of the details—is an authentic practice. I do it when I read text because I am interested in finding the major concepts before trying to link the smaller ones to them (especially if the text represents unfamiliar content). For English learners, it is an effective way to develop a structure that guides them in determining the primary points of the chapter or text piece. Separating primary points from supporting details is a particular challenge for English learners, especially if they are still learning to decode text in English and to understand vocabulary they may not previously have encountered, either orally or in their reading.

Main Idea Statements + Questions

The *main idea* of this excerpt is _____.
The third paragraph is *mainly about* _____.
The first paragraph *provides information about* _____.
This selection has to do *mostly with* _____.
The last paragraph of this article *contains information about*

_____.

This section of the newspaper is *about* _____.
A *good title* for this passage is _____.
Another possible title for this article is _____.

Figure 5–1

◎ Herringbone Procedure

By teaching explicit strategies, especially ones that students can practice in pairs or at table groups, teachers help learners grasp the abstract concept of the *main idea*. One such strategy is the herringbone procedure, originally developed by Tierney, Readence, and Dishner (1990). It consists of a short graphic organizer and is a concrete way of helping students find the comprehensive idea in a paragraph or passage. Students answer questions listed in the fishbone organizer, leading to the synthesis of all of the information in one newly created sentence, which becomes the main idea statement. In our center, we use a modified version of the graphic, illustrated in Figure 5–2.

After reading the excerpt in Figure 5–3, consider how threatening it might be to any student, much less an English learner, to be asked to identify the *main idea*. After all, there is a large chunk of information here, including many details. How does a reader isolate one main point from all of this text?

The following attempt by a student to identify the main idea of this passage clearly shows that he was uncertain about what information to include:

> This is about riding a bike on city streets where there are lots of fire engines, ambulances, and police cars. You can't see around giant-sized trucks and sports cars and SUVs that zip in and out of lanes. You are in a hurry like everyone else but you have less protection, so you should use your good sense. You have to know the rules of the road and obey them to be safe on highways or byways.

This student did his best to assimilate all of the information but ended up doing just that—including *all* of the information. He was not able to determine a simply stated comprehensive idea. However, in class when I modeled my own thinking as I read the text and then asked the student and his peers to help figure out the information that went into a fishbone organizer, they came up with the information shown in Figure 5–4.

By putting all the detail pieces together from the graph, students were able to determine this main idea sentence: "You (bike rider) have less protection than others while riding your bike on city streets, but you can protect yourself by having good sense and knowing/following the rules of the road."

Note that although the graphic organizer is set up for students to write the main idea across the middle line of the fishbone (as the "backbone" of the piece), many students prefer to place it underneath the graphic in order to have enough space, so we added the line below the fish. If the word order doesn't sound right (or is not syntactically correct), students can then move the words around for a clearer message, such as "While riding your bike on city streets with less protection

Blank Fishbone Graphic

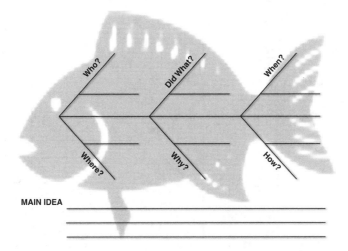

Steps
- Read the passage.
- Answer the questions on the graphic. (The answers to "why" and "how" relate back to the "did what".)
- Put the answers to the questions in one sentence.
- Revise the sentence, eliminating repetitive information and clarifying ideas.
- Read your final main idea statement!

Figure 5–2

Road Warriors, Listen Up: Some Rules for Streetwise Biking

When you ride a bike on city streets, you share the road with speeding fire engines, ambulances, and police cars. You see—but can't see around—giant-sized trucks with eighteen wheels instead of your two. Sports cars and SUVs zip in and out of lanes. Everyone's in a hurry, and there you are, with less protection than anyone else in a moving vehicle. Your best defense is your good sense. To ride a bike safely—on highways or byways—you've got to know and follow the rules of the road.

Figure 5–3

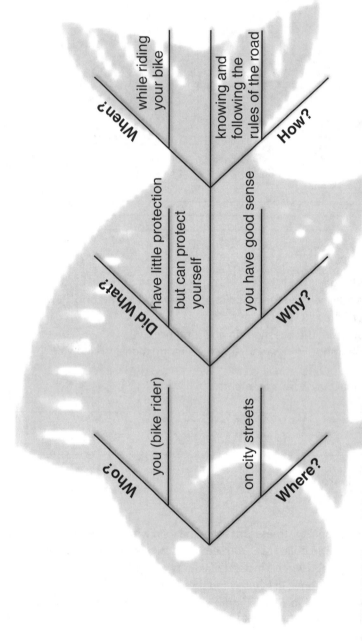

MAIN IDEA While riding your bike on city streets with little protection, you can protect yourself by using good sense and following the rules of the road.

Figure 5–4

than others have, you can protect yourself by using good sense and following the rules of the road."

It is important that the teacher does not encourage learners to expand the main idea statements into more than one sentence; if that happens, the temptation to include too many details will be strong, making it difficult for them to commit to one comprehensive idea. Gunning (2008) notes that the main idea provides a "framework for organizing, understanding, and remembering the essential details, not all of the details in the text piece," adding that without this framework, "Students wander aimlessly among details" (280).

The work these students did is a clear indication that these kinds of visual structures are powerful tools for comprehension instruction because they make memorable representations of abstract thinking processes more tangible. The next step for learners, as Alvermann and Phelps (2005) suggest, is to "give them occasional follow-up passages and read for the specific task" (200). Students used the fishbone graph with many different selections throughout the year in our center and experienced higher levels of success with it over time. They also developed a stronger ability to recall the details associated with the big picture, as they had a schematic structure within which to connect the pieces.

Fortunately, this graph can be used with single paragraphs or with longer text passages or selections that have interrelated paragraphs. A common way to find longer pieces such as this is for the teacher to identify chunks of text under subtitles in chapters. For example, the text piece in Figure 5–5, "The Development of Technology," includes two full paragraphs (representing a passage) under one subtitle.

The Development of Technology

Technology consists of all of the ways in which people apply knowledge, tools, and inventions to meet their needs. Technology dates back to early humans. At least two million years ago, people made stone tools for cutting. Early humans also made carrying bags, stone hand axes, awls (tools for piercing holes in leather or wood), and drills.

In time, humans developed more complex tools, such as hunting bows made of wood. They learned to make flint spearheads and metal tools. Early humans used tools to hunt and butcher animals and to construct simple forms of shelter. Technology—these new tools—gave humans more control over their environment. These tools also set the stage for a more settled way of life.

Figure 5–5

Ostensibly, the amount of detailed information in this two-paragraph selection would make it difficult for an English learner to sift out the main point of the entire piece. Figure 5–6 shows the results when the fishbone graph is used to answer the basic questions of *who, what, when, where, why,* and *how.*

Using the comprehensive idea created by answering the questions on the graph, the main idea statement looks something like this: "Since two million years ago, humans have applied their knowledge to develop more and more complex tools (technology) to meet their needs so they could control their environment and have settled lives."

The additional details in the selection (stone tools, carrying bags, hunting bows, metal tools, etc.) make sense because they connect to the comprehensive idea, but they are not part of the main idea statement. Also, the space reserved for the answer to *where* is left blank intentionally because that information is not included in the text piece. When this occurs, students simply leave spaces blank or put X's on the lines.

The idea that the graphic does not have to be "perfect" is important. Learners feel comfortable (which keeps their affective filters low), knowing that they can use the information that is provided to construct the main idea sentence, leaving blanks where necessary. Once students reflect upon their first response, they may see that redundant words can be deleted (and synonyms added) to create a more succinct main idea statement: "For two million years, humans have applied their knowledge to develop increasingly complex tools (technology), meeting their needs to control their environment and have settled lives."

Teachers can help with revisions of the initial main idea statements, modeling different versions on a whiteboard, overhead projector, or document camera, depending upon how important such rewrites are to the goals of the lesson. Then, when learners reread the passage, they are more likely to recall the important details, seeing how the smaller parts are connected to the larger overriding idea.

Testing Link

After students have begun to use comprehension strategies such as the herringbone procedure, it becomes a simple matter to transfer their competencies to test practice situations. McCabe (2003) notes that reading scores often "reflect test anxiety to a large degree, rather than true reading ability" (12). He adds that some students have had more opportunities to experience mastery in test taking and that careful selection and use of testlike material are critical. Teachers can use easy test material (authentic pieces from class readings) and choose short, manageable sections. As success with short portions is achieved, teachers should then gradually increase the length of the selections.

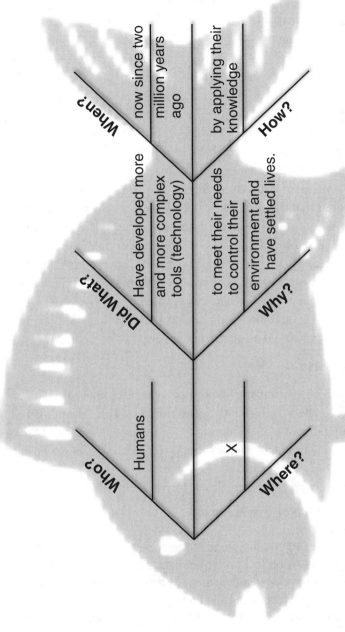

Who? Humans

Did What? Have developed more and more complex tools (technology)

When? now since two million years ago

Why? to meet their needs to control their environment and have settled lives.

How? by applying their knowledge

Where? X

MAIN IDEA   Since two million years ago, humans have applied their knowledge to develop more and more complex tools (technology) to meet their needs so they could control their environment and have settled lives.

Figure 5–6

Taking the final main idea sentence created for the passage on the development of technology, students can now easily apply the information to a question such as "What is the main idea of the passage?" Knowing that the *passage* is composed of both *paragraphs*, they recognize that the answer must represent the big idea of the entire selection and not just the main idea of one or the other paragraph—or detailed pieces of either (Figure 5–7).

Learners who use the fishbone graph for this test practice will see that statements A, B, and C are merely details from the passage and that statement D most accurately captures the comprehensive idea determined from the organizer. Also, they quickly recognize that the length of test answers is not a clue as to which statement would be the correct main idea, as C is the longest one and yet still represents only the "parts."

Some English as a second language (ESL) teachers tell me that since they began using the herringbone procedure, for the first time many of their English learners feel confident that they can figure out what their assigned text pieces are mostly about. Before the students learned the strategy, they felt overwhelmed, but they can now at least determine the most important information, paragraph by paragraph. One of our Literacy Center fifth graders, Elise, remarked that she thought it was "really awesome that the 'bones' remind me to include the *WHs* in figuring out the main points [*who, what, when, where, why, how, how long, how much, how many*] so that I can understand what I am reading!" A full version of the modified fishbone graphic that we use in our center is located in Appendix C.

Main Ideas Versus Titles

In assessment situations, particularly on norm-referenced standardized tests, students are often ask to choose which title (good title, best title—or perhaps alternative title) is most reflective of the content of a passage of writing. During an initial discussion with candidates in our Literacy Center about how to teach the

---

What Is the *Main Idea* of the Passage?

    A. Two million years ago, humans made stone tools for cutting.
    B. Early humans used tools for hunting animals and constructing shelters.
    C. In time, humans developed more complex tools, such as hunting bows made of wood, flint spearheads, and metal tools.
    D. Humans controlled their environment and became settled by developing technology, or complex tools.

Figure 5–7

concept of main ideas to students, we noted that there seemed to be a difference between the main idea of a piece of writing and its corresponding *title*. Although they are related, to be sure, there is a distinct contrast in their structures. Main ideas are written as statements or sentences, whereas titles are typically subjects or topics that reflect main ideas. Subjects or topics do not necessarily even contain verbs; they are short phrases or word groupings that represent the main idea of the text piece. However, students cannot develop (or choose good titles) if they have not already determined the main idea of the piece for which the title is written. So, with titles, the process includes two steps: find the main idea and then create a matching title.

The problem is that students today are quite familiar with how titles operate in the real world—and not so conversant with how they function in academic texts. The titles of magazine articles, videos, movies, and other types of marketed products are designed to sell; the goal is audience enticement. I recall a movie that came out a few years ago entitled *Not Just Another Teenage Movie*. The title was not meant to tell the paying public what the movie was actually about—but rather to get them to come to see it because they *didn't* know what it would be about (except that it was designed for teenagers, of course). If we consider other titles of books and movies such as *The Happening* and *The Visitor*, we can see that they are often meant to be provocatively clever but not specific enough to tell too much about the content. Sometimes the intent is artistic, of course, but in any case, the "rules" that apply to such selections are not the same as those for academic pieces. I remember how much I battled with the task of determining a title for my dissertation at the end of graduate school, being told that it should summarize the content focus as closely as possible. Unimaginative by any standards, the result was not memorable, but it was technically appropriate as a comprehensive statement of the dissertation work.

In academics, titles are intended to reflect the content—or main ideas—of the text pieces. Even in literature, there is a tendency to use figurative or symbolic language, while in expository text writing, the clearer the match to the subject matter, the better it is. Perhaps in the comic illustration in Figure 5–8, the frog was misled by the use of metaphor in the title of his book when he was hoping for it to be a more literal representation of the content.

Returning to the text piece about the development of technology in Figure 5–5 and reviewing its fishbone graph counterpart in Figure 5–6, we can determine which *title* would be the best, based on our identification of the main idea.

Testing Link

The first two examples in Figure 5–9 (A and B) reflect specific details in the passage, the third one (C) comes closer to the main point of the passage but does

Oh well, this is not at all
what I thought it would be...

Figure 5–8

not say why tools were developed by humans, and the fourth one (D) illustrates the motivation behind complex tool development, or technology, which is, in fact, the comprehensive idea. Therefore, D is the best answer.

◎ Triple Read Technique

Although the herringbone procedure can be used with any type of text, narrative or expository, an alternate main idea strategy for students to use is the triple read technique, which depends upon the selection having an expository organizational structure, which is classified as enumerative/descriptive. This means that the structure includes a listing of details about a subject that describes, gives examples or reasons, and defines concepts in order to support the main idea. One purpose of triple read is for students to identify the controlling, or main, ideas in text pieces to get the big picture as they read. In addition, they search for supporting details that provide evidence for the topic sentences (which, of course, reflect the main ideas). Figure 5–10 lists the steps originally created by Pearson (1993) as part of triple read, plus two steps added by teachers in our Literacy Center.

As the teachers in our center first began to use this technique with students, they recommended two additional steps, which we have included as a modification of the technique. The first one is an opportunity for the teacher or students (possibly in pairs) to read the entire text piece before analyzing the parts (topic

---

What Is the *Best Title* for the Passage?

A. Stone Tools for Cutting
B. Tools for Hunting and Shelter
C. Development of Complex Tools
D. Control of Environment Through Technology

Figure 5–9

Triple Read

- (*Added*) Read the selection aloud in class.
- Read the *topic sentences* (using a *think-aloud* procedure) to get the main ideas. *Sample* the text to be certain that the topic sentence has been located for each paragraph.
- Read the *details* to find support for the topic sentences; number the details.
- Put all of the main points and details into an *outline* form, using as few words as possible by paraphrasing and including only key ideas.
- (*Added*) Using the outline, rewrite the information into a "new" text piece, including appropriate transition words.

Figure 5–10

sentences and supporting details), as well as time for the teacher to preview selected vocabulary with students. The other step is to ask learners to rewrite the text piece with transitions after they have created an outline from it.

The selection in Figure 5–11 on the griots—West African storytellers—provides an effective source for an in-depth description of how to use the triple read technique. The passage under the subtitle "Storytellers Maintain Oral History" could be identified as the introduction, and the four-paragraph passage under "The Griots" could be chosen as the target text for the process of triple read.

In order to begin triple read, students read the overall text passage to get the comprehensive idea of the piece, relying upon support from the teacher to front-load terms needed for comprehension of the text and expansion of their vocabulary. Next, the teacher walks students through the identification of the topic sentences in each paragraph, using a think-aloud process. In a think-aloud, the teacher explicitly models reading processes by articulating them, or by "making thinking public" (McKenna and Stahl 2003, 179).

For example, looking at the first paragraph of this four-paragraph selection, the first sentence says that "West African storytellers were called *griots*." If students are asked what they expect the rest of the paragraph to say, they typically say that "what the griots did" will be described. They know from the introductory paragraphs that West African history was entrusted to storytellers, so they realize that what will follow will be positive remarks about the griots' contributions.

Before students identify the first sentence as the topic sentence, though, they must "sample" a bit of the text to determine if the role of griots, or storytellers, is actually discussed in the balance of the paragraph. To model the sampling

Storytellers Maintain Oral History

Although cities like Timbuktu and Djenne were known for their universities and libraries, writing was never very common in West Africa. In fact, none of the major early civilizations of West Africa developed a written language. Arabic was the only written language they used. Many Muslim traders, government officials, and religious leaders could read and write Arabic.

The lack of a written language does not mean that the people of West Africa didn't know their history, though. They passed along information through oral histories. An oral history is a spoken record of past events. The task of remembering West Africa's history was entrusted to storytellers.

The Griots

West African storytellers were called *griots*. They were highly respected in their communities because the people of West Africa were very interested in the deeds of their ancestors. Griots helped keep this history alive for each new generation.

The griots' stories were entertaining as well as informative. They told of past events and of the deeds of people's ancestors. For example, some stories explained the rise and fall of the West African empires. Other stories described in detail the actions of powerful kings and warriors. Some griots made their stories more lively by acting out events from the past like scenes in a play.

In addition to stories, the griots recited proverbs, or short sayings of wisdom or truth. They used proverbs to teach lessons to the people. For example, one West African proverb warns, "Talking doesn't fill the basket in the farm." This proverb reminds people that they must work to accomplish things. They can't just talk about what they want to do. Another proverb advises, "A hippopotamus can be made invisible in dark water." It warns people to remain alert. Just as it can be hard to see animals in deep pool, people don't always see the problems they will face.

In order to recite their stories and proverbs, the griots memorized hundreds of names and events. Through this memorization process the griots passed on West African history from generation to generation. However, some griots confused names and events in their heads. When this happened, specific facts about some historical events became distorted. Still, the griots' stories tell us a great deal about life in the West African empires.

Figure 5–11

process, the teacher reads the second sentence: "They were highly respected in their communities because the people of West Africa were very interested in the deeds of their ancestors." This sentence confirms that the paragraph is actually about the role of the griots as storytellers, so the students now underline the first sentence of the paragraph. We have them do this with a colored pencil, pen, or highlighter if they are using a photocopy—or on a heavy-duty transparency sheet or sheet protector that can be placed directly on top of a textbook page (see Figure 5–12).

The next step is for students to skip down to the second paragraph (without reading any more of the supporting details in the first paragraph yet) to see if the first sentence is operating as the topic sentence. The teacher reads, "The griots' stories were entertaining as well as informative." Asking the students if this

---

The Griots

<u>West African storytellers were called *griots*</u>. They were highly respected in their communities because the people of West Africa were very interested in the deeds of their ancestors. Griots helped keep this history alive for each new generation.

<u>The griots' stories were entertaining as well as informative</u>. They told of past events and of the deeds of people's ancestors. For example, some stories explained the rise and fall of the West African empires. Other stories described in detail the actions of powerful kings and warriors. Some griots made their stories more lively by acting out events from the past like scenes in a play.

<u>In addition to stories, the griots recited proverbs, or short sayings of wisdom or truth</u>. They used proverbs to teach lessons to the people. For example, one West African proverb warns, "Talking doesn't fill the basket in the farm." This proverb reminds people that they must work to accomplish things. They can't just talk about what they want to do. Another proverb advises, "A hippopotamus can be made invisible in dark water." It warns people to remain alert. Just as it can be hard to see animals in deep pool, people don't always see the problems they will face.

<u>In order to recite their stories and proverbs, the griots memorized hundreds of names and events</u>. Through this memorization process the griots passed on West African history from generation to generation. However, some griots confused names and events in their heads. When this happened, specific facts about some historical events became distorted. Still, the griots' stories tell us a great deal about life in the West African empires.

Figure 5–12

"sounds like" a topic sentence (one that will be supported by evidence in the rest of the paragraph), the teacher says that if it is, they should be able to tell just by *sampling* a bit of the paragraph. The next sentence says, "They told of past events and of the deeds of people's ancestors." Students are asked if this statement would begin to prove that the stories were entertaining and informative.

When it seems clear that it does (as past events and ancestral deeds were most likely interesting to the people), the students can now underline the first sentence as the topic sentence (using the same color as they did for paragraph one) and move on to paragraphs three and four to identify the topic sentences there. As the lesson progresses, students see that the teacher is showing them how to be conscious of one's mental processes, or using a "metacognitive teaching framework" as a model for them to follow (Pearson 1993, 11).

As it turns out, once students read the initial sentences in each of the last two paragraphs and sample the text, the first sentences do appear to be the topic sentences: "In addition to stories, the griots recited proverbs, or short sayings of wisdom or truth" and "In order to recite their stories and proverbs, the griots memorized hundreds of names and events." Therefore, students underline them (using the same color as in paragraphs one and two) so that the text piece now looks the way we see it in Figure 5–12.

After the topic sentences have been identified, the next step of the technique is for students to identify the facts, details, or examples that support the topic sentences. Using a think-aloud technique, the teacher directs students to return to the text, this time to find the details—typically examples or reasons—that help to support the topic sentences. In paragraph one, the description of the griots' role includes the fact that they were respected for what they did (storytelling) because West Africans were interested in the deeds of their ancestors. Therefore, students place a (1) by this idea and highlight it with another color, one they choose specifically to identify details. Second, the point that the griots kept history alive for each generation to come emphasizes their long-term importance, so a (2) can be placed next to this idea, and this detail is also highlighted with the same color used for "details."

Similarly, looking at paragraph two, students read the topic sentence about the griots' stories being both entertaining and informative and can now seek for the details that support this idea. There are two categories of information that would have human interest appeal to listeners: (1) past events and deeds of ancestors (what their relatives actually did, including by implication, any "skeletons in the closet"), along with descriptions of the actions of powerful kings and warriors, the heroes they may have feared or admired and (2) the making of stories more lively by acting out the events.

Highlighting these details in the second color, students then follow the same approach for the last two paragraphs. The final version of the passage with topic sentences and details might look the way it is shown in Figure 5–13 (without the colored markings).

The next step in triple read is for students to read the text one more time in order to put the main ideas (represented by topic sentences) and supporting details into an outline format. However, the key to this step is to encourage students not to write whole sentences. If they do, they will tend to copy from the text directly. Instead, they should write two to four key phrases that reflect a "title" of sorts, thereby having to think about what these words mean and committing their significance to memory.

The Griots

West African storytellers were called *griots*. They were (1) highly respected in their communities because the people of West Africa were very interested in the deeds of their ancestors. (2) Griots helped keep this history alive for each new generation.

The griots' stories were entertaining as well as informative. (1) They told of past events and of the deeds of people's ancestors. For example, some stories explained the rise and fall of the West African empires. Other stories described in detail the actions of powerful kings and warriors. (2) Some griots made their stories more lively by acting out events from the past like scenes in a play.

In addition to stories, the griots recited proverbs, or short sayings of wisdom or truth. (1) They used proverbs to teach lessons to the people. For example, one West African proverb warns, "Talking doesn't fill the basket in the farm." This proverb reminds people that they must work to accomplish things. They can't just talk about what they want to do. Another proverb advises, "A hippopotamus can be made invisible in dark water." It warns people to remain alert. Just as it can be hard to see animals in deep pool, people don't always see the problems they will face.

In order to recite their stories and proverbs, the griots memorized hundreds of names and events. (1) Through this memorization process the griots passed on West African history from generation to generation. (2) However, some griots confused names and events in their heads. When this happened, specific facts about some historical events became distorted. Still, the griots' stories tell us a great deal about life in the West African empires.

Figure 5–13

For example, using the information from the first topic sentence, the outline can begin with "Griots as Storytellers." Students can convert the second topic sentence into "Entertaining and Informative Stories." (See Figure 5–14.) The idea is to place key words and phrases in the outline that will serve as memory joggers for the eventual rewriting of the text in students' own words. In this way, teachers can urge learners to begin to paraphrase, rather than to copy down too much information directly from the text.

The teacher can demonstrate the outline on an overhead or document camera, talking students through the text, paragraph by paragraph. As they discuss the information, the class can use a Roman numeral system for placing the information in the outline. If the teacher feels the students are ready, the outline can contain even smaller supporting details (such as types of past deeds and events in Section II or examples of wise proverbs in Section III), but this depends upon students' levels of proficiency with the language and the importance of the smaller details related to the overall content goals of the lesson.

The Griots

I. Griots as Storytellers
   A. People's Interest in Ancestors' Deeds
   B. Generations of History Through Storytelling

II. Entertaining and Informative Stories
   A. Many Events and Deeds
      i. Rise and Fall of Empires
      ii. Actions of Powerful People
         a. Kings
         b. Warriors
   B. Acting Out

III. Wise Proverbs
   A. Talking Doesn't Fill Basket
   B. Hippo Invisible in Dark Water

IV. Names and Events Memorized
   A. History Passed On
   B. Some Confusion But Still Informative

Figure 5–14

My experience with the outline part of this strategy is that students enjoy determining all the information that they need before trying to identify how many levels they need for the numbering and lettering. They are often used to trying to make a round peg fit into a square hole when attempting to outline in classes, complaining that the information doesn't always fit the way they expect it to. Learners find this process to be easier because the numbering comes after the determination of the important information.

An optional, final step in the triple read process, added and recommended by the teachers in our Literacy Center, illustrates the reciprocity between reading and writing. Students discuss what they see in their outline and then try to rewrite the information into paragraph form without the use of the original text. This way, they do not copy the text verbatim but only paraphrase from the information in the outline. This approach ensures that learners work toward making sense of the ideas they write, rather than just parroting them back. Even students whose writing is less proficient than others in the class can do a satisfactory job of tying together the ideas in each paragraph. Teachers can also offer students a beginning list of transition words, which help to unify their ideas (a "starter" list is provided in Figure 5–15).

Transition Words

also, in addition	consequently
besides	nevertheless
in fact	on the other hand, on the contrary
for example	as a result of
first, next, then, last	similarly
initially, subsequently, in conclusion	in other words
meanwhile	of course
therefore, thus	indeed
to begin with	certainly
finally	for, and, nor, but, or yet, so

Figure 5–15

Figure 5–16 shows an example of one English learner's rewrite of his triple read outline from the passage on the griots. Though he is in an early intermediate ESL class, he still manages to bring together the details with the main points of the selection. He remarked that the color-coding of topic sentences and details helped him "a lot, because it made the big ideas more separated from the smaller ones, and then they all were making sense."

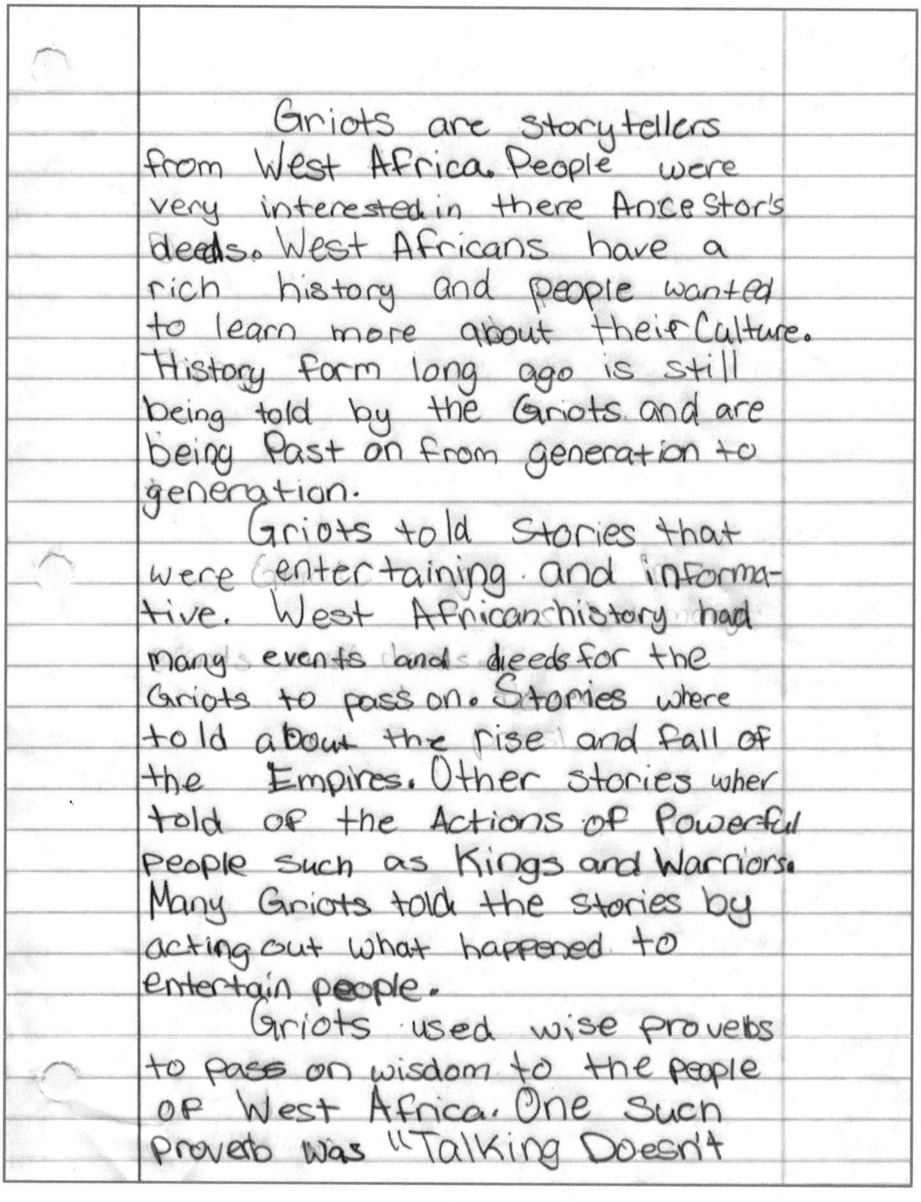

> Griots are storytellers from West Africa. People were very interested in there Ancestor's deeds. West Africans have a rich history and people wanted to learn more about their Culture. History form long ago is still being told by the Griots and are being Past on from generation to generation.
>
> Griots told Stories that were entertaining and informative. West African history had many events and deeds for the Griots to pass on. Stories where told about the rise and fall of the Empires. Other stories wher told of the Actions of Powerful People such as Kings and Warriors. Many Griots told the stories by acting out what happened to entertain people.
>
> Griots used wise proverbs to pass on wisdom to the people of West Africa. One Such proverb was "Talking Doesn't

Figure 5–16 *Student Sample—Triple Read*

Fill the Basket." This proverb
means that if you slack off
and don't do your work it
won't get done. Another similar
proverb teaches to watch out
because there may always be
something hidden.
    The Griots had to memorize
many names and events. Their
history was passed on by their
stories and plays. While the
Griots had confusion with names
and events but the imformation
passed on was still truthful to
West African History.

Figure 5–16 *(Continued)*

Over time, students do become comfortable with the text talk that they use
when doing this strategy and begin to see the benefits of turning the topic sentences and details into outlines. Not only do they become more adept at analyzing the organizational structures of expository text pieces, but they also transfer
these configurations into their own writing. Teachers often say that after their students learn the triple read technique, they stop asking how long their writing
assignments have to be; instead they ask how many supporting details they need
to have for each topic sentence!

Testing Link

A typical text question about this passage might be "What is the second paragraph
mostly about?" If students simply look for the topic sentence and then sample
part of the text to confirm it, they can determine the main idea. Then, in a test situation they can answer questions like the one in Figure 5–17.

1. The second paragraph in this selection is *mostly about*:
   A) the entertaining and informative stories that the griots told
   B) the actions of powerful people
   C) how some of the names and events became confused
   D) the wise proverbs told by the griots

2. What would be a *good title* for paragraph three?
   A) History Passed Down
   B) Wise Proverbs of Griots
   C) Acting Out Events and Deeds
   D) People's Interest in Ancestors

Figure 5–17   *Sample Main Idea Questions*

To answer question 1, since statement A reflects the topic sentence associated with paragraph two in this selection ("The griots' stories were entertaining, as well as informative"), students should identify it as the correct answer. The other choices contain information in the selection from various places, but only the first item accurately summarizes the main idea of that one paragraph. To answer question 2, students can look at the topic sentence in paragraph three ("In addition to stories, the griots recited proverbs, or short sayings of wisdom and truth") to determine that the title "Wise Proverbs of Griots" most closely reflects the main idea.

Commentary

It is important that strategy instruction that emphasizes relationships between main ideas and details in text is not limited to one or two examples throughout the year. A key to success for students is to apply strategies such as the herringbone procedure and triple read to a variety of materials so that the ability to identify such relationships generalizes across other types of texts (Gunning 2008). Consistently revisiting strategies in multiple contexts is advantageous so students can become ever more adept at implementing them; the goal is for learners to utilize strategies within all content areas, especially as text difficulty increases from grade to grade.

In the next chapter, the focus will be upon the use of signal words to identify sequences of events and cause-effect relationships. Fortunately, students typically have a large amount of schema for these two comprehension domains, so there is much to build upon. Transferring the concepts into academic contexts is the challenge, but with explicit support provided by their teachers, students can effectively learn to take their knowledge of these relationships (and how to identify them) from class to class as "transportable literacy strategies" (Fisher and Frey 2007, 210).

6

What Are Signal Words, Anyway?

Teaching Students to Understand Order of Events and Cause-Effect Relationships

When listening to people tell anecdotes, I am struck by the amount of "meandering" that they sometimes do when they recount events. For example, one of my friends has a unique way of backtracking several times throughout any story she is relating. "First, I didn't originally plan to go camping, but I was persuaded to join the group when I heard how low the cost of the weekend would actually be. Before I even knew about the opportunity, I had decided not to take a vacation because of the expense. You know how I am, kind of careful with money! I had already given up on doing anything at all, even though the past year was so very stressful. You remember how many family emergencies we had, just during the winter. Well, anyway…"

When people speak, they rely upon many nonlinguistic clues (gesturing, tone of voice, eye contact, etc.) with no particular concern that listeners might misunderstand what they are saying; they can easily clarify or elaborate if their audience requires feedback. However, in academic reading and writing contexts, such explicit help is not provided. If readers assume that a writer is relating events chronologically, they will not comprehend a text piece fully if the writer inserts "flashbacks" or adopts a back-and-forth discourse style similar to my friend's.

It is important to teach students that they need to use signal words to determine the *chronological order of events* in a text selection, even if the *order of the telling* is not the same as the actual order in which they occurred. Words such as *before that*, *in the meantime*, *afterward*, *while*, *prior to*, and so on are keys to the understanding of sequence. Too often, readers assume that the order in which a writer presents information is the actual order in which they occurred. By paying attention to signal words, they can verify whether this is the case.

Similarly, readers typically comprehend the concepts of *cause* and *effect* when they hear someone embed them into conversation but are sometimes mystified when they encounter them in texts, especially when the terms *cause* and *effect* are not used. For example, "My bad grade in math caused my parents to be very angry" is a statement that most students could relate to if a peer were to say it, understanding that the bad grade was the *cause* that led the parents to be upset—the *effect*. Yet, when students read the sentence "An ultralight plane had been flying for 40 minutes when a change of wind direction doubled its ground speed" in an algebra book, they do not automatically note the *cause-effect* relationship. This is because the signal word *when* is used to identify the cause-effect relationship, rather than the terms *cause* and *effect*.

In short, teaching students to identify signal words to understand sequences of events and cause-effect relationships to support comprehension is a priority. In this chapter, specific methods for making these processes "visible" will be presented (Barrentine 1999, 4).

Determining the Sequence of Events

A concept that is critical to readers' understanding of text is that events have a prescribed order in which they happen and that writers often achieve cohesion by using signal words. In the case of sequencing, the words can also operate as transitions (e.g., *after*, *at the same time as*, *before*, *during*, *finally*, *first*, *in conclusion*, *last*, *next*, *second*, *then*, *to begin with*, etc.). Questions or statements that contain these kinds of words help readers to identify such temporal relationships (Figure 6–1).

Questioning is a strategy that "propels readers forward" because when students ask themselves ongoing questions as they read, they are less likely to abandon the text (Harvey and Goudvis 2000, 22). Confusion about the order of events is a roadblock that keeps readers from moving ahead with confidence; they may ask themselves about the relationships among events but not be able to see them clearly. What many students do not see is that the events may be told by the author in an order that is different from the way in which they actually occurred chronologically. If the writer begins by describing the first event that actually

Sequence Statements + Questions

Which of these steps will be done *first*?

What happened right *after* _____?

Since that time, _____.

During _____, what happened?

The boxes below show some important ideas in this article. Which of the following events belongs in the *empty box*?

The boxes show some things that happened in the story. Which of these belongs in *box 2*?

The *last* thing that _____ (person) did was _____.

The *second* event that occurred was _____.

In the *beginning* of this story, _____ happened.

Before you can do X, you must _____.

At the very *end* of the procedure, you should _____.

When the story began, _____.

Figure 6–1

occurred and the second event next, readers have no difficulty identifying the chronological order of events (though the key words, like those listed earlier, still need to be taught explicitly). Yet, when a writer describes the events in a convoluted way, students may not see that the events are being related nonchronologically. If they are trying to comprehend the order in which the events truly happened for the purpose of understanding the story, or if they are answering sequence questions posed by a teacher (or on a test), then learners usually go by the *order of the telling*.

◎ *Sentence Strips + Timeline Strategy*

One interactive and especially effective comprehension strategy to use with students, especially English learners who may not be completely familiar with the specific discourse patterns of the English language, is called *sentence strips + timeline*. The object is to determine the chronological order of events in a text piece, even though the events may not be described or narrated in actual order of "real time" occurrence.

For example, if we read a passage on "How Banks Work" (Figure 6–2) and then analyze only the first five sentences of paragraph two (using paragraph one as an introduction), we can separate the sentences into four discrete events. To

How Banks Work

Why did Hamilton want to create a national bank? He believed that such a bank could help the economy of the new nation. It would create a partnership between the federal government and American business.

Let's say you deposited money into a bank account. Then you went back another day to withdraw some of the money. What happened in the meantime? Did the money just sit in the bank until you wanted it back? No—the bank used your money, and in doing so, helped fuel economic growth. In this way, money flows in a circular path from people like you into the general economy and back to you again. In the process, money can create goods and services, jobs, and profits, as the diagram explains.

Figure 6–2

identify each event, we recognize that there may be more than "action" in each sentence. It is helpful for learners to *scan* for verbs in order to identify individual events and then highlight these events in some fashion (via underlining, use of highlighters, numbering, etc.), as we see in Figure 6–3.

Once the events are numbered (with event 1 being coded as "E1"), we can see how many we are dealing with and can clearly identify the "order of the telling," or the order in which they have been presented in the text by the author. Then, we write each separate event on sticky notes, based in the order in which the writer described them to us. (See Figure 6–4.)

The next step, however, is to ask whether the *order of the telling* is the same as *chronological order*. That is to say, if readers are to comprehend the events in the sequence in which they actually occurred, they have to analyze the events. They cannot assume that the order in which the author writes the events is chronological.

Highlighted Events from Each Sentence

Let's say you <u>deposited</u> money into a bank account (E1). Then you <u>went</u> back another day to withdraw some of the money (E2). What happened in the meantime? Did the money just sit in the bank until you wanted it back? No—the bank <u>used</u> your money (E3), and in doing so, <u>helped fuel</u> economic growth (E4).

Figure 6–3

Using Sticky Notes

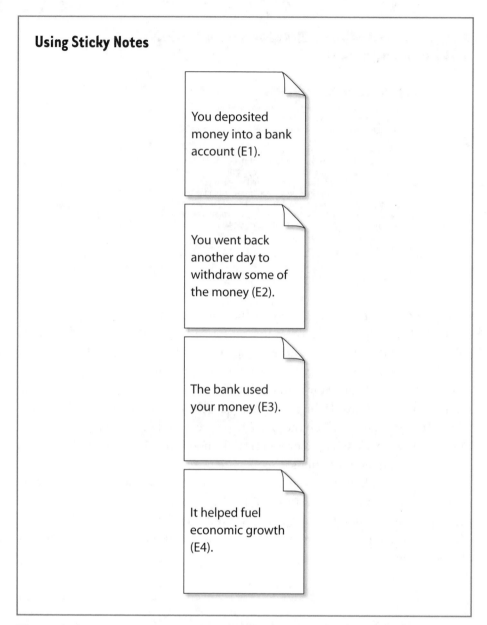

Figure 6–4

    To demonstrate how *chronological order* may be different from the *order of the telling*, the teacher uses strips cut from an overhead transparency sheet, listing the events on the strips and placing them on the projector. (For the teacher, these strips function in place of the sticky notes, which the students use.) During the placement of the strips, the teacher and students discuss the logic of the order.

Their task is to reorder the events (from the original order of the telling, as in Figure 6–4) to make sense of the selection if the strips do not represent chronological order. They do this by using dates, times, verb tenses, sequence words, and of course background knowledge. Students place their sticky notes on a blank sheet of paper or one containing a simple hand-drawn timeline. Graphic organizer "timelines" are also readily available through various publishers or can be constructed easily on a computer.

The teacher models the process, and the students follow. For example, the teacher asks learners to identify chronological event 1. Not yet validating that the first sentence (identified as E1) represents *chronological* event 1, the teacher writes that idea ("You deposited money into a bank account") on an overhead projector strip as the students write theirs on sticky notes.

Learners now focus on the second event (listed as event 2) to see if it is truly *chronological* event 2. They see this sentence: "You went back another day to withdraw some of the money." However, in the text, the information that occurs directly after event 1 is presented as a question ("What happened in the meantime? Did the money just sit in the bank until you wanted it back? No—the bank used your money") and includes sequence words (*in the meantime*). Therefore, the class takes note of the sequence words *in the meantime*, now recognizing that event 3 should replace event 2 chronologically. Therefore, the teacher and students move "The bank used your money" up to position two on the layout (projector, timeline, or blank paper; see Figure 6–5).

Moving on to event 3, the teacher asks the students if the next step should be that "Then you went back another day to withdraw some of the money." By now, being more critical readers and seeing that the *order of the telling may be convoluted*, or different from true *chronological order*, students may acknowledge on their own that when the bank used your money, it helped fuel economic growth because the banks gave the money to people to put into products, goods, services, and so on. (This inference would be based on the background knowledge of students in the class who understand the economic system, as well as the concepts of cause and effect.) Therefore, event 3 ("it helped fuel economic growth") needs to be moved to the position after the new event 2 ("the bank used your money"). The reordering of the strips results in the order seen in Figure 6–6.

Finally, one event remains to be placed in chronological order. Students can now see that between the time they deposited money in the bank and went back to withdraw some of the money, the bank utilized the funds, which is what banks do to spur the economy. (The class can discuss the idea that if everyone were to withdraw their money right away after depositing it, then the bank couldn't really use it.) Therefore, the withdrawing of the money becomes chronological event 4 (after the using of it and the fueling of economic growth), even though it was

Step One

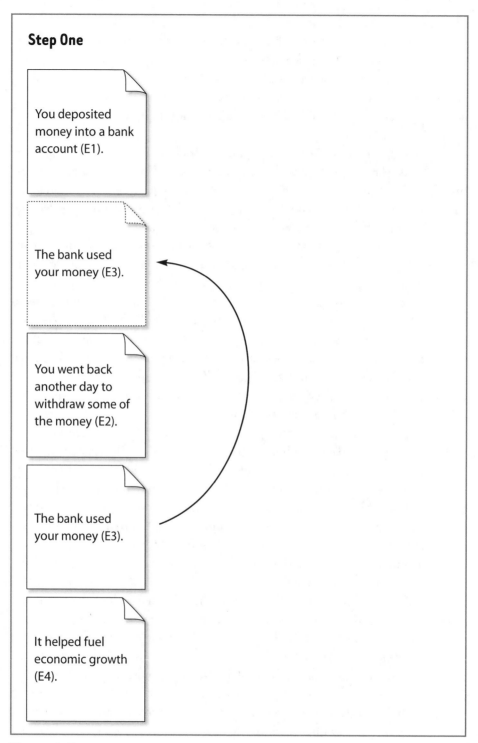

You deposited money into a bank account (E1).

The bank used your money (E3).

You went back another day to withdraw some of the money (E2).

The bank used your money (E3).

It helped fuel economic growth (E4).

Figure 6–5

Step Two

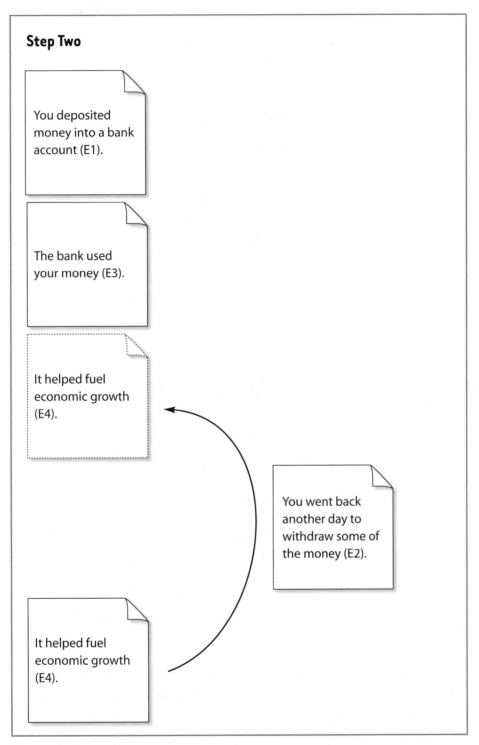

You deposited money into a bank account (E1).

The bank used your money (E3).

It helped fuel economic growth (E4).

You went back another day to withdraw some of the money (E2).

It helped fuel economic growth (E4).

Figure 6–6

Chronological Order

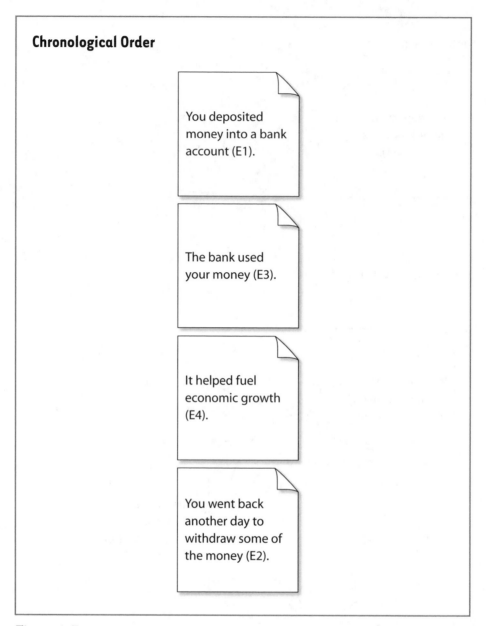

You deposited money into a bank account (E1).

The bank used your money (E3).

It helped fuel economic growth (E4).

You went back another day to withdraw some of the money (E2).

Figure 6–7

originally identified as event 2, based on the order of the telling. The final set of "renegotiated" sentence strips results in the order seen in Figure 6–7.

If this discussion sounds confusing, it is because talking orally about the order of events in text is not an easy task for anyone! For English learners, it is especially difficult because of unfamiliar vocabulary and syntax. The effort becomes much more manageable if we add a linguistic component (written sentence strips) and can move them around physically (a nonlinguistic approach) to determine the "real" underlying chronological order of events, thereby getting away from their presentational order, or the *order of the telling*.

The key is for collaboration to occur in class so that those students who do not see this logic will understand it through discussion. The timelines and sentence strips can be used in pairs at students' desks or tables as the teacher models them in front of the group. That way, there can be a considerable number of opportunities for English learners to seek clarification from their peers.

When analyzing this text piece, it may seem surprising that just a few sentences in a text piece can be so complicated. Though many readers have difficulty identifying the underlying chronological order when they encounter sequences of events in their reading, learners who speak English as their primary language are more easily able to recognize textual clues, including sequence key words, and they understand the subtle nuances of the language with more facility than English learners do. Therefore, strategies such as this one offer English learners tangible frameworks that help them comprehend texts containing otherwise confusing sets of events.

A final step for students after doing the sentence strips + timeline activity is to rewrite the text piece in chronological order, using the sticky notes, and then to add transitions containing sequence words such as those presented in Chapter 5. Figures 6–8 and 6–9 represent the directions for this activity, along with an example of a student summary of the rewritten sentence strips in *chronological order*.

Directions: Using the information from the strips you put into chronological order, rewrite the events using transition words such as these: *first, next, then, last*. Use appropriate sequence words to make your writing make sense.

_____

_____

_____

_____

_____

_____

_____

Figure 6–8 *Directions for Sentence Strip Activity—Rewritten Text*

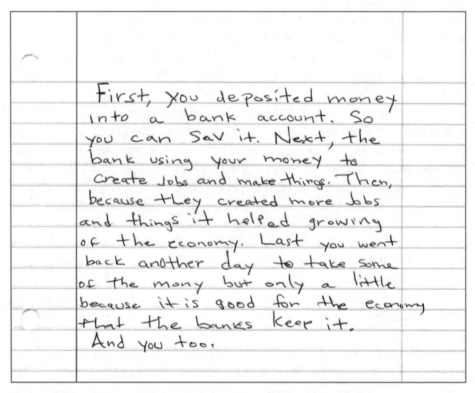

Figure 6–9 *Student Sample—Rewritten Text (Chronological Order)*

Not only does this extension of the strategy reinforce the idea that there is a deep chronological structure that underlies text, but by asking students to add sequence words in their own writing, we increase their chances of recognizing them when they encounter such words in subsequent reading endeavors.

Like all strategies, this one can be scaffolded for students over time. Teachers can select pieces that are longer, have more difficult English syntax, are written at higher reading levels, and contain a greater variety of "convoluted" (nonchronological) events. Eventually, learners should be able to tell the teacher the order in which to put the sentence strips from a text piece—perhaps after a period of practice within their groups. Over time, they will learn to develop the metacognitive ability needed to differentiate between the *order of the telling* and *chronological order* and to apply this knowledge to their comprehension of text. Figure 6–10 provides reminders to students as they engage in the timeline + sentence strips activity.

As students approach new readings in the future, they are much more likely to recognize when writers choose to introduce information in a nonchronological way, such as in flashbacks. In fact, when we showed students in our Literacy Center

Using the Timeline + Sentence Strip Strategy

1. Remember that the way in which someone tells a story does not neces-sarily show the true (*chronological*) order of the events that happened.
2. When you read, practice thinking about whether the events have really occurred in the exact order that they are told to you. There is the *order of the telling* and there is *true chronological order*, the way events would actually have occurred. Understanding true chronological order helps you to understand the story.
3. Focus on *sequence words*, such as *first, next, after, then, later, beforehand,* etc. They will help you keep the events in your head in correct order of their "happening."
4. Practice putting the events in chronological order to see if there is any event (or a set of events) that has been *told out of order.* Using a timeline + sentence strips approach is helpful.
5. Your teacher may ask you to respond to practice test items that ask about the *order of events in a story.* These items will help you comprehend text better and also to do well on real test items that ask you to demonstrate your understanding of *sequence,* or *true chronological order.*

Figure 6–10

the space man cartoon in Figure 6–11, those who hadn't been exposed to this activity immediately assumed that the six events occurred in the order represented by the figure, from left to right at the top and then left to right at the bottom. How-ever, those who had done the strategy as part of their literacy instruction were quick to point out that the "postcards" (their term) were out of *real* order; there-fore, they wanted to number them to indicate what the logical (chronological) order should be!

Being able to identify the correct sequence of events is also a skill often required of test takers, so this strategy, which supports better comprehension dur-ing reading, will easily transfer to testing contexts, as well.

Testing Link

It is not unusual for students to be asked to determine the sequence of events when they are taking tests. However, students may not recognize that they are being asked for *chronological order* and instead answer questions based on the *order of the telling.* Often, when they attempt to answer such questions, they immedi-ately focus on the order of events exactly as they are listed, as in the process dia-gram in Figure 6–12.

Figure 6–11 *Order of the Telling or Chronlogical Order?*

For example, the information in step 2 includes three separate events: banks use the money they receive in deposits; they lend money to people who want to buy homes or cars or to businesses that want to expand their operations; they charge interest to those who borrow the money. Related to the process diagram in Figure 6–12, what would students choose as the correct answer to test question 1 in Figure 6–13?

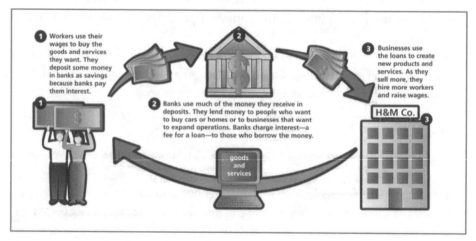

Figure 6–12 *Identifying Chronological Order*

Those who have not participated in a strategy such as sentence strips + time-line may not see that B is correct because the idea of lending money comes spatially in the text *before* the idea of people wanting to buy homes or cars. Yet, chronologically, banks lend money to people *after* people decide that they want to buy homes or cars.

Empty Box Format

A unique format for sequence questions is sometimes used on norm-referenced, standardized tests, which we refer to in the Literacy Center as the "empty box" type of question. Unfortunately, other than the boxes, no clues are provided to test takers about what skill they are to demonstrate; not even the term *sequence* is used, which is why, in my opinion, the format is misleading, even downright unfair. Test takers simply have to know that empty box questions are intended to elicit the underlying chronological order of events from a text piece.

Relating the empty box test practice question 2 in Figure 6–13 to the diagram in Figure 6–12, we can see that students are being asked to select the event that comes chronologically *after* "businesses get loans from banks" and *before* "They sell more."

1. By looking at step 2, we can tell that banks lend money to people who want to borrow it:
   A) before people decide to expand business operations.
   B) after people decide to buy cars.
   C) after banks charge interest.
   D) while people are considering whether to deposit money in the bank.

2. Identify the event that should go in the empty box based on the information in step 3:

Businesses get loans from banks.		They sell more.

   A) They hire more workers.
   B) Businesses need loans.
   C) They create new products and services.
   D) They raise wages.

Figure 6–13 *Sample Sequence Questions*

This prompting is indicated solely by the empty box positioned between these two events. However, the event they choose could come at any time after the getting of the loans (not necessarily *directly after* it) and at any time before the act of selling more (not necessarily *directly before* it). Most important, the "correct" sequence of events for this question is based on *chronological order*, not the *order of the telling*. In this case, the "creating of the new products and services" comes *after* the "getting of the loans from the bank" and *before* the "selling of more (products and services)." The "hiring of more workers" and "raising of wages" both occur at the same time that they "sell more" (based on the use of the sequence word *as*). Therefore, the correct answer is C, "they create new products and services."

In order to answer this question, students must first recognize what they are being asked to do and then do it correctly, understanding that their choice should reflect true chronological order. Without effective instruction from teachers related to such kinds of testing formats and explicit literacy strategies for sequencing, most learners would not do well on such items.

Recognizing Cause-Effect Relationships

It is compelling to think about the concepts of *cause* and *effect* and to wonder why they are so hard to locate and comprehend in texts. After all, our lives are built around multitudes of causes and effects that occur in everyday life. The concept of one event or agent leading to or causing another is not foreign to anyone. When I stub my toe and the pain radiates up my leg, I am fairly sure that the one event directly caused the other. What I may not have, especially if I am an English learner, is the language to describe this relationship.

An important task that readers must be able to perform to comprehend what they read is to recognize cause-effect relationships. Content-area history, social science, science, health, literature, economics, and government texts, among others, are rife with examples of causes and their related effects. However, perhaps surprisingly, the actual words *cause* and *effect* are rarely used. Instead, academic terms such as *resulted in, consequently, so, because, resulting in, as a consequence,* and *therefore,* to name only a few, often reflect the same ideas.

If we consider the possibility of a news anchor making a television announcement about the "consequences of the hurricane on the East Coast," we can see that if a reader or listener knows only the word *effects* (rather than *consequences*), he will not understand what the news anchor is saying. The same holds true in classroom contexts. When students are asked to identify *causes* or *effects*, the relationships are not always signaled by these two words. The text will typically include words that represent cause-effect concepts, but they will be synonymous rather than identical. In the following sentence, we can identify a cause and an effect, but neither the word *cause* nor *effect* is used: "Electric cars are powered by batteries, so they do not produce exhaust gases." Instead, the word *so* signals the *effect*—electric cars do not produce exhaust gases—which is *caused* by electric cars being powered by batteries. In many cases, students who have been taught to recognize cause-effect relationships only when the words *cause* and *effect* are used in the text simply miss them when authors substitute other words that signal such relationships.

Figure 6–14 includes many of the cause-effect signal words with which students should be familiar. However, it is important that students learn these terms as they participate in classroom activities; it is ineffective to ask them to memorize a list and then expect them to be conversant with the vocabulary. Instead, using

---

Some Possible Cause-Effect Signal Words

so, so that
that (meaning *so that*)
because, because of
causes
consequently, consequence
effect(s)
affects
contribute(s), contributed to
due to
as a result
for (meaning *because*)
leads to
originates with
make
create
then (<u>sometimes</u>, if it leads to an effect, meaning *so*)
and (<u>sometimes</u>, if it leads to an effect, meaning *so*)
when (meaning *because*)
as (meaning *because*)
influences
with (meaning *as a result of*)

Figure 6–14

examples of cause-effect relationships from students' own lives is a powerful approach, especially if the appropriate cause-effect terminology is presented concurrently.

◎ *Highlighting the Concepts*

To be certain that all students start on a level playing field, it is important to review the concepts of cause-effect before asking learners to identify them in textual contexts. One way for teachers to introduce the concepts is to give personal anecdotal examples that learners can relate to as a starting point and then ask students to add their own. For example, because I live in a community where dogs often run unleashed, I worry when I see animals dart across the busy street. So, I explain that the fact that the animals are unleashed causes me to worry that they could be hit by cars. Another way to say it is that *because* the dogs are running around unleashed, I worry that they could be hit by cars. I note that the word *because* signals this cause-effect relationship. Next, I ask students to describe some events in their own lives that have caused other events to occur, and we list them.

It's interesting—and often humorous—to ask students for examples of causes and effects in their real lives because they come up with some very unusual examples (sometimes leading us to learn more than we actually want to). One student offered this example: "I was grounded last weekend *since* I got 100% on the history test." "Wow!" her peers said to her. "Why would you be grounded for that?" She replied, "I didn't study, so Dad thought I cheated on it." Not only was her response funny, but it also included the signal word *so*, indicating another cause-effect relationship.

Providing students with a few selected signal words to start with is helpful. Then, as we saw in the example, we can ask them to use the signal words in examples that apply to their real lives or to the behavior of others whom they know or have heard about (such as celebrities or political figures). One way of keeping the affective filter low is to allow these kinds of choices. Some students are not as confident about sharing personal experiences as the young lady in our scenario was.

To choose a cadre of target signal words to begin with, teachers should look to classroom texts as the first resource. That way, as the signal words are used in real-life or everyday contexts, they can then be transferred to academic ones when students approach their assigned reading selections. For example, suppose that I have already determined that I will be asking students to read a selection entitled "A Cure for Air Pollution?" (Figure 6–15).

A Cure for Air Pollution?

Automobile emissions are responsible for at least half of all urban air pollution and a quarter of all carbon dioxide released into the atmosphere. Therefore, the production of a car that emits no polluting gases in its exhaust is a significant accomplishment. The only such vehicle currently available is the electric car. Electric cars are powered by batteries, so they do not produce exhaust gases. Supporters believe that switching to electric cars will reduce air pollution in this country. But critics believe that taxpayers will pay an unfair share for this switch and that the reduction in pollution won't be as great promised.

Electric Cars Will Reduce Air Pollution

Even the cleanest and most modern cars emit pollutants into the air. Supporters of a switch to electric cars believe the switch will reduce pollution in congested cities. But some critics suggest that a switch to electric cars will simply move the source of pollution from a car's tailpipe to the power plant's smokestack. This is because most electricity is generated by burning coal.

In California, electric cars would have the greatest impact. Here most electricity is produced by burning natural gas, which releases less air pollution than burning coal.

Nuclear plants and dams release no pollutants in the air when they generate electricity. Solar power and wind power are also emission-free ways to generate electricity. Supporters argue that a switch to electric cars will reduce air pollution immediately and that a further reduction will occur when power plants convert to these cleaner sources of energy.

Electric Cars Won't Solve the Problem

Electric cars are inconvenient because the batteries have to be recharged so often. The batteries also have to be replaced every 2 to 3 years. The nation's landfills are already crowded with conventional car batteries, which contain acid and metals that may pollute ground water. A switch to electric cars would aggravate this pollution problem because the batteries have to be replaced so often.

Also, electric cars will likely replace the cleanest cars on the road, not the dirtiest. A new car may emit only one-tenth of the pollution emitted by an older model. If an older car's pollution-control equipment does not work properly, it may emit 100 times more pollution than a new car. But people who drive older, poorly maintained cars probably won't be able to afford expensive electric cars. Therefore, the worst offenders will stay on the road, continuing to pollute the air.

Figure 6–15

(Continues)

Analyze the Issue
Do you think electric cars are the best solution to the air pollution problem? Why or why not? What are some alternative solutions for reducing air pollution?

Figure 6–15 *(Continued)*

When I read the selection myself, I scan for terms that may signal cause-effect relationships. In this case, I can identify the following eight examples in the first two columns of text: *are responsible for, therefore, so, because, produced by, when, when*, and *because*.

Instead of jumping into the text piece immediately, it is easier to ask students to use these terms in simple, "personalized" sentence frames (represented in Figure 6–16), which mirror the structures from the text. Teachers can write the frames on the board, type them onto handouts, put them on an overhead, or ask students to copy them from orally dictated statements.

When students fill in the sentence frames with personal information, they can then see how one event makes the next one happen (e.g., my hard work and energy caused me to receive a grade of "A" in math). Figure 6–17 represents one student's responses to the sentence frames from "A Cure for Air Pollution?"

Sentence Frames from "A Cure for Air Pollution?"
Page 421 Holt *Earth Science* (Allen et al. 2007)
(Frames from first two columns of this text)

_________________________ are responsible for _________________________.

_________________________. Therefore, _________________________.

_________________________, so _________________________.

_________________________. This is because _________________________.

_________________________ is produced by _________________________.

_________________________ when _________________________.

_________________________ when _________________________.

_________________________ because _________________________.

Figure 6–16

Sentence Frames from "A Cure for Air Pollution?"
Page 421 Holt *Earth Science* (Allen et al. 2007)
(Frames from first two columns of this text)

1. My hard work and energy are responsible for my good grades in math.
2. I love chocolate. Therefore, I buy 2 pounds of it every weekend.
3. I got good grades, so my parents took me to In-N-Out as a reward.
4. My shoes are muddy and wet. This is because I just finished washing the car.
5. Much noise is produced by little children on the playground.
6. I have to babysit my younger brother when my parents go out for the evening.
7. I get in trouble with my teacher when I try to "text" friends during class.
8. My face breaks out frequently because I eat a lot of French fries.

Figure 6–17

After students have filled out the frames in pairs or small groups, they can share the results orally with classmates. Auditory repetition of the structures helps ensure that the terms become familiar enough to learners so they can follow the next step of the process: identifying cause-effect relationships using the same signal words in the actual text piece.

To do this, students *scan* to locate the signal words introduced earlier and place the content information from the selection into the same sentence frames (Figure 6–18). Not only are the cause-effect relationships emphasized, but important content knowledge within them is also strengthened.

◎ *Validating Cause-Effect Relationships*

When English learners analyze cause-effect relationships, they can become confused because the term *cause(s)* often, but not always, precedes the word *effect(s)* in a sentence (or set of sentences). To help students recognize that there is no fast, easy rule to memorize about the way in which causes and effects are ordered, but rather to impress upon them that they need to "test out" such possible relationships, we can provide graphic structures for support. Such organizers provide students with opportunities to "construct their understanding of a subject in ways

Sentence Frames from "A Cure for Air Pollution?"
Page 421 Holt *Earth Science* (Allen et al. 2007)
(Frames from first two columns of this text)

1. Automobile emissions are responsible for at least half of all urban air pollution and a quarter of all CO_2 released into the atmosphere.
2. The emissions produced by automobiles are to blame for the majority of pollutants found in the atmosphere. Therefore, the production of a car that emits no polluting gas is a significant accomplishment.
3. Electric cars are powered by batteries, so they do not produce exhaust gases.
4. Critics believe that electric cars won't solve the emission problem, it will just move the source. This is because most electricity is generated by burning coal.
5. Most of the energy found in an electric car is produced by burning natural gas, which releases less air pollution than burning coal.
6. Nuclear plants and dams release no pollutants in the air when they generate electricity.
7. Supporters argue that a switch to electric cars will reduce air pollution and that a further reduction will occur when power plants convert to these cleaner sources of energy.
8. Electric cars are inconvenient because the batteries have to be recharged every so often.

Figure 6–18

that are less linear and therefore better suited for representing complex relationships" (Fisher and Frey 2008, 51).

Sentences containing words such as *when* and *because* are cases in point. In the text piece on "A Cure for Air Pollution?" the word *when* is used to mean *because*, and it is found in the middle of a complex sentence: "It is said that a switch to electric cars will reduce air pollution and that a further reduction [in air pollution] will occur when power plants convert to these cleaner sources of energy." The signal word *when* illustrates that the conversion of power plants to cleaner sources of energy is the *cause* that will lead to the *effect* of a further reduction in air pollution.

To validate whether we are correct about identifying the *cause* and the *effect*, we can place the information into a cause-effect chart and ask ourselves, "Does the cause that we listed make the effect occur?" It is important to do this for two reasons: (1) we need to verify that something is causing something else (not simply preceding it in time order) and (2) we need to be aware that some signal words can be placed at the beginning of sentences and some in the middle; however, the specific causes and effects do not change depending upon their order of presentation in the text.

Therefore, an effective step for students to take is to use a cause-effect graphic organizer. When they identify a possible cause-effect signal, they can try out their hypothesis by putting the events into a chart and checking to see if each listed cause truly led to the effect. Sometimes one event will simply precede another without causing the second one (e.g., I get up in the morning and then eat breakfast, but getting up doesn't *cause* me to eat breakfast). In this case, the relationship is sequential or correlational (Vacca and Vacca 2007). In the first example in the chart shown in Figure 6–19, the events in the sentence are placed into the correct cause-effect columns: "*When* power plants are converted to cleaner sources, air pollution will be reduced further."

For example, we can verify that the conversion of power plants to cleaner sources will certainly lead to a further reduction in air pollution. However, suppose the original text sentence noted, "*When* power plants convert to these cleaner sources of energy, there will be a further reduction in air pollution." In this case, though the signal word (*when*) is placed at the beginning of the sentence, the cause and the effect still remain the same even though the order has changed. Therefore, the information in the graphic organizer is still accurate.

Similarly, the word *because* is typically found in different locations in sentences, but regardless of where it occurs, the cause and the effect stay the same. The text statement that "electric cars are inconvenient *because* the batteries have to be recharged every so often" could just have easily have been worded, "*Because*

Signal Terms	Cause	Effect
when	Conversion of power plants to cleaner sources	Further reduction in air pollution
because	Batteries need recharging	Electric cars are inconvenient

Figure 6–19

the batteries have to be recharged every so often, electric cars are inconvenient." We can judge which is the *cause* and which is the *effect* by placing the events in the graphic organizer and testing them out; we can then easily see that the need to recharge batteries is the cause leading to electric cars being inconvenient, the effect. (Conversely, the inconvenience of electric cars does not cause the necessity of charging their batteries.)

As students become more adept at using the sentence frames provided by the teacher, they will be able to handle less support over time. In fact, another way to use the graphic organizers after a period of practicing this process is to skip the sentence frame step and ask students to scan immediately for cause-effect signal words in the text. Then, as students read, they can stop and respond by placing the signal words on the graphic organizer, along with some phrases from the content-area text that represent causes and effects. This kind of engagement with the text is representative of the findings of a study in which the researchers concluded that students became more active readers when they had a graphic organizer to aid them (Alvermann and Boothby 1986.)

Not only can students test out such relationships by using such a graphic organizer (with the student asking, "Does this cause really lead to the effect, or did it just happen at the same time?"), but they can also learn to identify when more than one cause leads to an effect (or more than one effect). In the second column of the article "A Cure for Air Pollution?" the example of electric cars being inconvenient because the batteries have to be recharged often is followed by another sentence telling readers that the batteries also have to be replaced every two to three years. In the cause-effect chart, then, we could place two causes (batteries having to be recharged often and having to be replaced every two to three years) and one effect (the inconvenience of electric cars) (Figure 6–20).

Being able to identify compound causes and effects in text pieces is an important skill that is necessary for overall comprehension. Frequently, especially in social studies and science texts, no one cause will lead to one effect. Instead, a variety of causes set the stage for a number of related effects. Without under-

Cause(s)	Effect(s)
Batteries have to be recharged often.	Inconvenience of electric cars
Batteries have to be replaced every two to three years.	Inconvenience of electric cars

Figure 6–20

standing these interrelationships, readers will have a poor or limited understanding of major content concepts.

As students learn to make cause-effect "hypotheses," they will also begin to differentiate between multiple meanings of words such as *since* and *as*, which can signal cause-effect relationships at times (and not at others) depending upon the textual context. If someone says, "It has been a long time *since* I saw you," there is no cause-effect relationship, as *since* does not mean *because*. Similarly, the statement "He acts *as* silly *as* a ten-year-old" does not contain a cause-effect relationship; yet the sentence "*As* I skateboard on a regular basis, I get better at it" does. Testing out these meanings in a cause-effect chart will clarify these differences in students' minds. Appendix D contains a simple organizer for identifying cause-effect relationships that teachers can adapt in many ways in various classrooms.

◎ *Rewriting the Relationships from the Graphic Organizer*

Knowing that reading and writing are interdependent processes, we should anticipate that as students recognize semantic and structural patterns in their reading, they will in turn apply the same processes in their personal written work. As we have seen, utilizing the cause-effect structures from texts, teachers can ask students to highlight signal words by writing them on a graphic organizer response sheet and then filling in the two parts—the cause(s) and the effect(s). They can do this *as* they read or *after* they have read. If students stop to take note of the cause-effect relationships as they read, the action represents what is often called a "through" activity—as it gets the students "through" the text with a focus on meaning. If they read the text first, then going back to fill in the organizer afterward (as a "beyond" activity), they reinforce the cause-effect relationships they were targeting as they read. These "during" and "after" reading phases are, according to Shanahan (1982), the times during which graphic organizer use is most effective.

A related step that can be taken beyond the organizer itself is to have students rewrite the cause-effect phrases into complete sentences, trying out multiple sentence structures, and positioning the cause-effect signal terms in different places. We can eventually see examples of the reciprocal nature of reading and writing when students begin choosing to integrate cause-effect relationships appropriately into their own writing in various contexts throughout the year.

◎ *Keeping the Process Authentic*

It is tempting to offer English learners every possible word that might represent a signal term for causes and effects, particularly as students begin to be successful at identifying such relationships. However, if teachers present a few basic signal words, choosing terms used in textbook contexts, rather than jotting down all potential signal words on isolated lists, students will be able to identify cause-effect relationships in meaningful contexts that also match important content objectives of the course. Over time, more difficult signal words, especially abstract ones (e.g., *with*, as in "With financial help from my older brother, I was able to buy a car"), can be added until students have a wide repertoire of terms that "jump out at them" as they read. If the signal words are consistently added to a list (or a chart on the classroom wall) as they come up in the context of classroom reading, by the end of the year, the chart should contain most of the terms from Figure 6–14, if not all of them. In this way, students have the benefit of recognizing the words in authentic reading as they appear and collaborating with the teacher and their peers in seeing how they function.

It is important to mention that cause-effect relationships occur in classroom contexts that one might not immediately consider. For example, in algebraic operations, students may need to recognize causes and effects before they can solve a problem. For example, problem 1 from this algebra text (Figure 6–21) includes the signal words *in order to*. Before students can even begin to solve the problem, they have to be able to identify what the cause-effect relationship is first. Metacognitively placing the events into a cause-effect framework (perhaps only through brief notations on scratch paper) will help them to see what is being asked before they can apply the correct mathematical operations.

In fact, in all three of these algebra problems, students need to recognize that the signal terms *in order to*, *when*, and *caused* represent cause-effect relationships

---

Algebra
Structure and Method, Book I
McDougal Littell, 2000
Pages 170–171

1. At 7:00 AM Joe starts jogging at 6 mi/h. At 7:10 AM Ken started off after him. How fast much Ken run *in order to* overtake him at 7:30 AM?
2. An ultralight plane had been flying for 40 min. *when* a change of wind direction doubled its ground speed. The entire trip of 160 mi. took 2 h. How far did the plane travel during the first 40 min.?
3. A ship must average 22 knots (nautical miles per hour) to make its 10-hour run on schedule. During the first hour hours bad weather *caused* it to reduce speed to 16 knots. What should its average speed be for the rest of the trip to maintain its schedule?

Figure 6–21

before students can determine how to solve the problems: in problem 1, the *cause* is Ken's speed, and the *effect* is his overtaking of Joe at 7:30 AM; in problem 2, the *cause* is the change of wind direction, and the *effect* is the doubling of plane's ground speed; and in problem 3, the *cause* is bad weather during the first four hours, and the *effect* is the reducing of speed to sixteen knots.

It is not difficult to find such relationships throughout content chapters and selections. What is important is that teachers notice them and call students' attention to the structures when they occur so that the process of identifying these words will become more automatic over time. Soon, students begin using such patterns more frequently, both orally and in their own writing.

"What do you mean 'it just happened'? Didn't we discuss cause and effect?"

Figure 6–22

Testing Link

As noted earlier, test questions often ask students to identify cause-effect relationships in passages. Some of these questions do not include the terms *cause* or *effect* but rather other signal words that are synonymous (or perhaps even none at all). The following questions from an excerpt on "Early Human Culture" (see Figure 6–23) represent characteristic cause-effect exam items:

1. What *influenced* the development of human culture (paragraph 1, sentence 2)?

2. What was a *cause* of the development of human language (paragraph 2, sentence 1)?

3. What was a *consequence* of human beings being able to talk to one another (paragraph 2, sentence 3)?

4. What is a possible *result* of the need for human cooperation in gathering and sharing food (paragraph 2, sentence 4)?

5. What *contributed* to the honoring of spirits of animals killed for food (paragraph 3, sentence 3)?

6. What *led to* insights into humans' daily life and shared beliefs (paragraph 4, sentence 1)?

World History: Ancient Civilization
McDougal Littell 2006 (Carnine et al. 2006)
Pages 52–55

Early Human Culture

What sets humans apart from other creatures? Art, language, and religion are special to humans and help *create* their culture.

Language

Human language probably developed *as a result* of the need for people to work together. One theory suggests that the need for cooperation during the hunt spurred language development. Hunters needed to be able to talk to one another *in order to* outsmart, trap, and kill animals for food. Another theory suggests that the cooperation needed to gather and share food *led* to the development of language.

Religion

Religion is the worship of God, gods, or spirits. Early humans probably believed that everything in nature, including rocks, trees, and animals, had a spirit. Some archeologists believed that early cave paintings of animals were made *to* honor the spirits of animals killed for food.

Art

Prehistoric art *gives* us insights into humans' daily life and shared beliefs. Early humans created art in caves and rock shelters. They also created art they could carry with them.

Figure 6–23

It is clear that with the exception of question 2 (which includes the term *cause*), most of the other items require students to understand less familiar cause-effect signal terms in order to be able to answer the questions correctly. Such proficiency takes time to develop, representing a process in which teachers should engage students throughout the year. Giving learners some help by offering them the paragraph and sentence numbers (as we see in these examples) is helpful at first—but deleting this assistance over time is realistic, as most test contexts will not provide this amount of support.

It is important to note that, there are also many cause-effect relationships in text selections that are *not* emphasized through the use of signal words. However, as learners become proficient at identifying such relationships, they will begin to spot them, even when no signal words are used. Alvermann and Van Arnam (1984) observe that the opportunities presented through graphic organizers activate comprehension strategies and metacognitive skills, along with prompting students to reread text passages in order to clarify understanding. It is reasonable to expect that readers will become more proficient at identifying cause-effect relationships as they encounter them over time in multiple text pieces—and eventually begin to recognize them without the support of the signal words. Students can simply place an X in the organizer where the signal words would be and continue to fill in the causes and the effects once they become sophisticated enough to identify less transparent cause-effect structures.

Eventually, as students approach new texts on their own, they can also transition to using a type of annotation as they read. They can write identified causes and effects on sticky notes in the margins, perhaps evening numbering the effects that are subsequently discussed after the causes are introduced (Irvin, Buehl, and Klemp 2007). Some students may even decide to color-code the sticky notes corresponding to each set of causes and effects!

Commentary

Teachers will find it easiest (and more authentic) to concentrate on locating signal words from their textbooks to illustrate sequence and cause-effect relationships to their students. Comprehensive lists should not be presented to learners with the expectation that they will memorize the terms; rather, the terms should be added to a list (or a chart on the classroom wall) as they come up in the context of classroom reading to emphasize such relationships in the content. In this way, students have the benefit of recognizing the words in actual reading selections as they appear and of collaborating with the teacher and their peers in seeing how the words function.

Next, we will address the issue of learning how to "read between the lines" to infer information from text and to determine the meanings of unknown words. These abilities represent "core intellectual skills that students need to conduct research, write papers, solve mathematical problems, read sophisticated texts, and take exams," and they are "arguably common to all classes" (Burke 2004, 92).

7

Get a Clue!

Teaching Students to Make Inferences and Determine Unknown Word Meanings

Sometimes it may seem as though our students are not reading carefully enough when they fail to understand a text piece that we tackle in class, even when we feel we have done a credible job of lowering the affective filter, developing background knowledge (including the front-loading of new vocabulary), providing linguistic and nonlinguistic contextualization, and teaching many big picture and specific reading strategies.

Yet, as educators who are proficient speakers of English, we may forget that what students know about the language may not be enough to navigate difficult texts to locate the information they seek. The questions we ask students about what they read can make them feel anxious, especially when the answers to such questions or the meanings of many unknown words are not clearly specified in the reading selections. This is because readers must often rely upon the background knowledge that they bring to the text, plus *clues* that are provided by the author, to make the meaning that is required of them. In this chapter, we will turn to strategies that help learners make use of such clues as they make inferences and derive new word meanings from textual context.

Making Inferences

One of the most frequent comments students make is that they cannot locate answers to the questions they are asked. One eleventh-grade English learner once even went so far as to throw a standardized test on the floor of my high school classroom, exclaiming, "It is just stupid." He went on to tell me that not one of the answers to the questions he attempted was even in the story.

Students who rely solely upon their scanning abilities quickly find that not all questions can be answered specifically by looking in a passage or selection for the exact answer. This is because inference questions are often posed, which depend upon the reader's skill in putting together clues to determine a plausible answer. Sometimes we hear this kind of interpretation referred to as "reading between the lines." Burke (2004) suggests that a core intellectual skill students need to conduct research, write papers, solve mathematical problems, read sophisticated texts, and take exams is "moving beyond what is given," or drawing inferences (93).

Not only was my eleventh-grade student frustrated by having solely one strategy to use (scanning for the exact answers, as if all the questions were detail questions), but his use of the word *story* also indicated that he expected it to be narrative in nature—when in fact it was expository. Gunning (2008) reminds us that when reading, students need to activate two kinds of schemata—prior knowledge and text structure—pointing out that the content of a text cannot be separated from the way the content is expressed. This testing incident highlights the need for students to have a wide variety of strategies that they can match to their purposes for reading, along with a familiarity of different text structures and organizational patterns.

When I work with large groups of teachers in workshop contexts, I am repeatedly asked what the ideal student age or grade is to begin teaching inferences. My answer is "kindergarten"! We make inferences many times throughout each day, often without being aware that we are doing it. This behavior is learned, based on our experiences, and it doesn't take long for little children to see that when Grandma is angry, she frowns, and that when Uncle Martin is tired, he doesn't talk much. Starting with real-life examples to illustrate the processing of inferring from clues is an engaging, interactive approach that will carry over into textual contexts quite easily. There are several approaches that teachers can consider for supporting their students in the process of making inferences. Three that we use in our Literacy Center are role-play scenarios, detective search, and the generative reciprocal inferencing procedure (GRIP).

◎ Role-Play Scenarios

The most powerful approach to teaching inferences is to start with what learners know about making inferences in their real lives because they quickly see that they must put together a variety of language clues in order to do it. Knowing that it is important to make learners feel relaxed and to provide strong scaffolding at the beginning of any new strategy, we use role-play scenarios that combine a number of linguistic and nonlinguistic features.

We begin by posing a question to the class, telling them that we will then act out a scenario that they will watch to figure out the answer to the question. We also remark that at no time will we specifically state the answer to the question, so they are to pay close attention to what happens in the role-play scenario. In fact, we direct them to jot down notes based on clues that they observe. Such scenarios represent context-embedded tasks in which English learners have access to a range of visual and oral cues, sources of comprehension support aside from written language (Finders and Hynds 2007).

For example, if the question posed is "Will Dr. Rodriguez renew her cell phone contract with the company she has now?" then Dr. Rodriguez moves to the front of the classroom with her cell phone. She begins to punch in a number on the phone—but because it does not seem to be working, she punches in the numbers harder, frowning as she does this. While waiting for the call to be picked up by the person whom she is calling, she taps her foot and grimaces. When the person she has called answers the phone, she speaks loudly. She then jumps up onto a chair and increases the volume of her conversation, sounding much more irritated than she did at the beginning of the call. She taps the phone a few times as she twists and turns to get better reception. Finally, she tells her friend that she will try to call later from a different location and tosses her cell phone into a trash can while saying "Arghhh!"

Students watch the scenario and are then asked to list every clue they noticed that might lead them to determine an answer to the question of whether Dr. Rodriguez will renew her cell phone contract. Sample clues that students list include the following:

punching in the number twice (the second time harder than the first)

frowning

speaking loudly

jumping up onto a chair

tapping her foot

looking upset

tapping the phone

twisting/turning around

saying she will call from a different location

throwing cell phone into trash can

saying "Arghhh!"

Once students have listed every clue they can recall, they share their answers, and the teacher makes a list on the board. At that point, class members are asked to use their combined information to answer the question, drawing of course on their own background knowledge of other similar frustrating situations that they have witnessed or experienced. The answer they come up with is that they are certain that Dr. Rodriguez will *not* renew her contract with the present cell phone company. After all, the phone does not get good reception, and Dr. Rodriguez is clearly dissatisfied! The teacher can now easily point out that the process they have just experienced is called *making inferences*—and that the more clues there are to work with, the stronger the inference is considered to be.

Of course, there are countless options for creating role-play scenarios. We have found that the more frequently we perform the scenarios with students, the better they get at finding the clues (linguistic and nonlinguistic) and the harder they try to find all of them. Additional ideas for the scenarios might include the following questions, though teachers are certainly creative and can come up with imaginative ideas that will appeal to their own students' interests.

- What is the weather like outside? (based on how someone is dressed and possible gesturing/comments as he enters the classroom)

- Is this student having success with his homework assignment? (based on a student's behavior as he sits alone at a desk)

- Do these two students agree on how to approach a class "team" project? (based on their interactions as they plan for the assignment)

- Will this girl and boy make a date for Saturday night? (based on positive or negative responses/interactions as they converse)

Of course, as students are exposed to various examples of role-play scenarios, they will want to be included in performing them, as well. This is a positive outcome that teachers can take advantage of so that learners participate in an entertaining, educational process and help create new scenarios for the class at the same time.

◎ Detective Search

The next step is to utilize the strategy of identifying clues to *infer* information in text. Irvin, Buehl, and Klemp (2007) note that strong readers make numerous inferences throughout their reading and that making an inference begins with a search for textual evidence. "Detective searches" (to use an obvious metaphor), which incorporate the use of inference signal words can help students learn to do this. As an analogy, students have to search for the clues, as a detective would in solving a crime. The teacher should begin by modeling the process for them with the long-term goal that later students will become more capable of finding the clues on their own. The first step is to introduce *inference* signal words.

Inference signal words, like cause-effect signal words, are signposts that tell readers what kind of information to target as they read. Figure 7–1 contains a list of inference signal words that are characterized by the nature of their "iffiness." That is to say, there is a measure of uncertainty about each one of them, so our students in the Literacy Center have developed a new term for them: "iffy" words. Though it is not a sophisticated way to explain the concept of using clues to determine information, it is comprehensible—and the terms we offer the students are excellent examples of academic language. Teachers may wish to start by introducing a few of them in the questions that they write for their students and then scaffolding, or reducing support, by adding more difficult ones later.

These words are characteristically embedded in well-written questions so that readers know the answers will not be directly stated in the text (as they are for detail questions). When teachers begin to use these inference signal words in questioning processes, they should make certain that enough clues exist in the text to support students' answers.

An effective way to choose an initial text piece is to find one that includes illustrations. Many recently published graphic novels relate well to state content standards, offering a variety of nonlinguistic clues that support the process of inferencing. For example, teachers might ask the questions, based on the Capstone Graphic Library excerpt about Clara Barton, that are shown in Figure 7–2.

Pointing out that because inference signal words (*most likely, probably, leads us to believe*) are embedded in the questions, a teacher may emphasize that the answers are not likely to be stated explicitly. Instead of letting students simply guess the answers to these questions, the teacher should remind students of the role-play process they engaged in earlier and ask them to list every clue in the

Inference Signal Words ("Iffy" Words)

according to	infers
appears	leads us to believe
approximately	may
assumes	might
believes	most likely
best clue	perhaps
can determine	possibly
can tell that	probably
could	seem
how we know that	should
if	suggests
implication	to show that
implies	would
inference	

Figure 7–1

text that they can identify related to each question. Students may read just a few pages of a graphic novel as a first step (or, if teachers are fortunate enough to have other technological sources, they can use a document camera to project the pages onto a whiteboard). Then, together, the teacher and class members should determine the clues needed to answer the questions.

For question 1 ("Most likely, why was it challenging for Clara to convince people about the need for the Red Cross in America?"), we can see from the first page of the graphic novel excerpt that people argued that they didn't "need the Red Cross," citing the opinion that there would never be another war (clue #1). In addition, the author tells us that few people had ever heard of the Red Cross,

Clara Barton: Angel of the Battlefield

(Lassieur 2006)
Graphic Library
Capstone Press, 2006

For the following questions:

    A. Read the question carefully and underline the "iffy" words in the question.
    B. Write down each clue that can be used to answer the question. Use bullets.
    C. Answer the question using all of the clues you listed. Write in complete sentences.

1. Most likely, why was it challenging for Clara to convince people about the need for the Red Cross in America?
2. What information probably persuaded people to support Clara's efforts?
3. What leads us to believe that Clara needed much help to ensure the success of the American Red Cross?

Figure 7–2

making Clara's task even more difficult to get the word out about its benefits (clue #2). Also, we see that she gave lectures for several years (clue #3), wrote letters to congressmen (clue #4), and gave out pamphlets to people (clue #5). Clearly, it was a long-term effort for her to convince people of the importance of establishing the American Red Cross. Students would be asked to underline these clues (if using copies of the text) or list them on a response sheet so that they can be put together to form a reasonable answer to the question about why Clara's move to help people understand the need for the Red Cross was so challenging.

Similarly, to answer question 2 ("What information probably persuaded people to support Clara's efforts?"), students may note the advantage of having a Red Cross (it would help victims of natural disasters like floods and hurricanes—clue #1). They would see that people needed help right away, so the Red Cross could organize instant relief (clue #2). Also, the fact that the United States was the only civilized nation not to have joined the Red Cross was a possible factor in getting people to listen (clue #3).

The final question ("What leads us to believe that Clara needed much help to ensure the success of the American Red Cross?") will prompt students to notice that Clara stated that she "can't keep doing this alone" (clue #1), that people responded by saying "yes" (clue #2), and noted that they would help her because America needed the Red Cross (clue #3). Readers may also point to the reference about Clara's group of supporters, the people with whom she founded the Red Cross on May 12, 1881 (clue #4).

It is important that students do not jump ahead to answering the inference questions before they find all of the clues so that they fully engage in the process of locating evidence to support their answers.

In pairs, students can continue to analyze the illustrations and use the language clues to answer predetermined inference questions for other pages (not shown). They should list the clues they find before they attempt to answer the questions so that they are convinced of having enough evidence for their positions. At the beginning, if teachers ask only one or two questions per page (instead of many at the end of a selection), students stay solidly within the meaning-making framework, so that they do not move on to the next page without understanding previous questions. Figure 7–3 contains the steps for doing such detective searches.

Certainly, readers bring their prior knowledge to bear upon their answers to inference questions; therefore, teachers may wish to help students make connections to their own experiences and perspectives as they answer them. However, we need to keep in mind that there is always a range of possible acceptable answers, based on the textual clues. Calkins (2001) has referred to the practice of reminding students to find that balance between background and textual information as

Detective Search—Making Inferences

1. Choose a passage that lends itself to asking inference questions. Be sure the passage is at the independent or instructional level of the students.
2. Write a few inference questions that utilize inference key words (iffy words). Be sure that the textual clues to answer these questions are present in the text.
3. Ask the students to find the clues to support the answers without writing the answers yet. (Highlighters or highlighting tape is especially useful for this purpose.)
4. Based on the *textual clues* and *some background knowledge*, students answer the inference questions.
5. Scaffolding: Passages can get progressively longer over time; clues can be more dispersed, rather than all in one place in the text; and there can be fewer clues to answer each question.

Figure 7–3

"holding readers accountable to the text" (353–54). She observes that the meaning in a text is cocreated by the reader and the author, stating, "It can be absolutely true that readers bring meaning to the page and also true that there is a meaning that skilled readers are expected to find on the page" (353–54).

When explaining this to students, I often draw a line on the board, showing that there is a continuum within which answers can fall (from the use of mostly background knowledge on the left to a complete use of textual clues on the right), based on the combination of prior knowledge and text. The middle part of the continuum is where students' interpretations will most accurately capture the essence of the author's meaning while still integrating the schemata students bring to the reading task.

I recall one instance when my high school students had just read a text piece about a young man who lost his expensive new backpack at school. He arrived home without speaking to his parents who were sitting in the kitchen, locked himself in his room, threw himself onto his bed, didn't come down for dinner, and thought about various ways he could earn enough money to replace the backpack his parents had generously purchased for him. One question asked at the end of the selection was, "How is this young man *most likely* feeling right now?" Choices included *hungry, happy, depressed,* and *angry*. Though *angry* and *depressed* are possible answers (within the ballpark, so to speak), the clues indicate that he was feeling remorseful, especially since he was considering odd jobs that he could take to replace the backpack. Therefore, *depressed* is the better answer. However, many of my students chose *happy*. When I asked them why, they said that because he had lost his backpack, he was lucky. He didn't have to do his homework that night!

I realized then that students sometimes believe that making inferences means putting yourself into another person's situation, which is not an accurate interpretation of the process. Making inferences means using textual clues, combined with what one knows (background knowledge), to determine what is occurring in a text. If students are asked how a character is *probably* feeling, they need to look at the clues first, tempering their perspective with how they may have felt at times in their lives, but they should not simply place themselves into the character's situation—that is, hypothetically change places with him. As a result of their response to this question, we went back to the text, using highlighting tape to emphasize each clue that indicated how the boy might be feeling. (Such tape is available at teacher supply shops and is enjoyable to use once in awhile when a text piece cannot be marked upon with highlighters.) Using the combination of clues, we then determined that although some of the students in my class might feel happy if their backpacks were lost, the young man in the story, in fact, did not; instead, he felt depressed.

Once students become involved in seeking out clues to answer inference questions, they recognize that they are learning a strategy that will help them in all content areas. Teachers can choose selections from different subject areas, offering longer pieces as the year progresses and asking questions for which there are fewer clues available. It is important to recognize, however, that learning to make inferences from text is a procedure that takes time. No text is ever fully explicit, and readers must constantly make inferences to understand what they are reading (Graves, Juel, and Graves 2007), but practicing strategies for learning to use textual clues proficiently is a long-term process. In a study whereby students learned methods for making inferences, no significant changes were noted until after four weeks of teaching. However, at that point, the effects were long-lasting—and even literal comprehension improved (Dewitz, Carr, and Patberg 1987)!

©2004 Jonny Hawkins

Figure 7–4

In the text piece on the social effects of the Great Depression, "Stresses on Families" (Figure 7–5), the challenge is substantial, especially for English learners, because the clues are solely linguistic, with no illustrations or captions. Also, it is likely that some students may not have a broad range of experiences related to scrounging for food or watching their parents struggle to retain jobs. With little prior knowledge to draw from, the textual clues become even more critical in helping readers make correct assumptions about what is occurring.

1. Did some people *probably* stay in unhappy relationships during the Depression? Why or why not?

2. What does the author *imply* about people's access to privacy during this time?

3. *Most likely*, why did school districts fire women who got married?

America: Pathways to the Present
Prentice-Hall (Cayton et al. 2003)
Chapter 22, "Crash and Depression"
Section 2, "Social Effects of the Depression"
Page 748

Stresses on Families
Living conditions declined as families moved in together, crowding into small houses or apartments. The divorce rate dropped because people could not afford separate households. People gave up even small pleasures like an ice cream cone or a movie ticket.

Men who had lost jobs or investments often felt like failures because they could no longer provide for their families. If their wives or children were working, men thought their status had fallen. Many were embarrassed to be seen at home during normal work hours. They were ashamed to ask friends for help.

Women faced other problems. Those who had depended on a husband's paycheck worried about feeding their hungry children. Working women were accused of taking jobs away from men. Even in the better times of the 1920s, Henry Ford had fired married women. "We do not employ married women whose husbands have jobs," he explained. During the Depression, this practice became common. In 1931, the American Federation of Labor endorsed it. Most school districts would not hire married women as teachers, and many fired those who got married.

Figure 7–5

A first step for students is to recognize the inference signal words in the three questions: *probably, imply, most likely.* The next step is to seek out clues that will substantiate a logical answer to each one. Using a graphic organizer similar to the one we used to validate cause-effect relationships is an effective way for learners to see that there are usually multiple clues that lead to the forming of an inference. (A copy of the generic one we use in the Literacy Center is located in Appendix E.)

For example, a teacher might pose question 1, identify the iffy, or signal, word (*probably*), and then direct students' attention to the following clues in the passage: divorce rate dropped because people could not afford separate households; people gave up even small pleasures. Then, students would fill in the graphic organizer, as illustrated in Figure 7–6.

In the same way, students can determine the answer to question 2 by noting the signal word (*imply*) and then looking for the clues that, when combined, lead to a reasonable inference that can be written on the organizer: families moved in together; they crowded into small houses or apartments.

Similarly, paragraph 3 in this passage contains numerous clues that would help to answer question 3 (signaled by *most likely*) about the firing of married women. Working women were accused of taking jobs away from men; during the Depression, the practice of firing married women whose husbands had jobs

Inference Signal (Iffy) Words	Clues	Answer to Question
probably	Divorce rate dropped because people could not afford separate households; gave up even small pleasures.	Financial reasons forced them to stay together.
imply	Families moved in together; they crowded into small houses or apartments.	They had little privacy because many people lived together.
most likely	(Students list clues.)	(Students determine answer.)

Figure 7–6

became common and was endorsed by the American Federation of Labor. (There are additional clues in paragraph 2 that students might notice, as well.) Students could identify these clues in small groups and place them into the graphic organizer to answer the question. As they become expert sleuths, they will be able to follow the detective process more independently.

Unfortunately, most students do not have access to expendable texts in which they can highlight clues. To begin teaching inferencing strategies, it is helpful for teachers to use an overhead projector, document camera, or computer to model the highlighting in front of the class to find the clues. Subsequently, teachers can offer students reusable heavy-duty overhead write-on transparencies or page protectors to place over textbook pages, providing students with overhead pens as highlighters. Additionally, laminated copies of appropriate, short (representative but not lengthy or overwhelming) photocopied text excerpts can be used so that the marks can be erased. Teachers who wish to use publishers' materials should check with the textbook companies to be sure that they obtain permission to reproduce copies of excerpts for classroom use only. Another approach is to simply ask students to write down the clues on a sheet of paper before answering the inference questions.

The process underlying the detective search is reminiscent of the well-known "author and you" procedure that Raphael (1982) originally developed as part of the question-answer-relationship technique. In both cases, readers recognize that they have to think about what they already know, what the author tells them, and how this information connects. In detective searches, though, we rely upon the use of inference signal words as a way to emphasize that readers will need to use this process.

◎ GRIP

GRIP is a method that teachers can use to scaffold the process of inferencing for students. Originally developed by Reutzel and Hollingsworth (1988), it is a "generative" procedure in that both teachers and students create, or generate, inference questions about texts. It is "reciprocal" because they also take turns answering them. (See Figure 7–7.)

There are four phases to this procedure: teacher/teacher; teacher/students; students/teacher; and students/students. During the first phase, the teacher develops inference questions and then in front of the class models the finding of textual clues to answer them. In the second phase, the teacher generates the inference questions, but the students practice finding the clues and answering the questions with the support of the teacher. Phase 3 involves the students' creation of inference questions, which are then answered by the teacher (who looks for the clues

GRIP: Generative Reciprocal Inferencing Procedure

Procedure moves from *teacher modeling to independent learning.* It is a highly scaffolded process, which occurs over time.

A. The teacher asks questions, provides clues to the answers, and answers the questions.
B. The teacher asks questions, the students provide clues for the answers, and the students answer the questions.
C. The students ask questions, the teacher provides clues to the answers, and the teacher answers the questions.
D. The students ask questions, other students provide clues to the answers and also answer the questions. Reverse roles often.

Demonstration with chapter excerpt:

A. Teacher/teacher/teacher
   1.
   2.
B. Teacher/students/students
   1.
   2.
C. Students/teacher/teacher
   1.
   2.
D. Students/other students/same other students
   1.
   2.

Figure 7–7

the students have pre-identified). In the fourth phase, groups of students develop questions for other groups to answer and then trade places so that their peers can do the same for them.

How quickly students move from one phase to the other depends upon their success with the procedure. It is reasonable to assume that the second phase would occur almost directly after the first one as students can rarely sit still long enough for the teacher to be the only one engaging in the activity; they will want to try it.

However, before asking learners to write inference questions for the teacher (phase 3), several weeks or even months might elapse before they are familiar enough with inference questions and their format to be able to write them on their own. Students usually need a great deal of practice answering inference questions before they can write them with specific textual clues in mind. Otherwise, they tend to write detail questions, which lead readers to search for an exact answer in the text.

The same is true of phase 4 in which students write questions for other classmates. By the time students write inference questions for others, the teacher has relinquished most of the control over the process, so they should be capable of generating the questions independently. The idea is for students to use a metacognitive approach whereby they predict what clues their classmates will need to find in order to answer the questions they pose. Fortunately, whichever end of the reciprocal process they are on, they practice identifying clues either way!

An advantage to this technique is that it can be used with all types of texts across many different content areas. Starting with a sizeable amount of teacher guidance in the first two phases, students eventually accomplish the feat of writing and answering inference questions without any support other than the clarification of their classmates.

When we use GRIP in the Literacy Center, we depend upon our students' recognition of the inference signal words. Of course, just as we saw with the cause-effect questions, signal words are not always used in every inference question. If our learners originally identify a question as a detail question (because it does not contain signal words), we tell them that after they find they cannot locate the answer specifically, they should label it an inference question. When this occurs, we laughingly tell them to "get a GRIP!" What we are saying is that this isn't going to be an easy question, but rather one that requires searching for the clues. It's a joke now in our center—but the process truly works!

Context Clue Strategies

Another challenging task we face when we work with English learners is helping them to learn new vocabulary words as quickly as possible so that they have access to grade-level content information. We know that a wide repertoire of vocabulary knowledge is a major contributor to comprehension, but the fact is that we can't front-load every vocabulary word that students might not know before they read each text selection. We would never get to the actual reading if we did that, nor would we have time to teach our students the strategies they need. We can only select the most important content terminology and present it prior to the reading of the text itself. Graves (2006) maintains that most vocabulary is learned from context, saying, "No other explanation can account for the huge number of words that students learn" (23). Only a small percentage of words are taught through direct instruction.

Fortunately, there are signals in texts that tell students they can determine a beginning or partial meaning to specific unknown words *as* they read. Often, students are not aware of these signals, so they may not actually recognize the support they are getting from the text to determine the meanings of these words. These signals act as clues for readers. The earlier we can teach our students to observe these clues, the faster students will be able to analyze the meanings of unknown words as they read. Given that secondary texts contain a large amount of technical vocabulary, such clues are extremely helpful in defining terms that are integral to students' understanding of the content. We will discuss three kinds of signals that will help readers—especially English learners who are just beginning to navigate texts and who need additional support with vocabulary: apposition signals, definition signals, and suggested meanings.

◎ Apposition Signals

One type of clue is the *apposition* signal. "In apposition to" actually means *placed next to*, so it makes sense that apposition signals alert readers that a word meaning will be placed directly next to the possible unknown word. A kind of apposition signal is the use of commas placed directly after a difficult word. English and language arts teachers may recognize this type of usage as an appositive. Therefore, in a sentence such as this one, the appositive defines the term *electrical energy*: "The electrical outlets in our homes allow us to use electrical energy, the energy of moving electrons." The reader sees the comma after *electrical energy*, followed by a renaming of the term—*the energy of moving electrons*. This is a beginning definition of *electrical energy*. By recognizing this and moving forward in the text, readers do not need to stop and ponder what the term means, thus continuing on with uninterrupted comprehension.

Another apposition signal that may be unfamiliar to students is the use of parentheses. Actually, when I ask secondary students what they do when they see parentheses, they tell me that they usually skip the information between them. They believe that it is either redundant or just a pronunciation reference; in either case, they choose to bypass it for the most part. However, if we look at a sentence that says, "Hunter-gatherers were nomads (people who move from place to place)," we can see that what comes between the parentheses contains important information for readers; in fact, subsequent ideas in the text will more than likely depend upon the reader's knowledge that nomads are people who move from place to place. Seeing that the parentheses encapsulate a beginning definition of the

Apposition Signals

, ,	commas
( )	parentheses
— —	dashes

Figure 7–8

word *nomads* is critical if the reader is to continue reading with sufficient comprehension.

A third kind of apposition signal is the use of dashes after a word that is potentially unfamiliar to readers. For example, we may read a short story in which "a caring young boy becomes frustrated—very upset—that the bank is taking advantage of older people by charging them money for cashing their checks." Through the use of the dashes after *frustrated*, the word is defined well enough that the reader does not have to stop to look it up in the dictionary or ask someone what it means, which might detract from a fluid comprehension process. In short, these three apposition signals are important clues for students to recognize. (See Figure 7–8.)

◎ *Definition Signals*

A second type of signal that occurs frequently in texts is the definition signal. Such signals are words, or clues, that indicate a definition is contained within the sentence, usually directly after or before a vocabulary word that might cause difficulty for readers. Figure 7–9 contains most of the definition signals that readers will encounter.

Most of these words are explicit enough that once teachers point them out to students and help them to begin noticing how they are used as signals in classroom texts, the words are easily identifiable. For example, in an earlier passage on the West African storytellers (Chapter 5, Figure 5–11), we encountered some of these clues. Two of the sentences in the selection included the following: "An oral history is a spoken record of past events," and "West African storytellers were called *griots*."

Careful readers will recognize that the definition of *oral history* is being given (a spoken record of past events), emphasized by the signal *is*; and the definition of *griots* is also provided (West African storytellers) through the use of the signal *called*. In the second case, the difficult word (*griots*) comes after the signal, rather than before it.

Definition Signals

or	who is, who are
that is	called, are called
is, are	known, known as
means	which is, which are
which means	

Figure 7–9

However, in addition to the more common terms that may seem somewhat logical to learners (my favorite signal being *means*, which for almost any reader who is paying attention identifies that there is a definition coming), there are two that are used primarily in academic contexts. Because students do not hear them used in everyday conversations, they may not recognize that they are being offered definitions to unknown words when they appear in texts. One of these is *or*. Sometimes a writer will use *or* in conjunction with commas to indicate that a definition will follow.

For example, in the following sentence from the same selection on storytellers, we see that the writer included the word *or* to highlight the fact that the definition of *proverbs* is presented directly after the word (short sayings of wisdom or truth): "In addition to stories, the griots recited proverbs, or short sayings of wisdom or truth." Students generally think of the word *or* as an indication of a choice, rather than another way to say the same thing. Clearly, though, the use of *or* in these sentences represents a different meaning in each context: "Would you like to have hot dogs or hamburgers?" is quite different from "I am ravenous, or extremely hungry." In the first example, there is indeed a choice. In the second, the word *or* signals another way to describe *ravenous*, but there is no choice between being *ravenous* or *extremely hungry*; they are the same. Knowing that commas usually accompany the word *or* when it is used this way is helpful to students.

The second signal that causes problems for students is the term *that is*, which is almost archaic in its usage as a context clue signal. We often hear, "Yes, that is right," but rarely do we hear someone say, "I am feeling diffident right now, that is, very shy." The term *that is* as a signal is more commonly found in technical contexts such as social studies or science. For example, this sentence contains a definition for an object that readers might not recognize: "One of the most useful achievements of Tang China was the perfection of the magnetic compass, that is, an instrument which uses the Earth's magnetic field to show direction." Because the concept of a magnetic compass might need additional clarification, the writer chose to include *that is* to signal the forthcoming definition.

Aside from these two signals, with which students may be unfamiliar, the others from the list in Figure 7–9 are fairly easy to distinguish. What is important is finding them in authentic classroom texts and analyzing how they function.

◎ Suggested Meanings

The last type of signal that readers need to look for in order to determine the meanings of unknown words when they read is more implicit and abstract than the other two. These signals are actually just words or phrases in the surrounding text that serve as clues about what a difficult word might mean. In fact, when readers use them to define a word in the selection, they are in essence making inferences about the definitions they need in order for the text to make sense to them. The typical approach that is "taught" in English classes is to ask students to use the clues in the surrounding text to figure out the meaning of a word—or what are more simply referred to as *context clues* in most classrooms. Context clues are, in essence, a subset of inferencing.

For example, in the text passage "Stresses on Families," we see the word *declined,* which has no obvious apposition or definition signals to emphasize it. However, because we can find the clues that surround it (families moved into together, they crowded into small houses or apartments) and we know that the word *declined* describes *living conditions*, we can estimate that declined means something like "got worse." Clearly, these clues are far less obvious than apposition and definition signals—but they are important for students to learn to recognize, which they will be able to do with practice when teachers ask them to search for *suggested meanings.* Sometimes these words are even used in conjunction with the other kinds of signals, which makes the process of using them even more manageable.

Applying Knowledge of Context Clues

One way to make the process of using context clues into a routine is to choose a sample text piece from the classroom curriculum (see Figure 7–10) in conjunction with a simple graphic organizer.

When beginning to teach students how to use context clues, it is important for the teacher to preselect important words from a text that has obvious context clues so that learners can be successful to begin with. For example, using an earth science excerpt called "A Future to Preserve" from the *National Geographic Reading*

A Future to Preserve

National Geographic, *The Oceans Around Us*, pp. 24–25

We know that oceans are essential to our survival. Without them, our planet would be very different—with burning hot days and freezing cold nights. As new technologies help us explore our underwater world, we are learning more about what we can do to protect it.

When we think of the ocean, we often think of vast stretches of water and waves. But areas along the coast are also more important parts of the ocean. Why? Because many forms of ocean life are born in coastal areas. Young animals often need the protection of plants growing along the coast before they can venture out to open water.

A major problem threatening the oceans is **pollution**. We used to consider the ocean a good dumping ground because it was so big. Now we know better. Chemicals, pesticides, and sewage can harm fragile sea life. Countries all over the world are beginning to pass laws to limit pollution.

Another problem affecting the oceans is **overfishing**. Did you know more than 20,000 species of fish live in the ocean? Even though that number sounds like a huge supply, sometimes humans overfish in certain areas. This means that we take more fish out of an area of the ocean than nature can replace. If some species of fish become **extinct**, or die out, this can affect other animals that depend on that type of fish. Eventually, the whole balance of the ocean can be upset.

The baby green sea turtle is a member of an unfortunate group called **endangered species**. This means that the number of green sea turtles is dwindling. If the decline continues, the turtles may become extinct. These magnificent animals have survived many extreme climate changes. But human activity has destroyed many of their nesting sites. And many turtles have become food for humans or drowned in fish nets.

The good news is that people all around the world are working together to protect the sea turtle and the ocean it calls home. You can help by learning about the oceans. Then you will be able to make good decisions to protect this valuable resource and the life within it for many generations to come.

Figure 7–10

Expeditions series on page 24 (Figure 7–10), we notice several technical vocabulary words whose definitions we can easily locate through such clues: *overfishing, extinct, pollution,* and *endangered species.* Then, we place some of these words in a context clue chart, adding the page, column, and paragraph numbers, as appropriate. It is up to the students, with varying degrees of support from the teacher or classmates, to determine the clues and the probable definitions of the unknown words (Figure 7–11).

Depending upon how new this process is to students, the teacher can model how to use the signals to determine the meanings of these important scientific terms or give learners an opportunity to do so somewhat more independently in pairs or small groups. (Appendix F contains a master copy of this chart for teacher use.) Once learners become proficient at using different kinds of context clues, they can even set up such charts for other students to fill out in a reciprocal manner similar to the suggested procedure for phase 4 of the GRIP procedure. The

Context Clue Applications

Word	Page	Column	Paragraph	Clues	Meaning
overfishing	24	X	4	"means"	taking more fish out of the ocean than nature can replace
extinct	24	X	4	", or"	die out
pollution	24	X	3	suggested: "dumping ground"; "pass laws to limit it"	harmful chemicals, pesticides, sewage
endangered species	24	X	5	"called" "means"	unfortunate group # is dwindling (declining)

Figure 7–11

eventual goal is that students will transfer context clue strategies into their own fluent reading process without having to stop to write any notes at all.

It is important that teachers do not expect students to possess a full understanding of new words learned from context but instead to highlight additional occurrences of the same words when they appear later in other text selections. As Graves (2006) suggests, "We learn a little from the first encounter with a word and then more and more about a word's meaning as we meet it in new and different contexts" (25). This is true of target vocabulary words taught through direct instruction methods, as well.

Testing Link

In testing situations, students are frequently asked to determine the meanings of unknown words. If the question is simply a vocabulary question—one that asks for a word meaning without providing any surrounding context—then learners either know the word or they do not. However, if there is context present, then test takers need to recognize that they can use their knowledge of context clue procedures to determine the definition. Often, inference signal words are contained in test questions or statements, as well.

From the sample test questions in Figure 7–12, we can see that knowledge of different clues can support students in identifying the definitions of unknown words. Statement 1 contains apposition signals for *fossils* (commas around the definition "the solidified remains or imprints of once-living organisms"); statement 2 contains suggested meanings for *sources* ("evidence includes fossils as well as comparisons among different groups of organisms"), and statement 3 contains definition signals for *present* (*or* preceding "in that particular place"). Such clues can serve students well in determining the meanings of words in testing contexts, as well as during authentic reading processes.

In addition, one suggestion that we make to learners when they encounter such test items is to determine the meaning of the unknown words before they even look at the answer choices. That way, they will not be sidetracked by the cleverly written distractors (other choices that may seem correct at first glance because they are created to deter readers from the right answer). In fact, Graves (2006) recommends that readers "play and question" (99). When students figure out what unknown words might mean through context, they should substitute their guesses for the difficult words to see if they make sense.

This would be an important step to take for multiple meaning words also, words that have many different meanings in the world of possibilities but only one meaning in a specific context (e.g., I *bat* my eyelashes, the baseball player has an expensive *bat*, the *bat* flew around the cave, my mom *bats* flies away with her bare

1. Fossils, the solidified remains or imprints of once-living organisms, are found in the crust's layers.

   In this sentence, the word *fossils* means:

   A. remainders of organisms that used to be alive
   B. old people
   C. rocks in a collection
   D. elephant tusks made of ivory

2. Evidence that living things evolve comes from many different sources. This evidence includes fossils as well as comparisons among different groups of organisms.

   The word *sources* in this paragraph probably means:

   A. people who give information
   B. dictionaries or encyclopedias
   C. magazines, periodicals
   D. origins or places

3. Choose the definition below that best matches the way in which the underlined word is used in the excerpt.

   Most fossilized organisms had skeletons or shells buried in sediment that is very fine. Also, oxygen, which promotes decay, cannot be <u>present</u>, or in that particular place. If oxygen is present, much of the organism will not fossilize.

   A. gift received by someone who is being honored
   B. to offer or put forth ideas
   C. in that area, nearby
   D. lost completely, unattainable

Figure 7–12 *Sample Context Clue Questions*

hands). For example, if readers are not using context clues, they might simply choose an answer such as *gift* for the meaning of *present* in statement 3 of Figure 7–12. However, by substituting *gift* for *present* (the idea they have in mind from background knowledge), students then see that the sentence does not make sense: "Oxygen, which promotes decay, cannot be *gift*, or in that particular place." By using the clues, however, students can see that *or* tells them the meaning should reflect "in that particular place," meaning existing in a certain place. By following this step metacognitively as they regularly begin to determine unknown meanings from context clues, students are also reminded that the actual goal is to create meaning from the text, not just to outguess a test developer.

Commentary

Whether teachers work with secondary English learners in the context of English as a second language or Specially Designed Academic Instruction in English (SDAIE) classrooms—or in mainstream content area and language arts classrooms—the need to teach effectively is the same. Vacca and Vacca (2007) suggest that "many students in today's diverse classrooms have trouble handling the conceptual demands inherent in reading materials when left to their own devices to learn with text" (28). Teaching students to recognize textual clues that help them make inferences and determine word meanings through context are strategies that can be demonstrated and practiced within the regular course of instruction. Such explicit attention to these elements yields benefits in the long run, both in terms of access to core content and performance on tests.

As we have seen in the first seven chapters, the task of comprehending grade-level content for English learners is doubly difficult because they are also aiming for the goal of full English language and literacy development. Therefore, it is imperative that teachers recognize students' diverse needs, pay special attention to the development of academic language within the classroom (including signal words), and model explicit comprehension strategies, scaffolding them as needed.

In the next chapter, we will consider some of the assessment tools we can use efficiently to identify the goals that teachers may choose to set for their students, remembering that the most effective way to proceed is to use materials that are already part of the classroom curriculum. Also, it is important to teach all strategies throughout the year, reviewing them consistently but scaffolding the processes to achieve higher levels of sophistication in increasingly more challenging textual contexts. To sum it up, "Independence develops by design, not chance" (Alvermann and Phelps 2005, 10).

8

Using Assessment Tools That Lead to Effective Instruction and Student Growth

There is no question about it. We are in an era of "high-stakes testing." Ever since the 1960s, when the National Assessment of Educational Progress became institutionalized as part of a widespread assessment plan for children in fourth, eighth, and twelfth grades, the pendulum began to swing toward more accountability, culminating in the mandated testing of reading required by No Child Left Behind to demonstrate the "adequate yearly progress" of students and schools. Unfortunately, as Afflerbach (2007) notes, the idea that more testing will lead to better schooling and that "students' reading test scores are a reflection of teacher and school goodness" became accepted by many (132). He clarifies that tests "are considered to be *high stakes* when their results are used to make important educational and life decisions" (131).

In this chapter, we will concentrate on ways to use assessment data to provide information about students that will assist us in becoming better teachers. In general, reports given to instructors containing standardized, norm-referenced test results are not helpful in telling us what our students can actually do; they are more useful for letting us know how one student stacks up against another (or a teacher, school, district, or state compares/contrasts with others). Other kinds of assessments, especially those that are easy to administer and interpret—and are typically informal in nature—contribute more practical information that we can analyze to plan better instruction and offer students what they need in terms of effective literacy strategies.

Assessment Woes

Every classroom teacher has painful tales to tell about interactions with students who are forced to take tests. I vividly recall one instance of giving a standardized, norm-referenced state test to a class of tenth-grade English learners. They vociferously questioned why they had to take such tests in English because the reading level of a tenth grade test is, well, tenth grade, of course. Complaining to me that they could do better on the test if it were a little bit easier, they were emphasizing what we already know about English learners. Their reading levels are typically not commensurate with those of native speakers of English, especially if they are in beginning or intermediate levels of English as a second language (ESL). Therefore, though they are gradually making progress that we may view as developmentally appropriate, they can't demonstrate what they do know about the content in a language context that is simply too advanced for them right now. In my opinion, they were understandably distressed.

Prior to my position at the university level, I was an English, reading, and ESL teacher in three secondary schools in Southern California. Over the course of twenty-two years, I taught grades 7 through 12. No matter what classes I was assigned to teach, I had many English learners as students. Though they were characteristically highly motivated and orally responsive in class, they often struggled when they were asked to read and write. The playing field, so to speak, was not a level one for them.

As I became a more seasoned teacher and eventually a doctoral student specializing in language and literacy, I learned that it takes as many as five to eleven years for English learners to develop cognitive academic language proficiency (CALP, a concept discussed earlier in Chapter 1), depending upon whether they are literate in their primary language, or L1 (Cummins 1980; Collier 1987). It became clear that it was up to me to teach my students the academic language and necessary literacy strategies for handling different types of reading tasks in school. I appreciated the opportunity to continue to work with English learners and slowly learned to identify approaches to help them develop CALP. Many of these steps included utilizing the strategies presented in the previous seven chapters, but some of them involved using assessments effectively to inform instructional practices. A side benefit was that by providing appropriate, essential strategy instruction and teaching the "secret language of school" to my students, they also became better able to "show what they know" in testing contexts.

Comfortable Contexts for Instruction and Testing

Good teachers are very well aware that there is a strong correlation between positive instructional contexts and student responsiveness. In Chapter 1, we discussed the importance of lowering the affective filter for English learners as we ask them to interact in classrooms. For testing situations, it is even more critical to help students maintain reasonable stress levels so that their potential anxiety does not unduly affect their performance. Emphasizing the importance of hard work and doing well is certainly appropriate, but teachers who worry so much about test results that their students become frenzied create a negative psychological setting for everyone. Airasian (1996) suggests that teachers encourage students to do their best but find the middle ground between overemphasizing the importance of testing (thereby heightening anxiety) and underemphasizing it (diminishing pupil motivation). As test dates approach, teachers should do the following to minimize stress:

- Give students advance notice.

- Provide opportunities for test preparation (especially in the case of a chapter or unit test).

- Minimize interruptions so that the testing environment is quiet and comfortable.

- If the test contains questions presented in unfamiliar formats (such as the empty box format we saw in Chapter 6), pupils should be given practice with the new structures prior to testing. English learners are contending with language issues, as well as content information, so even though they may have subject-specific background knowledge for a test, they may not recognize what the questions are asking them to do.

Kohn (2000) comments that the significance of test scores, in general, is dubious. He explains that test anxiety has grown into a subfield of education psychology, and its

"They've all tested positive for stress."

Figure 8–1

"prevalence means that the tests producing this reaction are not giving us a good picture of what many students really know and can do" (5). He points out that the more a test is made to "count," the more that anxiety is likely to rise and the less valid the scores become.

Not only does apprehension play a role for many students, asserts Kohn (2000), but others simply do not take tests seriously for a variety of reasons. They may just "guess wildly, fill in ovals randomly, or otherwise blow off the whole exercise, understandably regarding it as a waste of time" (5). In such cases, the result is, once again, that the scores are not meaningful. The cautionary tale is that unless teachers know their students very well and do what they can to create supportive environments, testing results do not have the potential to tell us much at all.

English learners also benefit from accommodations, which may include extra time to take an assessment or linguistic modifications that make the items more easily understood. Afflerbach (2007) provides an interesting example of how such adaptations can support English learners. For example, the question "What word describes how Elizabeth feels at the party?" is less complex, more straight-forward, and likely to confuse fewer students than the question "What word does the author utilize to describe how Elizabeth feels at the party?" If such a question is part of a norm-referenced, standardized state or national test, then teachers cannot ethically change the wording, of course, but if it is asked within the context of a class discussion, they should opt for opportunities to make linguistic changes. If the point of the question is to ask students to make an inference about what Elizabeth is feeling based on clues from a story, then knowing that the student can use an appropriate reading strategy to determine the answer (e.g., detective search) is more important than insisting upon the use of a high-level word such as *utilize* in the question itself. With time, English learners will acquire more sophisticated vocabulary, but the priority is for them to practice using literacy strategies. If the word itself is high utility, that is, used frequently in academic contexts, then teachers can also model context clue strategies (described in Chapter 7) to introduce it. For example, "What word does the author *utilize*, or *use*, to describe how Elizabeth feels at the party?" In this example, students are provided the support they need to understand what is being asked of them while also being exposed to the meaning of the difficult word.

Limited Reliance upon Norm-Referenced Testing

Whenever I talk to secondary teachers about the testing that takes place at their schools, there is general agreement that (1) there is too much of it and (2) it is not valuable to them in planning meaningful instruction for their students. For the most part, the intent of district and state testing mandates is to determine how well students are doing in relation to others. This is why reports often include stanines and percentiles or percentile bands. If a student scores within the fifth stanine or close to the 50th percentile, we can say that he is scoring about average, compared to the other students in his grade level. If he scores lower or higher than the 50th percentile, that tells us he is doing not as well as his peers in the same grade level or he is doing better than they are. Of course, the score tells us nothing about whether the test taker was hungry, tired, upset, sleep-deprived, or just anxious, in general. We take the raw score and mathematically convert it into a "derived" score, using it to show how the student performed relative to others. However, we rarely have the leisure to question the test's validity—or capacity to demonstrate what the student actually knows—in the first place.

Classroom teachers should be aware that the terms *standardized* and *norm-referenced* actually have different meanings, though they are frequently used interchangeably. *Standardized* simply means that everyone taking the test follows exactly the same guidelines in terms of what the directions are, how the directions are given, the response format for the students, the time allowed for the taking of the test, and any other requirements that may accompany a specific type of test or its administration variables (e.g., using a dictionary for a writing test, etc.).

Norm-referenced, on the other hand, tells us that the test was originally field-tested, or *normed*, by giving it to a large sample of similar students at a particular grade level and then generalizing the results to the entire population of students at this grade level. Therefore, the goal is to tell us how one student (perhaps a tenth grader in a science class) scores compared to other tenth graders. The problem is that while we may understand that one student scores lower than the average student at this grade level, no diagnostic information is given to us to tell us how to help him reach grade-level proficiency. Stanines and percentiles do not reveal patterns in the student's responses that might conceivably lead us to conclusions about appropriate instruction for him. Cizek (2005) sums it up well with the observation that that the current generation of high-stakes tests is "incapable of delivering on the promise of providing high-quality information that teachers can use for individualizing instruc-

COME IN JUSTIN, I JUST FINISHED MARKING YOUR EXAM.

Figure 8–2

tion for any particular student" (47). Without actually analyzing a student's responses in relation to what he typically demonstrates in other contexts, it is difficult to account for any one performance on any given test.

Kohn (2000) belabors the limitations of norm-referenced, standardized testing when he points out that the very nature of most high-stakes tests (i.e., short reading passages with a single, predetermined correct answer to be picked in a multiple-choice format) reflects an outdated conceptualization of reading and how to measure it. Noting that "the best way to judge schools is by visiting them and looking for evidence of learning and interest in learning" (47), rather than by analyzing test scores, he maintains that testing is "becoming" the curriculum. We should, he maintains, begin by determining what students ought to know and then address the question of assessment; instead "the tail of testing is wagging the educational dog" (35).

Similarly, Afflerbach (2007) observes that high-stakes tests are hardly ever a teacher's first choice for a reading assessment that provides useful information. In short, standardized (norm-referenced) tests provide limited information about what readers can do; therefore, teachers who want more diagnostic information about their students are turning to more authentic forms of assessment.

Assessments That Provide Useful Information

The best reason to test is not to differentiate among test takers, but rather to use the results to determine what students need, instructionally. Sometimes teachers can simply observe that students need support with a particular skill or strategy. Other times, it is helpful to use a more systematic—but still relatively informal— approach to identify what they need.

Why should teachers consider more testing when so much assessment is already mandated? Because some test data can point to areas of instructional need, thereby telling us what literacy strategies to target. As emphasized in the first seven chapters of this book, teachers can embed this strategy instruction into any kind of content area, from ESL, Specially Designed Academic Instruction In English, and language arts classes to science, social studies, art, home economics, government, and physical education. (Yes, some schools actually do have texts for P.E.!)

Teachers can opt to use a variety of assessment instruments (outside of the required summative, or end of grading period or year, assessments that are state- or district-required) in order to be sure that classroom instruction is appropriate and efficient. These assessments should have the potential to be diagnostic in nature and yield information about students' reading levels, as well as their success with different reading tasks. Such information helps teachers identify specific literacy strategies to introduce as they teach content. Many informal tools that are relatively simple to administer and not costly in nature can be used to ensure that time is not spent on material that students already know or written at levels that may be too easy or too difficult for them.

Data from assessments can easily be aligned with literacy goals within the curriculum. Afflerbach (2007) points outs that all reading assessment should be conducted with the purpose of helping students achieve in reading and emphasizes that truly informative assessment allows us to pinpoint the strengths and needs of our students.

However, in our Literacy Center, we are committed to the idea that the results of any one instrument should not be the sole basis for making decisions about students' literacy programs, and we make every effort to use multiple measures to validate our findings. Therefore, in setting up our curriculum, we selected a manageable variety of assessment tools, including the following:

1. interest inventories

2. informal reading inventories (IRIs)

3. formal survey and diagnostic reading tests

4. other informal instruments such as writing samples, checklists, and observations

Though other assessment tools are also used in the center, these four categories represent the most efficient in terms of helping content-area teachers who want to find out more about their students' needs.

◎ *Interest Inventories*

Recognizing that student interest is a key factor in whether students comprehend what they read, we knew that the teachers in our center first needed to have a handle on what activities the students enjoyed during and outside of school. Sometimes, asking students about their favorite stories and books leads nowhere, as few students who come to our center are avid readers and cannot identify such choices; so having a sense of their interests and hobbies can often aid in the selection of interesting reading materials when no established pattern of reading practices is available.

Gambrell and Gillis (2007) remark that students are more motivated to engage in literacy activities when they have "positive affective responses" to the content or processes. They suggest that one way to increase the potential for high levels of literacy motivation is to provide choices in reading materials for students so they can pursue their own interests or at least offer "text to topic" choices that link class readings to individualized assignment options (53). Using interest surveys or attitude inventories is an effective way to gather information about how students feel about reading, whether they view themselves as readers, and what their hobbies and leisure pursuits include. Many such assessment tools are available through different publishers, some of them embedded within IRIs.

Ekwall-Shanker Reading Interests Survey

The Ekwall-Shanker Reading Inventory (Shanker and Ekwall 2000), to be described in more detail in the following section on IRIs, contains a Reading Interests Survey. This survey includes three sections: open-ended questions (e.g., related to attitudes about school, books, and teachers); reading interests (e.g., topics and genres); and reading experiences (e.g., library visits, favorite books, reading habits of family members). The survey is easy to administer, and students can fill in the cloze blanks and checklists on their own, or teachers can read the items aloud. It is important to remember that students are not being tested on reading and writing skills but rather prompted to provide information about their reading habits and interests. The Ekwall-Shanker Reading Inventory also contains a more sophisticated version of the survey, appropriate for older students. Learners are asked about their educational goals, feelings about school, attitudes toward their classes and instructors, and the age at which they learned to read. They are also queried about what "reading" means to them and how it affects their lives, delving into many personal aspects of literacy.

Motivation to Read Profile

An inventory that we favor, primarily for its ease of administration and also because it spans a wide range of questions related to the categories of "self-concept as a reader" and "value of reading," is the Motivation to Read Profile, developed by Gambrell and colleagues (Gambrell, Palmer, Codling, and Mazzoni 1996). It includes two basic instruments, a Reading Survey and a Conversational Interview. Figure 8–3 contains eight sample questions from the twenty-item Reading Survey portion, providing an overview of the content and format. All of the survey questions (rated on a scale of 1 to 4, with 4 representing the most positive answers) typically take only about fifteen to twenty minutes to administer. Each student has a separate score for "self-concept as a reader" (SC) and perceived "value of reading" (V), adding up to a raw score out of forty for each and a full survey raw score out of eighty. The interview also takes fifteen to twenty minutes to administer and

Motivation to Read Profile

Name: _____   Date: _____

Sample 1: I am in _____.

☐ first grade   ☐ fourth grade   ☐ seventh grade   ☐ tenth grade
☐ second grade   ☐ fifth grade   ☐ eighth grade   ☐ eleventh grade
☐ third grade   ☐ sixth grade   ☐ ninth grade   ☐ twelfth grade

Sample 2: I am a _____.
☐ boy
☐ girl

1. My friends think I am _____.
   ☐ a very good reader
   ☐ a good reader
   ☐ an OK reader
   ☐ a poor reader
2. Reading a book is something I like to do.
   ☐ never
   ☐ not very often
   ☐ sometimes
   ☐ often
3. I read _____.
   ☐ not as well as my friends
   ☐ about the same as my friends
   ☐ a little better than my friends
   ☐ a lot better than my friends
4. My best friends think reading is _____.
   ☐ really fun
   ☐ fun
   ☐ OK to do
   ☐ no fun at all
5. When I come to a word I don't know, I can _____.
   ☐ almost always figure it out
   ☐ sometimes figure it out
   ☐ almost never figure it out
   ☐ never figure it out

Figure 8–3

6. I tell my friends about good books I read.
   ☐ I never do this.
   ☐ I almost never do this.
   ☐ I do this some of the time.
   ☐ I do this a lot.
7. When I am reading by myself, I understand _____.
   ☐ almost everything I read
   ☐ some of what I read
   ☐ almost none of what I read
   ☐ none of what I read
8. People who read a lot are _____.
   ☐ very interesting
   ☐ interesting
   ☐ not very interesting
   ☐ boring

From Gambrell, L. B., Palmer, B. M., Codling, R. M., and Mazzoni, S. A. (1996, April). "Assessing Motivation to Read." *The Reading Teacher*, 49(7), 518–533. Reprinted with the permission of the International Reading Association.

Figure 8–3 *(Continued)*

contains both scripted and open-ended responses dealing with narrative and expository text genres, as well as "general reading" behaviors and opinions about reading.

The strength of this assessment is that it combines information from a group-administered survey instrument with an individual interview, providing a useful tool for exploring more fully the personal dimensions of students' reading motivation. Gambrell and Gillis (2007) note that it is not uncommon to find inconsistencies between how students (especially adolescents) respond to survey questions and what they say in more conversational contexts, recommending that survey data be supplemented by other forms of data collection such as interviews whenever possible.

Secondary Reading Assessment Inventory—Interest Inventory

The Secondary Reading Assessment Inventory for middle and high school students (Cook and Babigian 2000) contains an eight-question Interest Inventory that prompts students to share their interests in reading, indentify the "target" times when reading is easy or difficult for them, and list the kinds of pleasure reading materials that they read on a regular basis. Students are also asked how they believe teachers can best help them with their reading.

This inventory is simple to administer and can be given to a whole class at the same time. From it, teachers can get an initial sense of how students feel about reading and their general reading habits (if any). The information can also provide guidance for the purchase of class books for independent reading at home or sustained silent reading in school. The questions are worded clearly, without any embedded idiomatic expressions that might be confusing to a reader who is translating the information literally, so English learners understand how to respond to them, even if they may typically have some difficulty with academic language.

Other Interest/Attitude Inventories and Surveys

Another interest inventory that we use in the Literacy Center was actually devised by our own reading specialist candidates. Called The AIM (Attitude/Interest/ Motivation) Secondary Reading Inventory, it is a compilation of each student's "favorites" (movie, TV show, music, book, video game, memory) and includes a listing of places that students have visited and enjoyed, hobbies and outside activities that they do regularly, statements about their reading practices, and information about the literacy strategies they use. Because we offer a class for secondary students, who are not always forthcoming about sharing personal information, our teachers created this specialized tool to provide greater insight into their students' reading practices and preferences. Many students can easily fill out this inventory on their own, but some English learners in particular may need clarification about directions or vocabulary definitions. Because many of the questions are open-ended, there are opportunities for them to provide unique, personalized responses. However, this assessment can be administered on a group basis, which is a benefit for content-area teachers who may have large class sizes. The full inventory is provided in Appendix G.

In addition, the Elementary Reading Attitude Survey (McKenna and Kear 1990), or what we informally refer to in the center as the "Garfield survey," is a possible instrument that can be used successfully with older English learners primarily because it features nonlinguistic contextualization—but the questions are not too childish. When students respond to the questions, they are asked to circle the "Garfield" cat figure that represents their attitude. For example, in response to the question "How do you feel when you read a book in school during free time?" a student might circle the Garfield who is happy (hands waving in the air), satisfied (with a smiling face), detached (disinterested), or upset (with a scowl). Students receive 4 points for a happy Garfield and only 1 point for an upset Garfield. The first half of the survey relates to students' attitudes toward recreational reading, and the second half relates to their feelings about the academic aspects and challenges of reading. Raw scores can be analyzed informally or converted into percentile ranks using a table, so teachers can easily use the data to get a sense of their students' viewpoints.

The Elementary Reading Attitude Survey consists of twenty items and can be administered to an entire class in about ten minutes. The creators of this survey remark that is important to emphasize to students that they should respond according to their own feelings, not as Garfield might respond! It is helpful, they mention, to point out the position of Garfield's mouth, especially in the middle two pictures, which is a way of providing nonlinguistic contextualization for comprehension support. Because the Garfield pictures are funny and the wording is straightforward and simple, it is an entertaining inventory that students seem to enjoy—and does not represent the usual school task.

One source that teachers may find useful is a text entitled *Using Metacognitive Assessments to Create Individualized Reading Instruction* (Israel 2007). It contains several informal questionnaires and surveys related to how students see themselves as readers and what strategies they use consciously as they approach text. They include the following: Index of Reading Awareness, Reading Strategy Awareness Inventory, Metacognitive Awareness of Reading Strategies Inventory, Metacomprehension Strategy Index, and Differentiated Analytic Reading Self-Assessment. Such tools go far beyond the typical interest inventory, probing into learners' feelings about their relationships to literacy and acknowledging the behaviors they exhibit during the reading process. We have plans to use these surveys with our upper-grade students in the Literacy Center, as they hold the promise of helping us reach deeper levels of understanding about students' perspectives on literacy and the particular challenges they face.

In addition, to determine if our older students know the importance of linking specific reading practices to purposes for reading, we frequently give them a "preassessment" activity entitled Flexible Reading. As illustrated in Figure 8–4, students are asked to match specified purposes for reading with four choices of approaches: scanning, skimming, reading, or study-reading. Teachers do not frontload any definitions of these academic terms for learners if the goal is to assess their knowledge, but rather simply let students read the brief definitions at the top of the page before deciding upon an appropriate reading method for each option. For example, in the case of statement 1, "cuddling up with a book just for enjoyment," learners who know the differences among skimming, scanning, reading, and study-reading would likely choose "read" as the answer. Similarly, they would also see that in statement 2 (getting statistics from a football game) the reader is searching for target information only, so they would choose "scan" as the answer.

As a way of assessing whether students understand the importance of selecting strategies that correspond to their purposes for reading, this activity, used as an instrument, is revealing. Once students have filled in their answers, teachers can immediately determine which strategies to present in their classrooms. Students need exposure to the idea that good readers approach text "flexibly," that is, matching purposes to practices that are most efficient in helping them to reach their goals.

One advantage to having this assessment tool available is that is can also be used to assess students' understanding of the four different practices after various strategies for skimming, scanning, reading, and study-reading have been taught. Used this way, it is more summative in nature. As Graves, Juel, and Graves (2007) point out, "Part of teaching students strategies is teaching them to apply a strategy only when it is needed" (273).

Many students experience insights during class discussions about potentially acceptable response(s) to each statement; for some items, more than one answer might be appropriate, depending upon the background knowledge of the reader. Appendix H contains the full Flexible Reading activity for teachers to duplicate, either for preassessment or postassessment purposes. (Answers are provided for discussion purposes.)

Flexible Reading

Scanning:	Briefly locating target information
Skimming:	Reading main ideas located in topic sentences (typically placed first or second in the paragraph)
Reading:	Reading all of the material at a natural or normal pace
Study-reading:	Reading material in-depth, usually utilizing a note-taking approach, study guide, or graphic organizer

If your purpose is to:	You would:
1. Cuddle up with a book just for enjoyment	Read
2. Get the most important statistics from the latest football game in order to discuss them with your friends	Scan
3. Find the main ideas in an article that explain the importance of the ozone layer	Skim
4. Memorize information for a unit test in history about the Mayan civilization (which you know very little about)	Study-read

Figure 8–4

Additional Interest Inventory Applications

Because we are not limited in the text materials that we can use in the center, it is easy for our teachers to take information from interest inventories and apply it to personalized instructional programs for students. However, knowing what learners enjoy is important for content-area classroom teachers also. Not only do the results of such inventories help to identify students as class "experts" in particular subject areas (insects, space, the Civil War, skateboarding, romance stories, etc.), but they also provide a sense of students' behaviors and attitudes related to reading. Do they hate to read aloud in class? Do they use previewing strategies before reading an assignment? Do they read anything outside of class for pleasure? What are they interested in doing outside of the classroom? Having access to such information is important as students are asked to respond to the various literacy demands in school.

When teachers are able to offer choices of assignments, incorporate content that links to students' interests, or purchase appealing materials to supplement basic texts (e.g., graphic novels in history, literature, and science), levels of engagement rise. We can combine knowledge about students' affective perspectives with what we know about their cognitive abilities such as word recognition skills, comprehension strategies, study strategies, and reading levels in order to help set objectives for class or small-group lessons. One step to take in learning about our students' reading abilities is to utilize IRIs.

◎ IRIs

IRIs offer excellent sources of information about how students read. They tell us a great deal about students' reading levels, their ability to recognize words (in and out of context), and the kinds of comprehension questions they can respond to most successfully. The emphasis here is on "learning about the skills, abilities and needs of the individual in order to plan a program of reading instruction that will allow a maximum rate of progress" (Roe and Burns 2007, 1).

Our initial plan for the Literacy Center was to start by choosing several IRIs, with the idea that they offer teachers (who are the reading specialist candidates and tutors) baseline information about particular students to whom they are assigned for the term (tutees). We recognized that other tests, both informal and formal, could also be administered later to validate initial findings. When teachers arrive at the same diagnostic conclusions through the use of a variety of instruments, they can feel more confident that they are not basing instructional decisions on flimsy evidence, but rather on multiple sources of information. This process is referred to as "triangulation," or using several data sources that "say the same thing about a student when making educational decisions about that student" (Northwest Evaluation Association 2009). Typical components of IRIs include graded word lists, passages that can be read orally or silently by the student or to the student, retelling rubrics, and comprehension questions.

The advantage of beginning an instructional process with an IRI is that word lists can be administered quickly, providing the teacher with information about the student's placement level—that is, the level at which to begin giving the reading comprehension passages. After a student has read two or three passages at her level and answered the questions, the teacher generally has some knowledge of the patterns in the student's word recognition and comprehension processes. Afflerbach (2007) notes that reading inventories "help us focus on the processes and products of student reading: the meaning that is constructed and the tools that students use to construct this meaning" (47).

A principal feature of IRIs is that they help us identify three "reading levels" for each student (Roe and Burns 2007):

- independent: the level at which learners can read with understanding and ease without assistance

- instructional: the level at which students can read with understanding with the teacher's assistance

- frustration: the level at which students are unable to function adequately because the reading material is too difficult

Students should be doing in-school and at-home pleasure reading at their independent levels, in-class work at their instructional levels, and no work at all at their frustration levels (which is why the term *frustration level* was coined in the first place).

Students may have different independent, instructional, and frustration levels when they read silently instead of orally. For English learners, silent reading may be advantageous for keeping the affective filter low. "Some students will read silently and comprehend text at levels higher than oral reading as silent reading does not have the considerable public performance requirement of oral reading" (Afflerbach 2007, 36).

Of course, not many teachers have the time to use IRIs with all (or even most) of their students. Because IRIs are administered individually, it is worthwhile to choose the students who are struggling the most for this assessment. The special time allocated to these learners makes this kind of process constructive and affirming. For a short period of time, the test taker is the recipient of the teacher's complete attention. Contexts may differ, but the personal attention teachers show students during IRI test administration can help learners feel comfortable. Teachers have more opportunities to infuse their personal styles into the testing process as they interact closely with each student who takes an IRI—and there is also more interpretational wiggle room. Conditions are only partly standardized (the examples, directions, and range of possible answers), reflecting the idea that there is "no single best way to give an IRI" (McKenna and Stahl 2003).

Ekwall/Shanker Reading Inventory

The Ekwall/Shanker Informal Reading Inventory published by Allyn and Bacon (Shanker and Ekwall 2000) was the first IRI that we chose to make available to teachers in our center. This instrument is actually a compilation of ten separate tests and offers a wide variety of choices for teachers who may need extra information about their students beyond what they would get from the administration of reading passages and the accompanying miscue analyses (coding of errors during oral reading). Certainly, the first step a teacher would take would be to give tests 1 and 2, which includes the San Diego Quick Assessment or Graded Word List (to determine placement on the reading passages to follow) and the reading passages tests, which contain two sets of reading selections for pretesting and posttesting purposes: A–B and C–D.

The reading passages (preprimer through ninth grade) provide information about a student's independent, instructional, and frustration levels and, if administered orally, also offer specific data about word recognition abilities, which teachers can analyze by following the directions for the coding of oral reading errors. In most secondary classes, however, there is no opportunity for content-area teachers to follow up with the teaching of word recognition skills, so this information would primarily be used as a basis for referring students to reading specialists or reading intervention programs.

However, students' answers to the comprehension questions can offer critical insights into the types of strategies that should be emphasized during content-area instruction. Although there are only three identified categories of questions in this test, the patterns in students' responses provide a starting point for teaching literacy strategies. The (F) questions are *factual*, or detail questions, the (I) questions are *inference* questions, and the (V) questions are *vocabulary*, or context clue questions. Students' responses will quickly tell the teacher what strategies to model during class (e.g., scanning for detail questions, detective search for inference questions, and context clue strategies for vocabulary questions, etc.) so that over time and with repetition, learners can answer such questions more successfully.

As an aside, the Ekwall/Shanker is also an effective resource for teachers who do have the leisure to work with struggling readers one-on-one. It includes emergent literacy tests, such as phonemic awareness, concepts about print, and letter knowledge. If a student cannot achieve a score of "independent" on the lowest reading passages, the instructor should consider administering these subtests. Also, if it appears that the learner may not have a satisfactory repertoire of sight words, other subtests offer options for assessing basic sight words and sight word phrases. Some subtests provide information on a student's application of phonics skills in context, and others highlight facility with the decoding of such features as initial consonants, blends and digraphs, ending sounds, vowels, vowel teams, phonograms, and special letter combinations.

Finally, it is possible that although a student is able to "sound out" a variety of unknown words, he would benefit from learning to break longer, multisyllabic (or what our students sometimes refer to as more "scary" words) into chunks. In this case, the teacher may wish to administer structural analysis subtests, including word parts, inflectional endings, prefixes/suffixes, compound words, contractions, and syllabication.

In summary, the Ekwall/Shanker Reading Inventory is an excellent assessment resource and contains many small subtests that a teacher can give quickly—but there is no practical way to administer this inventory as a group test. Even the comprehension questions in the passages are typically given to students in a one-on-one situation because they are open-ended and may require some prompting from the teacher. The authors of this inventory include a full section on the interpretation of test results, along with sample analyses of hypothetical student profiles. Test summary sheets are also available for photocopying, so in addition to being provided with suggestions for using the assessment data, teachers have the opportunity to develop an organized record of the results to inform classroom literacy instruction.

The Roe and Burns Informal Reading Inventory

The Roe and Burns Informal Reading Inventory (Roe and Burns 2007), published by the Houghton Mifflin Company, is a second inventory that we chose to purchase for our Literacy Center. This is partly because it contains a systematic process for detecting the decoding problems of struggling readers who are functioning far below grade level, but mainly because it tests the widest variety of comprehension skills that we have seen in any inventory.

Comprehension questions include the following domains: main ideas, details, sequence, cause-effect, inference, and vocabulary (context clues). The larger the number of passages that students read, followed by such questions, the more we can learn about students' strengths and weaknesses within the different domains of comprehension. Four forms of the test are included in the inventory (A–D) so that passages can be administered for various purposes or as alternative forms (oral reading, silent reading, listening). We ask the teachers in our center to consider using this inventory as a second source of information after giving the Ekwall-Shanker Informal Reading Inventory.

Initial information from the Ekwall-Shanker Informal Reading Inventory on the graded word lists and reading passages usually points to possible independent, instructional, and frustration reading levels and highlights students' strengths and possible weaknesses in decoding and comprehension. Giving the Roe and Burns Informal Reading Inventory as an additional assessment assists instructors in validating these findings, thereby more solidly justifying instructional goals that emerge for class or tutorial instruction. (The reverse can also be true—administering the Roe and Burns and then the Ekwall-Shanker—depending upon the preference of the test administrator.)

Often, teachers see that an older student's decoding ability is excellent. Students can whiz through the oral reading passages, sounding as though they are quite proficient. Yet, when they are asked questions at the end of the passages, they are unable to answer many of them. What does this really mean? First of all, it might simply indicate that the learner feels put on the spot as he is taking the test—and is focused on the performance aspect of the task. He sounds out the words but can't concentrate on the meaning of the passages as he reads them. It could also indicate that the student has problems with reading comprehension but is actually a fairly good decoder. We call these learners "word callers" (Harris and Hodges 1995), as they may be able to sound out the words almost perfectly—but do not understand what they read.

One way to see if performance anxiety is at work is to ask the student to read some alternative passages silently and then ask the comprehension questions. If he does better, it may indicate that he is more comfortable reading silently and probably possesses higher levels of comprehension than he was able to demonstrate on the oral passages. If not, it may be that his word recognition ability is simply much better than his comprehension. This is frequently true of English learners whose first language is highly phonetic (such as Spanish speakers); they can transfer their knowledge of the alphabetic system into English as their second language but are perhaps still developing CALP. They sound fluent but are not making sense of what they read.

It is not unusual to find that students who read below grade level do have problems comprehending what they read. This is why it is a good idea to look closely at their answers to the comprehension questions, both on the Ekwall/Shanker Reading Inventory (which primarily tests recall of details, along with a lesser emphasis on inference and vocabulary questions) and/or on the Roe and Burns Informal Reading Inventory (which focuses on a wider variety of comprehension areas and includes a Comprehension Skills Analysis Chart for documentation). The areas in which learners make the largest percentage of errors can then become instructional emphases, guiding teachers to select literacy strategies such as those described in earlier chapters to address these needs.

Secondary Reading Assessment Inventory

A third IRI that we use in the center is the Secondary Reading Assessment Inventory, which is discussed earlier in this chapter in the section about interest inventories (Cook and Babigian 2000). This assessment tool includes comprehension passages that are, relatively speaking, more interesting to older students than many others on the market and spans grades 6 to 12. Question categories include the following: topic (subject matter, main idea); recall (details); inference; evaluation (background knowledge and personal response); and vocabulary (context clues). A large proportion of the selections are expository in nature, and students may answer the questions in writing without any additional prompting from the teacher, which is an advantage for whole-class testing purposes. (Individual students can read alternate forms of the passages aloud at a later time if the teacher suspects that they may have severe problems with reading.)

There is no time limit for reading the passages and answering the questions (which is true also of the Ekwall-Shanker and Roe and Burns IRIs), but because it can be group-administered, students do not need to wait for others to finish before completing their own work. As we would expect of an IRI, the Secondary Reading Inventory offers information on students' strengths and weaknesses in word recognition (if the text is read aloud) and comprehension, whether it is read aloud or silently, including the domains of main idea, details, cause-effect, inference, context clues, and evaluation (personal response). Of course, the assessment also helps to identify students' independent, instructional, and frustration levels.

Other IRIs

Other well-known IRIs are the Classroom Reading Inventory by Wheelock, Silvaroli, and Campbell (2009), published by McGraw-Hill, and the Qualitative Reading Inventory-4 by Leslie and Caldwell (2005), published by Pearson Education. The Classroom Reading Inventory has only three types of reading comprehension questions (facts or details; inferences; and vocabulary, or context clues) with two forms (A and B), but it is easy to administer and the passages span a wide variety of topics. The Qualitative Reading Inventory-4 offers retelling opportunities in addition to the typical comprehension question format and includes the option of identifying the three reading levels for two different categories of selections: expository and narrative. Therefore, teachers can gain information about the types of texts with which students perform best.

No matter which IRI is used, teachers are certain to glean important diagnostic information about their students that is unavailable using standardized, norm-referenced assessments. However, in the spirit of triangulation, it is always recommended that more than one method of assessment be used, if possible. In fact, there are effective, if sometimes unconventional, ways to use survey and diagnostic reading tests that will yield helpful information about students.

◎ *Formal Survey Tests*

Although it is ideal to have the time to administer an informal inventory to a student on a one-to-one basis, we know that the act of reading aloud is a risky undertaking for less confident students, and they may forget what they are reading when they have an audience. In addition, the procedures for many of the inventories require that readers do not "look back" at the text when they are answering comprehension questions, which may be a good way of determining students' levels of recall but are not truly representative of authentic practice in real life.

One way of checking to see if an IRI has overestimated or underestimated a reader's abilities is to give a survey test. Such a test does not demand a large portion of instructional time (usually less than forty-five minutes) but offers another perspective on the student's "real" reading level. Survey tests are technically group tests that can be administered to many students simultaneously, so they are more efficient than most IRIs. In the same amount of time needed to gather information about one student, group-administered procedures gather information from a whole class (Airasian 1996).

Typically, when people think about giving survey tests to students, they automatically choose the grade-level test that matches the grade the students are in (for example, a ninth-grade test for a ninth-grade student). However, as diagnosticians, we are less concerned with percentiles and stanines than we are with discovering what learners can really do—including the identification of their independent reading levels (or grade equivalencies [GEs]). To find out what students are capable of doing, we have to make sure that the test can actually "capture" their true reading levels by not being too hard or too easy. This means that we may have to administer an out-of-level test.

The first question teachers in our center ask is how to determine which out-of-level test they should give to their students. The answer lies in the results of the IRI (or from preassessment information from another source). For example, if the information from the IRI shows that a tenth-grade student's instructional reading level is seventh grade, then asking the student to take a seventh-grade survey test is the next step.

The rationale for choosing a seventh-grade test is that the student can actually read it. It may be the case that he will score one or two grade levels below seventh grade, or conversely, one or two grade levels above seventh grade. In any case, the GE will certainly be closer to his actual reading level than if the student were to take a test written on his true grade level (tenth), which he cannot understand. If a student does not understand the reading selections (i.e., they are at his frustration level), then the results obtained from the test may tell us that he is doing better or worse than his peers, but they do not tell us anything about his actual reading proficiency.

Once a teacher knows the level at which a student can understand written text, the process of selecting materials for instruction becomes much easier. It is also appropriate to make some determination of how much the student will need to improve in order to be able to handle true grade-level reading. Although we recommend out-of-level testing for diagnostic purposes, we do need to supply a word of caution here: results from these tests should not be used for interpretation of percentiles or stanines, as the sample of students on which they were normed by the test company does not represent the same age and grade as the test taker, so comparisons between the student and his peers are not valid. If derived scores such as stanines, scaled scores (sometimes called extended scaled scores), and percentiles are reported based on an out-of-level test, they represent mathematical extrapolations at best and are not legitimate indicators of where a student places in relationship to others in his grade level.

The results that are useful and considerably more valid lie in the specific answers the student chose on the survey test. The teacher can do a quick "item analysis" to see what kinds of questions the student could answer easily—and which ones were more difficult. From these data, patterns may emerge, which often parallel the kinds of items missed on the original IRI. When more than one test points to a student's particular strengths and weaknesses, teachers can have more confidence in the findings. In addition, if teachers share their findings with students, it is likely that learners will be apt to devote efforts to improving in their identified areas of need. In this case, the survey test represents "a type of formative assessment that is not only a powerful measurement tool but also a powerful instructional tool because it allows students to observe their own progress" (Marzano 2007, 24).

It is important to point out that some test companies actually do include such item analyses for us; they list item numbers, with the corresponding reading skills beside them. This information makes the diagnostic process much easier, and a good deal faster, for teachers. (For example, the Gates-MacGinitie offers a word recognition component in the form of a grid on the grades 1 and 2 tests. It is a simple process for the test administrator to identify which questions the student has missed on the phonics subtest and to match them with the phonics skills that the student needs.) However, there is no such analysis available for the comprehension portion of the test matched to question types. This is one reason that we use the Types of Questions handout (Appendix I), which links to the strategies presented in Chapters 1 through 7. Teachers become skillful at identifying the items students miss and matching the items to the types of questions that indicate specific domains of comprehension. This information leads to the selection of strategies linked to these domains that can be presented and modeled during content instruction (e.g., recognizing the signal words that highlight an important cause-effect relationship in a text piece about ecology).

What is truly noteworthy is when students themselves begin to analyze the items they missed. One of our ninth graders exclaimed, "I missed two main idea questions and two inference questions, but I got all the detail questions right!" In response, an eighth grader remarked, "I always get the main ideas questions right because I am great at doing the herringbone!" (She is also great at identifying the gist of selections because she possesses the strategies for getting main ideas as she reads—and that is the true achievement!)

Gates-MacGinitie Survey Test

We have found that giving the Gates-MacGinitie Reading Test, Fourth Edition, Forms S and T (MacGinitie et al. 2000), combined with the results of at least one IRI, gives us a reasonable starting point for gauging a student's independent reading level. The Gates-MacGinitie is considered to be a *survey test* for the general assessment of student achievement in reading. Having identified a student's independent reading level based on an IRI, we can then select the out-of-level Gates-MacGinitie test that most closely matches it. For example, if an eighth-grade student tests at the sixth-grade independent reading level on the Roe and Burns, we would then give the Level 6 (sixth grade) Gates-MacGinitie Reading Test, remembering that when we give an out-of-level test, we cannot report stanines, scaled scores, percentiles, or any other scores derived from the original "norming" sample of the population in our reporting of results because the student is not actually being compared to other students at his grade level.

However, we can look at the GE and see what kinds of items the student missed. A GE related to a particular raw score on a particular form and level on a test will always correspond to the same GE. For example, if a seventh grader received a GE of 6.7 (sixth grade, seventh month of the school year) on the Level 6–9 test in the spring (designed for sixth through ninth graders), it would be reasonable to say that he was reading about average for a seventh grader.

Teachers must be extremely careful not to place too much stock in the GE because one raw score point one way or the other can change the results drastically. For example, according to Manual for Scoring and Interpretation (what we call the "norms" booklet), a student who gets a score of 21 on the sixth-grade comprehension subtest is reading "at" 4.5, or the equivalent of a fourth grader who is in the fifth month of school. If this student were to earn one more raw score point on the same test (a score of 22), he would be reading at 4.6, a difference of one month. Yet, a student who gets 32 is said to be reading at 7.4, while with one more point earned, a 33, the score would relate to a GE of 7.8, a difference of four months. This is because the scores bunch up in the middle, where 68 percent of all students score, on the bell curve. There are more "average" students in the middle of the distribution than there are at either end of the scale, very low or very high. Therefore, small differences in raw score points toward either end make a greater overall difference in grade equivalency scores. If we acknowledge that students often do not try their best on school tests to begin with, then the knowledge that 1 raw score point can make such a difference in the interpretation of GE also leads us to be wary of accepting such interpretations as definitive.

In addition, if the maturity and difficulty of the test content are too high or too low (e.g., a sixth grader taking a third-grade test), then the validity of the result is questionable, as well. For example, if a sixth-grade student gets a score of 3.8 on the third-grade test, we should recognize that because the third-grade test represents what third graders should do, the 3.8 can only be a ballpark GE, telling us that the sixth grader is reading at least a couple of years below grade level on a test designed for third graders with third-grade interests and abilities. (Of course, this is also assuming that the student didn't find the test so "babyish" that he didn't perform his best on it to begin with!) Still, such information may be helpful in noting where to begin with students—and in understanding why they cannot read their sixth-grade textbooks!

The test materials that teachers need for the Gates-MacGinitie include the following: student test booklets, the Manual for Scoring and Interpretation, and the Directions for Administration. Typical types of test questions in the comprehension subtests include the following categories: details, main ideas, inferences, sequence, cause-effect, and context clues. Analyzing the kinds of questions their students answered (such as those identified in Appendix I), both accurately and inaccurately, helps teachers to set appropriate instructional literacy objectives for classroom lessons. With practice identifying key words in the questions and classroom modeling of strategies by the teacher, students can learn to identify comprehension domains and select appropriate reading strategies to use, depending upon their purposes for reading (identifying events in sequence, recalling a detail, finding the main idea, etc.).

◎ Diagnostic Reading Tests

Though survey tests typically include vocabulary and comprehension subtests (and often even word recognition components at the lower grade levels), diagnostic tests usually supply us with an even greater number of subtest breakdowns and an analysis of question categories that highlight specific information about students' reading abilities.

We typically use the tests designed for grades 3 to 8 for our struggling upper-grade students, choosing an out-of-level test if we know that the grade-level test represents frustration level for them. Our choice, once again, may depend upon the results of an IRI, or we may have other preassessment information that is provided to us from a previous teacher or assessment that was given earlier.

The Stanford Diagnostic Reading Test

One diagnostic test that we use regularly is the Fourth Edition of the Stanford Diagnostic Reading Test, Forms J and K (Karlsen and Gardner 1995). Depending upon the level that is used (from first grade through high school), subtests include phonetic analysis, vocabulary, comprehension, and scanning. Each question is aligned with a skill or item cluster for easy analysis. For example, the comprehension subtest in each level is broken down into *recreational* reading (pleasure reading, primarily narrative), *textual* reading (content reading, primarily expository), and *functional* reading (real-life reading skills such as prescription labels, rules for the pool, how to get a library card, etc.). This information does point to the kinds of texts with which students are most successful, but for the most part, they do best at functional reading, followed by recreational and then textual reading. There are not a lot of surprises.

Similarly, the comprehension questions are categorized into *initial understanding*, *interpretation*, and *critical analysis and process* strategies. However, it is sometimes difficult to see why particular questions fall into these four categories as determined by the publishers, so our teachers are usually more comfortable matching the Types of Questions (Appendix I) to missed items to see where students may have problems.

The Stanford Diagnostic Reading Test is simple to administer, and it offers phonetic analysis at the lower levels (red and orange, from 1.5 to 3.5) and vocabulary and comprehension at the higher levels (green, purple, brown, and blue, from 3.5

to 13.0). There is also a scanning subtest for the purple, brown, and blue tests. Teachers need the test booklets, the Directions for Administering, the Teacher's Manual for Interpreting, and the Multilevel Norms Book. The cost of these materials is not prohibitive, and the information they can provide is well worth the investment. There are alternative forms of the test available (J and K) for pretesting and posttesting purposes.

An advantage to owning diagnostic tests for classroom use is that teachers can look back at the students' responses, whereas once the administration of a district, state, or national test has been completed, the booklets are whisked away, not to be seen again until the next testing cycle. In the meantime, teachers have no information about how their students did—and even when the "results" are returned, the "bell curve" information is really not helpful for knowing how to help students. Unfortunately, with the development of the standards-based reform movement and its emphasis on high academic standards and expectations for all students, more English learners are mandated to participate in such standardized assessments "sooner and more broadly than in the past" (Garcia, McKoon, and August 2008, 258). Teachers need to rely less upon assessment results that are "cloaked in secrecy" (Calkins, Montgomery, and Santman 1998, 95) and turn instead to tools that help us identify general patterns as beginning points for class instruction (Leslie and Caldwell 2005).

◎ Other Informal Assessments

A powerful (and often underestimated) method of identifying the literacy strategies we need to teach in content-area classes is to observe students as they work. As they approach the first reading of an assigned chapter, what do most of them do? If they want to get the big picture before they deal with a whole chapter, what steps do they take? Do they understand that they should try to get the big picture first? If we ask students to make an inference, do they tell us that the answer is not in the book? If we prompt them to state what a selection is mostly about, do they summarize it (with embellishments) instead of focusing on one comprehensive idea?

Collins and Cheek (1999) note that the best way for teachers to identify students' strengths and weaknesses in reading is to use a variety of nonstandardized tools. These include observation, word recognition inventories, writing samples, learning centers, and any other avenue for analyzing students' performance as they engage classroom tasks, display literacy strategies, and create projects. Barrentine (1999) recommends that teachers pay close attention to "the artifacts of daily reading experiences," such as story reflections, illustrations, character maps, Venn diagrams, and graphic organizers. Anecdotal record keeping, interviews, and surveys also help educators to "trace a reader's developing ability to comprehend and discuss text confidently" (4). These practices also illustrate what is difficult for readers, how they process print, and what reading strategies are employed.

Airasian (1996) adds that watching students as they carry out assignments (performance-based assessment) is an effective way of determining sound instructional practices in classrooms. When teachers glean information from these kinds of less intrusive measures, then they are allowing assessments to "emerge from the classroom rather than be imposed upon it" (Cobb 2005, 25).

Commentary

In short, there are many effective avenues for finding out what our students need, as well as what they can already do. With such information in hand, teachers can easily embed appropriate and engaging literacy instruction into their classroom curriculum. A summary listing of the instructional recommendations described in this book (Strategies and Instructional Goals) is provided in Appendix J for easy reference.

The next chapter will address the idea of immersing students in "real reading" processes—including pleasure reading—so that they do not "lose their edge in reading" by slipping further behind their peers who read avidly with more fluency and sophistication (Leonhardt 1993, 35). The most powerful instruction includes the teaching of explicit strategies combined with many opportunities for engagement in authentic reading events.

9

Offering Real Reading Opportunities in All Classrooms

How teachers approach reading in middle school and high school classes is a touchy issue. Students want to focus on content at this point without the burden of having to demonstrate that they can read, and teachers would prefer to teach the subject areas in which they are experts. Neither group wants to face the fact that, for many students in grades 6 to 12, reading is still a struggle. English learners bring another set of challenges to the classroom since by the very nature of their ongoing language development in English, they are not yet proficient in reading and writing at grade level.

According to Opitz and Rasinski (1998), silent reading should be the "mainstay" of any effective reading program (xi). It is faster than reading aloud and provides individual time to reread without burdening other readers who may have a different pace.

Also, researchers found that when compared with oral reading, silent reading enables students to be "more attentive during reading" and "more responsive during discussions" (Galda and Graves 2007, 91). Students could more easily recall information from the text and locate specific textual information to support answers. "The more silent reading we can motivate our students to do—both in class and out of class—the better they will become at this activity that will engage them throughout their lives" (Galda and Graves 2007, 91).

Interestingly, we know that at least for the upper grades, silent reading is also the most *authentic* kind of reading we can ask students to do. This is the way adults read in the real world. Nobody stops us at street corners while waiting for lights to turn green, demanding we read aloud from specific passages of text. Nor are we typically asked to volunteer to read aloud to our friends and associates at social events or in the workplace. It simply does not happen. Adults read where, when, and how they want or need to. If students were to do primarily silent reading in secondary classrooms, then their in-school reading practices would match the kind of reading that readers typically do outside of school.

So why is it that so much of the reading that takes place in sixth- to twelfth-grade classrooms is oral?

Typical Reading Practices in Secondary Classrooms

Secondary teachers have a great number of responsibilities in addition to teaching subject matter content, not the least of which is class management. When faced with a classroom of learners who possess a wide range of reading abilities, the easiest way to be sure that everyone stays on the same page, literally, is to ensure that classroom reading is done aloud. When teachers allow students to read silently, they worry that students may not comprehend the reading—or even attend to the print in the first place. They believe that having students read aloud is the best way to ensure that the content is covered and that everyone has access to the material in the reading selection. However, there are numerous disadvantages to having students read aloud as the primary reading method in a classroom.

◎ *Round-Robin Reading*

When reading a novel or text chapter is the focus of an English or content area class period, it is not unusual to see a "round-robin" structure used. This is a practice in which students take turns reading aloud, one after the other, until everyone has had a turn, and then the process begins again. Defined by Harris and Hodges in *The Literacy Dictionary* (1995) as an "outmoded practice" (222), round-robin reading is often the method of choice because it provides a built-in class management system. Teachers can always be certain if students are following along on the same page at the same time. Also, most educators, particularly content-area experts, do not possess a wide repertoire of reading strategies to replace it. Yet, if we look at the practice itself, we can see that there are several serious disadvantages to having students take turns reading aloud in front of their peers (Opitz and Rasinski 1998):

- Students' main goal becomes recognizing the words in their assigned part of the text correctly and reading fluently in front of their peers in order to avoid embarrassment.

- Students often count down to the section they will be responsible for while other students are reading, thus losing any sense of the text that has come before and not focusing on the meaning-making process during their own reading.

- "Sounding out" to seem proficient is the goal for the moment.

- Participation in a round-robin activity gives students a view of reading that is not accurate. Even educated professionals feel put on the spot when asked to perform in front of colleagues. When Opitz and Rasinski (1998) asked a group of teachers to engage in round-robin reading, one admitted that he was not paying attention to those who were reading aloud before his turn came, saying, "I was trying to figure out your pattern so that I could prepare the part I thought you would have me read" (ix).

Many times, I have asked my graduate students to read a short excerpt or even just some directions for administering a test, and the response I get from them is less than enthusiastic. After all, they haven't practiced, and they might make a "miscue" on a word or two in front of their colleagues, which causes discomfort, to say the least.

For English learners in our classrooms, the ramifications are even more serious. Not only will the affective filter potentially be raised during the process of round-robin reading, but learners' confidence can be undermined to such an extent that they eventually shy away from participation in class reading activities altogether.

Another negative result of round-robin reading is that it may hinder students' ability to develop listening comprehension. Trelease (2001) explains that listening comprehension is the "reservoir" for reading comprehension; it is the pool of language that readers use to draw from when they read. Eventually, if enough words are "poured into it" as a result of many different listening experiences, the reservoir starts to overflow into the speaking vocabulary, the reading vocabulary, and the writing vocabulary (39). However, if readers are concerned about their own performance and not focused on what others are reading, the potential benefits of hearing new vocabulary read aloud are lost. Paired reading, small-group reading, and silent reading can be much more valuable and productive.

◎ *Popcorn Reading*

A preservice teacher with whom I once worked told me that she would never compel a child to read aloud if he didn't want to. When asked what she did instead, she noted that she allowed her students to do "popcorn reading," a practice whereby students raise their hands if they want to read aloud and are randomly called on by the teacher. Because there is no particular order to this process, the hands extended into the air at various intervals represent popping kernels that teachers select one by one, identifying each reader to have his turn.

When I prompted this teacher to estimate what percentage of her students participated in this activity, she said that four or five of her students were always the ones who did the reading (about 17 percent), while the rest just sat quietly. Noting that the majority of the students, especially the English learners, were simply left behind, I asked her why she continued the practice. Her response was that it "got the assigned reading done" even though she had no way of knowing if those who did not participate in the oral reading understood what was read aloud. This is a typical example of how class management issues and the need to cover the curriculum can dictate the reading practices teachers choose.

◎ *Advantages to Having Students Read Aloud*

There are certainly some advantages to having students read aloud, but they depend upon how sensitively and effectively the teacher handles the process. One obvious benefit is that it gives the teacher an opportunity to assess students' reading abilities. This is an important component of elementary school reading programs, but most secondary teachers are not equipped to help struggling readers (nor do they typically take on this role voluntarily) even if they are able to identify weaknesses in students' reading patterns. Unless appropriate instruction based on the assessment information follows a read-aloud opportunity, the assessment practice is meaningless.

Another advantage to having students read aloud might be that the teacher can see what reading strategies the students are using. Again, the value of this information depends upon what the teacher plans to do with it. If teachers can use this knowledge to help students develop strategies beyond what they are already using, then hearing students read aloud may sometimes be appropriate. For example, if teachers have taught students think-aloud practices ("I might just skip this word that I don't know right now and hope that the clues in the rest of the sentence or paragraph will help me to figure it out"), then the oral aspects of popcorn reading may serve as a model for other students. However, it is not appropriate to use a think-aloud approach for all reading assignments, as it would be extremely irritating for everyone in the long run. Instead, there may be other instructional options that would benefit and interest students more than the time spent reading aloud. In addition, as noted earlier, when students are asked to read on a volunteer basis only, teachers have no way of ensuring that everyone participates.

Finally, it may sometimes be motivational for students to read aloud during class. Many secondary students, especially English learners with whom I have worked, simply like to read aloud once in a while, particularly if they are sharing or performing something about a topic of interest. Letting them read aloud can whet their appetites for language, allowing them to see that speaking is related to the other language skills, leading to the development of listening comprehension and vocabulary, fluency, expression, and phrasing (Armbruster and Wilkinson 1991). However, there is a difference between planning for a read-aloud activity to meet a specific motivational purpose (e.g., taking parts in a play, creating a hypothetical newscast, or participating in script reading for readers' theater) and defaulting to a round-robin technique on a regular basis for lack of a better alternative. Combs (2004) notes that teachers should avoid practices such as round-robin and popcorn reading unless oral language or speech is the purpose of the activity, maintaining that reading aloud emphasizes errors, provides poor reading models, and discourages metacognitive and comprehension strategies, such as rereading.

In summary, teachers should carefully consider the reasons they ask their students to read aloud in class. There is no documented comprehension benefit for the students who participate in the process (unless instruction matched to their areas of need directly follows the activity), but there are many motivational drawbacks, not the least of which may be personal embarrassment during their own time to read and off-task behavior while others are reading. Instructors may want to consider "constructive alternatives" (Harris and Hodges 1995, 222).

◎ *Reading Aloud to Students*

It seems logical that in order to develop language proficiency, English learners need to hear models of fluent reading, including the prosodic elements of pitch, volume, and phrasing. Certainly, they do need repeated exposure to language that is read aloud. However, if demonstrations of reading aloud only occur when classmates do it—peers who are also not yet proficient—they may not have access to the "kind of proficient reading that we would like them to emulate"

(Trelease 2001, 49). Therefore, other instructional practices should be included regularly in classrooms, one of which is the practice of the teacher reading aloud *to* the students.

In the well-known *Read-Aloud Handbook*, Trelease (2001) advocates the practice of reading aloud to students from babydom throughout the high school years. He notes that whereas an adult only uses nine "rare" words (per thousand) when talking with a three-year-old, there are three times as many in a children's book and more than seven times as many in a newspaper. The point is that "oral communication is decidedly inferior to print when building vocabulary" (17).

If we chatted informally with high school teachers, most would tell you that they do not usually read aloud to their students for the purpose of stimulating interest about the content. Instead, they may read from the textbook when they feel the students cannot handle the difficulty level on their own—but they rarely bring in supplementary materials to read aloud such as periodicals, primary source materials, or biographies in order to broaden their students' background knowledge and vocabulary and to create excitement about the subject matter. The justification is that there is little time within an already jam-packed curriculum to bring in the "extras." Yet, read-alouds can stimulate student enthusiasm and help develop background knowledge on key topics that are being studied in class.

It is a common belief that by the time students get to secondary school, they have already learned to read and should do so on their own. Educators may even ask the same question that we hear from parents so frequently: "Why *should* we read to kids? Doesn't it rob them of opportunities to practice?" One reason is that, as discussed earlier, the listening comprehension is the "reservoir" for reading comprehension (Trelease 2001). If teachers read aloud from a source that is too difficult for most of the students to read on their own (at their frustration level), they are still being exposed to new vocabulary words and concepts that will aid them when they encounter these words on their own.

Second, hearing something read aloud passionately and powerfully is motivational. In our Literacy Center, I am always surprised when students tell us how much they love it when we read aloud to them as we "model" specific reading strategies. They appreciate the strategy instruction, yes, but they also feel pampered when we read aloud to them. When students are lucky enough to have teachers who plan read-alouds that are provocative and engaging, they become enticed to want to read the same things—and just as proficiently—as the adults do.

Finally, and perhaps most critical of all, hearing effective read-alouds can spark students' interest in reading and spur them on to read voluntarily outside of school. Often, in classes where teachers have read aloud to students, the students begin to seek out reading materials similar in topic, genre, or style to what their teachers have chosen. In my own experience as a secondary teacher, even when I have read only excerpts from books during class time, I often have to put students eager to read the books on waiting lists afterward. A short read-aloud can generate that much interest.

One book that holds secondary students' attention is Eve Bunting's *A Sudden Silence*. Set in Laguna Beach, an area known to many high school kids in southern California, the story revolves around a pair of brothers, one who is deaf and is hit by a car, unable to hear the squeal of brakes in time. Fraught with guilt over not having been able to warn him in time, his hearing brother embarks on a path to find the driver to ensure that justice is done. I use this text as a way to introduce setting and the plotline, but once I start reading it to students, they simply do not want me to stop. I now own about fifteen copies of the book, which I check out to students who are looking for a wonderful real-life story of teenagers and the issue of drunk driving. I know for a fact that many of my students read the book in one night—a real testament to the power of reading aloud!

Richardson (2000) comments that authors are good at what they do "precisely because they possess an intuitive knowledge of the human condition—that they know about the pain and joy of life" (5). In thinking about my students' responses to *A Sudden Silence*, it seems clear to me that somehow the story speaks to them about drunk driving in a way that I could not. Read-alouds can be the best introduction to the content in our classes and help us start conversations about a variety of topics through a shared experience of text (Richardson 2000).

◎ *Teacher Read-Alouds of Assigned Selections*

It is important to emphasize that the kind of read-aloud practices encouraged in this chapter are not the same as teachers choosing to read assigned textbook chapters to students in lieu of having them read the text on their own. I am told regularly by secondary teachers that because students, especially English learners, read far below grade level, the only way to get the content across is for teachers to do the reading for students. However, if we think of the rationale behind this well-meaning practice, we begin to see a circular problem. Assuming that students cannot handle textbook reading because of the difficulties that such reading presents, teachers read aloud to them; in turn, students have even fewer opportunities for becoming more adept at textbook reading, which is the only way that they will get better at it.

It is true that expository, or textbook, reading presents specific challenges to students that narrative, or storylike, reading does not. In the first place, the writing is more factual (some say "dryer"), and technical vocabulary related to the subject matter is used in place of simpler, more conversational language. Different structures are used to convey the information, as well. Instead of containing a narrative plotline with conflicts and character development, expository text structures include the following types of patterns: sequential or chronological order, comparison and contrast, cause and effect, definition or explanation, enumeration, or simple listing (Roe, Stoodt, and Burns 2006).

Students who were lucky enough to be read to when they were younger recall the story lines of *The Three Little Pigs*, *The little Red Hen*, *Rainbow Fish*, *The Grouchy Ladybug*, *The Velveteen Rabbit*, or *Chrysanthemum*. They often express sentimental thoughts about the times their mom, dad, older sister, grandmother, or favorite uncle read to them, curled up in a favorite chair or tucked into the covers, just before bedtime. They learned how stories flow; how they have a beginning, a middle, and an end; and ways that conflicts are resolved. Of course, everyone also lives happily ever after—at least until readers move beyond third-grade stories!

Such "story schema" is wonderful preparation, academically and motivationally, for the act of reading in general—but it is not enough when students reach the first textbook and find that there is no "story" to follow, but instead, an unfamiliar structure and much more difficult language. Reading about the Earth's layers compels us to think about the main ideas of the content and some of the most important supporting details in order to understand it. If a reader is seeking "story-ness" in a description of volcanic eruptions, he is probably not going to find it, much to his distress. English learners, especially, need to have explicit support with various textbook reading structures because in addition to the language challenges they face, they may not be familiar with the organizational patterns that help to facilitate comprehension, a point that was addressed in Chapter 2.

Other Effective Interactive Structures for Reading

Teachers who want their students to have access to the core curriculum, that is to say, to ensure that students can all comprehend the content, must take extra steps to demonstrate how to read content-area text. The introduction and practice of academic language (the secret language of school), plus the use of specific content-area literacy strategies, as described in earlier chapters, go a long way toward achieving this aim. However, there are alternative classroom reading structures that work well for secondary teachers, providing students with the necessary support and practice they need to read difficult texts while not taking the ownership of reading away from them. These structures include paired and small-group reading, ReQuest, and scaffolded reading.

◎ *Paired Reading*

Paired reading is generally thought of as a strategy used in elementary schools where one more "expert" reader is paired with a less proficient one as they read a specific assignment. However, it is an effective and efficient strategy that can be used with older readers, as well. When students do paired reading, ask them to do the following.

- Read the same text piece either aloud or silently.

- Stop at predetermined points in the text to clarify their understanding before moving on to the next section.

- If either partner has questions about the content, he asks his partner and together they try to resolve any unclear issues.

- Students do a "respond" activity together, such as answering questions, filling in a graphic organizer, or responding in any number of other ways (including taking notes, creating illustrations, identifying character traits, listing causes, etc.).

- Students resume reading.

In paired reading, students learn to collaborate with each other while they engage in a "through" activity that emphasizes the purpose of the assignment. Though a respond activity at stopping points is not mandatory with this process, it is helpful to include one to keep learners focused on the task at hand. The respond activities also help the teacher to monitor students' comprehension along the way.

If the reading is oral, one partner reads aloud while the other one listens, and then they change roles for the following chunk of text. The idea is that each partner is responsible for the comprehension of the other, but they know that they may ask the teacher for help at any time if both partners are confused or need clarification. The role of the teacher is an active one; it is absolutely necessary to circulate and provide assistance and feedback while students are engaged in the paired reading activity, whether there are written respond components or not.

Also, the teacher needs to predetermine the appropriate stopping points at which pairs switch roles. The text may be broken down logically to begin with, especially if there are subtitles. Otherwise, the teacher's choices depend upon how much learners can read before they lose focus, the difficulty of the reading selection (including the readability level and the number of technical vocabulary words), and the purposes for reading. For intermediate English learners, one long paragraph at a time may be sufficient. If a stop-and-respond activity is included, pairs can work together (e.g., answering questions, asking questions, making comments, filling in a graphic organizer, etc.), and then the partner who did not read the previous section begins reading once again until reaching the next stopping point.

Perhaps students are seeking the underlying causes of a war, the kinds of tools that a civilization developed, the steps in a science experiment, or multiple shifts in the setting within a novel. It is important for the teacher to preview the text and decide where reasonable stopping points for finding this information would be.

Students in the partnership should typically consist of one more proficient reader and one less proficient reader, but there is no hard-and-fast rule about it; with older readers, the purpose of paired reading is to offer a relaxed, successful context where students can ask for clarification from their partner and not be embarrassed to read aloud in front of him or her. As they take turns reading, the less public structure is not as likely to lead to the humiliation that struggling readers sometimes feel by not performing well enough or by simply being left out (Combs 2004).

When students engage in paired reading, it is noisier in the classroom than when one student reads aloud at a time or when students read silently. However, in my experience, when students have set purposes for reading and time to do the work with a partner, they will focus on their own task and tune out the other distractions. They feel less "put upon" than when they have to read aloud in front of the entire class, recognizing that they are getting valuable help from a peer, which can help them to succeed in doing the assignment; they are not as likely to wander off task or socialize endlessly as a way to avoid a task that may seem too challenging for them. Consistent teacher monitoring can help students keep track of their goals and encourage them as they move forward. The paired reading structure can also be expanded to small-group activities, where three or four students take turns reading aloud.

© ReQuest

Another engaging, interactive option that secondary teachers may find beneficial is the ReQuest procedure, created by Manzo (1969). The procedure involves having the teacher read the first portion of the reading selection aloud, then stopping for the students to ask questions of the teacher. This "reciprocal" questioning approach encourages learners to ask questions that will help them to understand the text, putting the teacher (rather than the students) on the spot in an atypical role reversal. After students ask questions about the first part of the text, the teacher asks the students questions. Then, the students predict what they think the next portion of the text will be about. Manzo (1969) notes that if the predictions are "reasonable," the teacher and students can move to the next step—silent reading of another selected portion of the text and another exchange of questions, with the students asking questions first (125).

The ReQuest procedure has built-in motivation for students who have grown disillusioned with the typical initiate-respond-evaluate discourse form responses that are typically asked of them in school (as discussed in Chapter 3), where teachers know the answers before they ask the questions (Afflerbach 2007). This school-based question-answer framework clearly gives students the message that authentic and purposeful questions and answers are not important or required. In the ReQuest procedure, students have control over what they would like to emphasize, which gives them higher levels of motivation for the activity and naturally leads them in setting their own purposes for the reading.

Teachers should keep in mind that if students' questions are unclear or not relevant to the text, it is important to point this out to them and to ask for clarification or restatements. Then, when it time for instructors to ask questions, the teacher should strive to effectively model various questioning formats.

Of course, as students become better at participating in ReQuest, they should strive to ask increasingly sophisticated, higher-level questions than when they first begin to use ReQuest. They may perhaps ask inference questions rather than detail questions—or create questions about the sequencing of events dealing with underlying chronological order rather than the order of the telling. Through prompting, demonstration, and much practice, teachers can be role models, supporting students in these efforts.

It is not necessary for the ReQuest procedure to be implemented during the entire reading of a text piece, but rather only until the teacher feels that students have a handle on the topic, organization, and major technical concepts of the selection relating to the subject matter. Once the ReQuest procedure ends, students may simply finish the reading assignment in pairs or small groups, or perhaps even simply by reading silently.

◎ Scaffolded Reading

Scaffolded reading allows students to work collaboratively with their teacher and peers to understand text. This strategy allows more support to be provided from the teacher and peers at the outset and less during the middle and end of the reading event. True to its name, during this activity, many opportunities for clarification and elaboration are available as the teacher reads the introductory parts of the text aloud and peers take turns reading in small groups or pairs. But the eventual goal is for students to be able to read the last part of the text independently. Here's how it works:

- The teacher to determine the "chunks" of text that will be read (stopping points), dividing them up with the idea of providing increasingly less support for students as the reading progresses.

- The teacher reads the first predetermined text passage aloud, making sure to front-load important vocabulary ahead of time.

- In groups of three or four, students take turns reading aloud until they get to the next predetermined stopping point (identified by page and paragraph numbers or by sticky notes that students place in the margins of their texts).

- Groups then break into partners who engage in paired reading for the next section of text.

- Each student should be responsible for reading the last chunk of text on her own, independently and silently.

Stopping points are selected based on concept difficulty and students' background knowledge. Though groups may be formed by the teacher to combine struggling, average, and better readers, everyone receives the benefit of the teacher reading aloud (and setting the stage) at the beginning. Support is ongoing with constant peer interaction and teacher feedback available, whenever necessary, right up until students begin to engage in the silent reading portion at the end of the selection. The focus is on comprehending the material, not just sounding out the words, so students rely upon the help of their peers in the small-group and paired reading formats. Knowing that they will have their own section to read silently at the end motivates students to set purposes for reading and stay fully involved in the meaning-making process.

Activities like these are designed to ensure that students focus on chunks of text as they read long selections, allowing for stop and respond opportunities along the way to ask questions, clarify, or receive additional elaboration. Teachers who offer these kinds of reading structures to students typically report that their students stay on task more consistently, are less hesitant to read, and are more successful in terms of content comprehension.

A modification that can be added to interactive reading strategies such as scaffolded reading is "radio reading," a preparation activity suggested by McEwan (2007) as a way of allowing learners to practice, ahead of time, reading the portions they will be assigned in class. Students can read the portions orally at home or in practice groups so that they can prepare sections of texts for later in different group contexts. Not only will such practice opportunities lower the affective filters for English learners, but they will also contribute to the development of expression and fluency.

Free Voluntary Reading

An important and less performance-based type of reading is free voluntary reading. We know that in order to read better—to increase one's reading ability and independent reading level—real reading of text, silently and individually, needs to be done habitually. Although we can meet the needs of many of our students by setting up reading experiences in positive ways during class, the only sure way of ascertaining that our students will continue to become better readers is to encourage them to develop the habit of reading for pleasure. Independent reading can occur at home after the school day has ended or during school, as a planned activity.

In-school free reading programs are not a new idea. In fact, they have existed since the arrival of individualized reading programs in the 1950s and 1960s and have been labeled in a wide variety of ways: free voluntary reading, self-selected reading, and sustained silent reading (SSR). What the programs share in common is the objective to develop each student's ability to read silently without interruption for a predetermined period of time (McCracken 1971). Free voluntary reading refers to any in-school program where part of the school day is set aside for reading (Krashen 2004). It is the umbrella term under which the other two in-school reading programs fall. Two types of free voluntary reading are self-selected reading and SSR.

◎ *Self-Selected Reading*

Self-selected reading may incorporate accountability measures such as student-teacher conferences. As students meet with their teachers, they discuss difficult vocabulary or concepts from their books, read aloud parts of their books to the teacher or engage in retells, or summarize their reading in ways that enable the teacher to monitor their comprehension. Rarely do we see self-selected reading activities occurring in upper-grade or content-area classrooms. Secondary teachers do not have the time to conference with students about their reading—nor do they feel confident knowing how to address comprehension issues they may identify during discussions with students. These are behaviors generally left to developmental reading teachers or reading specialists in secondary schools; they have not historically been the domain of content experts.

◎ *SSR*

SSR, on the other hand, does not include any accountability measures, nor does the teacher do prescribed follow-up activities to meet students' skill needs. Book reports, quizzes, and comprehension checks are avoided in favor of simply allowing students to enjoy what they read. Notably, while students read, the teacher reads, too. A researcher once commented that SSR has been around for as long as people have been reading, explaining that whenever people select something to read for their own purposes, spend more than a few minutes reading it and comprehending whatever they want, SSR is occurring (Manning-Dowd 1985). Unfortunately, the opportunity to read for pleasure in a comfortable environment during school time on a regular basis—the kind of reading that is most beneficial at the secondary level—is typically not included in today's curricula.

Why is SSR so important? The percentage of time that secondary students actually spend interacting with print is a small fraction of the overall school day. For students who struggle, it may represent an even smaller portion, as they often resort to avoidance techniques that allow them to skip the "reading" part and deal with the assignment at hand, using as little textual information as they can just to get by.

Originally, when free reading was incorporated into early programs after World War II, its purpose was to allow students to have the drill and practice necessary to learn to read. It was thought that students needed a special time period to apply and transfer the isolated skills learned during the regular instructional period or reading group (Oliver 1970; McCracken 1971). With the influence of work by cognitive psychologists, sociolinguists, and psycholinguists, reading came to be viewed not simply as an act of decoding the print on the pages but as a process requiring a meaningful transaction between reader and text (Rosenblatt 1969; Goodman 1994). The idea that students who read a great deal tend to become better readers gained prominence, along with the notion that the best way to develop reading ability is not through isolated skill-and-drill practices, but by reading itself. This view of reading with its highly personalized meaning-making emphasis is articulated by Smith (1988, 3): "The purposeful nature of reading is central, not only because one normally reads for a reason...but because the understanding which a reader must bring to reading can only be manifested through the reader's own intentions."

Since the report of the National Reading Panel (2000) was published, providing time for students to read during school hours has

"You mean that's all you ever read, designer labels?"

Figure 9–1

been called into question. Touting the idea that there is no research to support the practice of SSR, critics have noted that free reading studies do not follow the strict scientific research design models that are being required in this age of accountability. Ideally, they would like to see SSR tested out using a design where students are randomly assigned to schools and randomly assigned to treatment groups within these schools. This is not how schools operate in the real world. Instead, schools either offer opportunities for students to read during school or not, believing that when people read more, they get better at reading and that when they get better at reading, they read more. Classes do not stay intact; students move from class to class and school to school, and some even move to other countries for awhile (and then back again). Any attempt to impose a "rat lab" approach to an SSR study will not work. We need to look at what happens when kids read and then decide whether a small allotment of time per day in school devoted to real reading is worthwhile.

◎ SSR Philosophy

Anyone who has seen an SSR program successfully implemented at a school can tell you how committed students become to having time to read for pleasure; these observers can document numerous outcomes that show that learners are reading more frequently—and better—than ever before. In an age of technology and infomercials, distractions are plentiful, and adolescents are teased by the quick-fix pleasures of games, television, and other technological options, so they rarely give reading a chance. In our Literacy Center, we always begin our initial conversations with new students who come for tutoring with questions about what they like to do and whether they like to read. We give them different kinds of interest inventories (as described in Chapter 8), but we do not always glean as much information as we would like. Most tell us about their passionate interests in soccer, dance, karate, baseball, fashion, sharks, video games, pop culture, or hockey, but few reply that they enjoy reading about any of these topics—or reading anything, for that matter.

When we share with students and their parents the idea that free reading is a behavior that will help them become better readers, they are surprised. Students come to us because they do not read well, expecting an elixir that will immediately solve the problem so they will become more proficient, yet no one seems to think of having students actually engage in real reading practices. The key is to determine what they might like to read about and offer them opportunities to read materials at their independent reading levels—not to assign the classics and expect the failure that will surely follow.

It is important to add that in our center we do not use the well-known Accelerated Reader program that includes compulsory computer quizzes, designed to check students' understanding of every book they read. Believing that holding students to such accountability requirements may actually add to their "aversion" of the reading process (Thompson, Madhuri, and Taylor 2008), we strongly advocate a "pure" approach to SSR, where the idea of reading for pleasure is emphasized.

Krashen (2004) feels so strongly about free reading that he has identified it as the "missing ingredient in language arts, as well as in intermediate second and foreign language instruction" (1). Labeling it the "bridge" between a basic foundation in a language and higher levels of proficiency, he maintains the necessity of reading for pleasure in order to increase reading, spelling, grammar, vocabulary, and writing. These findings are supported by Elley's (1992) study of twenty-seven countries, in which a steady trend upward in achievement was seen in the populations that engaged in the greatest amount of free voluntary reading.

In a study carried out with older, avid readers (e.g., baby boomers) who were asked what they liked to read as youngsters, many of them said that they launched their reading habit by reading comic books, magazines, and series books such as Nancy Drew, Little House on the Prairie, and Reader's Digest (Russikoff and Pilgreen 1994). In fact, most respondents commented that they were devotees of popular, or "light" reading, as opposed to "classic" or literary materials. Krashen (2004) notes that light reading is a genre that "schools pretend does not exist," but he suspects it is the avenue through which nearly all of us learned to read (92).

Years from now, we will probably hear that graphic novels, manga (Japanese print comics with unique, stylized art work), Internet stories and articles, and series books such as Harry Potter, Twilight, A Series of Unfortunate Events, The Spiderwick Chronicles, Diary of a Wimpy Kid, and Zombie Butts (popular books by Andy Griffiths) initially sparked the interest of adult avid readers. No matter what the nature of this "light" fare will be, its value is in its ability to stimulate interest, leading to a lifetime reading pattern. Leonhardt (1996) comments that even though students may "enter reading" through a particular interest (e.g., sports), through years and years of reading they develop "many, many other interests" (9).

A problem that adolescents face is that they have difficulty finding materials that are interesting and are written at appropriate reading levels. Bean (2002) observes that teens are engrossed in discovering their identities and life pathways, often considering the curriculum of school to be irrelevant. However, independent reading offers opportunities for them to connect with texts that have significance and are manageable for them.

In a Southern California study with high school English learners, students were provided with access to a wide variety of reading materials (including nonfiction materials, novels, magazines, newspapers, and comic books), written at their independent reading levels (Pilgreen 2000). Teachers helped these high schoolers make reading selections for daily SSR opportunities and provided a comfortable and quiet environment for pleasure reading to occur. No tests, quizzes, or other tasks were assigned. Many learners noted that they didn't know "reading could be so fun and easy," and one young lady said that there was no other place where she and her friends could read "the stuff we prefer." Within one semester (sixteen weeks), the students' average reading level rose more than one and a half years. Clearly, helping students make "matches" between their interests and reading materials—and offering time for real reading to occur—can result in tangible levels of achievement. The key is determining what they want to read.

Many noteworthy authors are now helping educators learn more about the reading preferences of both young men and women in the field of adolescent literacy: Newkirk (2002) offers *Misreading Masculinity: Boys, Literacy, and Popular Culture*; Hahn, Flynn, and Reuben (2008) edited *The Ultimate Teen Guide (More Than 700 Great Books)*; Ayers and Crawford (2004) compiled *Great Books for High School Kids*; Pearl (2007) developed *Book Crush for Kids and Teens, Recommended Reading for Every Mood, Moment, and Interest*; Silvey (2006) presents us with annotated descriptions of books from a variety of genres in *500 Great Books for Teens*; Sprague and Keeling (2007) offer a theme-based text for young girls entitled *Discovering Their Voices: Engaging Adolescent Girls with Young Adult Literature*; Brozo (2002) produced a compendium of the reading practices and preferences of older boys entitled *To Be a Boy, to Be a Reader: Engaging Teen and Preteen Boys in Active Literacy*; and Smith and Wilhelm (2002) authored a text with insightful perspectives on the evolutions and patterns of boys' reading selections called *"Reading Don't Fix No Chevys": Literacy in the Lives of Young Men*. Finally, for those who are lovers of popular young adult author Scieszka (2005), his edited book *Guys Write for Guys Read* contains "a bunch of pieces by a bunch of guys . . . all about being a guy" (11). Boys in our center love the stories, but the teachers enjoy the book just as much as a way to understand what captures the attention of young men. There is certainly no paucity of information about what adolescents are doing and what they might be interested in reading about.

However, when considering reading materials for English learners, teachers must be cautious and selective. Choices should be "appropriate for the age and interest level" of the students (Vardell, Hadaway, and Young 2006, 735). Noting that the task of matching books and readers is more complex than it sounds, Vardell, Hadaway, and Young (2006) make the case that the typical grade-level

(GE) suitability criterion may not apply. Teachers must know something about the maturity level of the learners, as well as their backgrounds (family, culture, language, and knowledge) and interests, which can vary tremendously from student to student. An English learner who is reading at the third-grade level is not likely to enjoy materials that are targeted for third graders, yet a nonfiction trade book on insects or a high-interest, low vocabulary mystery novel might be ideal. Companies who offer a broad continuum of well-written and beautifully illustrated books that appeal to older students are Rosen, Artisan Press, Capstone Press, and National Geographic. Although the readability levels of these materials are manageable for intermediate English learners, the content is sophisticated, offering students many choices to match their individual preferences.

Harper and Bean (2007) also point out that "compared to previous generations, adolescents as a group are showing greater complexity, intensity, and diversity in their literacy practices" (327). The idea of literacy has, in fact, changed enormously in a very brief period of time. Students are reading information on websites, e-books, and email, and they are participating in discussion boards, chat rooms, and instant messaging activities. Hughes-Hassell and Podge (2007) state, "We have to expand our definition of reading" (28). Although the rules for writing and responding to such various sources of literacy may be different from typical classroom guidelines, these kinds of offerings can be enticing to students who have found themselves on the periphery of literacy activities in our classrooms. Vasudevan (2007) remarks that these new media provide "multiple ways in" for such young people (253), reminding us to consider ways of bringing such "texts" into our curriculum whenever possible.

At a time when few students own library cards and libraries have cut their services and hours dramatically (Constantino 1998; McQuillan 1998), schools should be allocating funding to purchase reading materials that match the interests and reading levels

"CAN I CARRY YOUR COMPUTER DISKS TO SCHOOL?"

Figure 9–2

of their student body, including technology to support different kinds of reading practices. Krashen (2004) points out that many people, not just adolescents, do not read well enough to handle the complex literacy demands of modern society, advocating the need for more reading in schools. What better place to implement a practice that will help students do better in all of their subjects, enabling them to be productive members of society who can read voting pamphlets, magazines and newspapers, computer information, labels and directions, websites, online texts, novels, and technical information? In my view, SSR should be established as a routine part of every school day in every school. As Trelease (2001) maintains, "The more you read, the better you get at it; the better you get at it, the more you like it; and the more you like it, the more you do it" (3). It's cyclical!

Commentary

Literacy demands are changing, and supporting students effectively means engaging them in a variety of experiences with text to promote language development and reading proficiency. Simply giving students assignments does not help them to construct meaning (Roe, Stoodt, and Burns 2006). Preparing them and guiding them through texts so that they will learn effectively facilitates the process. As Deshler and colleagues (2007) suggest, there is a wide range in the types of texts that secondary students are expected to read and write, including literature, scientific and technical writing, math notations, history documents, Internet sources, and reference materials. Because of the changes in literacy demands after fourth grade, the nature of literacy instruction needs to become increasingly "discipline-specific" (19).

It is true that, as Freeman and Freeman (2009) remark, teachers often feel "a sense of urgency" when working with older struggling readers and writers because such learners have "a great deal to learn and not many years to learn it." As long as teachers use effective strategies to make content comprehensible, English learners can learn academic language while they learn academic content; the two processes are inextricably related (176).

Many options are open to content-area teachers who want their students to achieve in school. Keeping in mind that it is essential to know how to read multiple kinds of texts, we must "demystify" the process for students, especially English learners who are grappling with both content and language, including what I have termed the "secret language of school." The steps to take are clear: providing learners with appropriate, explicit strategies in instructional contexts that are supportive and interactive; encouraging students to do as much real reading as possible, both in school and outside of it; and engaging students with interesting and meaningful activities. As one content-area researcher succinctly puts it, "Reading remains one of the most efficient and powerful tools for learning. It is our job to facilitate successful reading experiences so that all of our students will become mature, expert readers and lifelong learners" (Combs 2004, 19).

APPENDIX A Definitions of Text Terms

chapter	a main division of a book or text
title/heading	the name of a book, work of art, piece of music, text, chapter, article, poem, document, etc.
subtitle/subheading	secondary or additional title of a book, work of art, piece of music, text, chapter, article, poem, document, etc.; secondary or additional heading within these works to indicate new section
paragraph	a distinct section of a piece of writing, typically beginning on a new indented line; contains one primary (main) idea and other related ideas
paraphrase	the act or result of restating the meaning of something spoken or written in another form
passage	an extract from a book or other text piece; may consist of one or more paragraphs
excerpt	a short extract from a book, text, article, motion picture, piece of music, etc.
column	a vertical division of a page, chart, etc., containing a sequence of figures or words
section	a subdivision of a book, article, text, etc.
page	a leaf of a book, periodical, etc., what is written or printed on this
illustration	a picture, painting, drawing, photograph, cartoon, etc., that illustrates a book, magazine article, text, etc.

caption	a title or brief illustration appended to an illustration
font/print	a set of type of one style, or "face"
boldface type	type that is printed in a thick, black style, or "face"
italic or italicized type	type that is printed in a style, or "face," that has sloping letters (like early Italian writing)
font size	a set of type of one size; can be any style or "face"
graph (line, bar)	a diagram showing the relationship, usually between two variables, each measured along one of a pair of axes
graph (pie)	a circular diagram, typically showing the relationships among specific variables
chart	a sheet of information in the form of a table, graph, or diagram
table	a set of facts or figures, systematically displayed, especially in columns
figure	a diagram or other illustrative drawing
map	typically a flat representation of the Earth's surface, or part of it, showing physical features, cities, etc.
summarize	a brief statement that contains the essential ideas of a longer passage or selection
diagram	a drawing showing the general scheme or outline of an object and its parts; may also indicate processes related to an object or phenomenon
introduction	an explanatory section at the section at the beginning of a book, text, etc.; a preliminary section in a piece of music
conclusion	a summing up of any kind of material

transition	a word or phrase that signals a change from one idea (or set of ideas) to the text
quotation	a passage or remark that represents a specific statement (or part of a statement) by another person
indentation	space preceding a line of type, so that the type begins farther from the margin than other lines; used to mark a new paragraph
title page	a page that precedes the main part of a book or text; contains the title, author's name, date (or copyright) and, if appropriate, publisher information
table of contents	a set of topics, listed with a corresponding page numbers, indicating the different sections of a book or text
preface	an introduction to a book, stating its subject, scope, etc.; the preliminary part of a speech
handbook	a short manual or guide book
glossary	an alphabetical list of terms, with definitions, relating to a specific subject or text, typically placed at the end of a book
index	an alphabetical list of names, subjects, etc., with references, typically placed at the end of a book
bibliography	a list of books, articles, etc. (containing author and publisher information) referred to in a book, article, or chapter
author index	a list of the authors referred to in a book or other text

APPENDIX B Detail Key Question Words

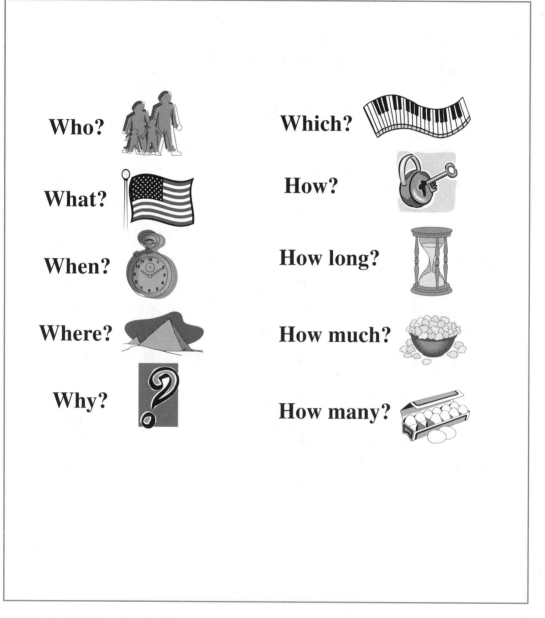

Who?

What?

When?

Where?

Why?

Which?

How?

How long?

How much?

How many?

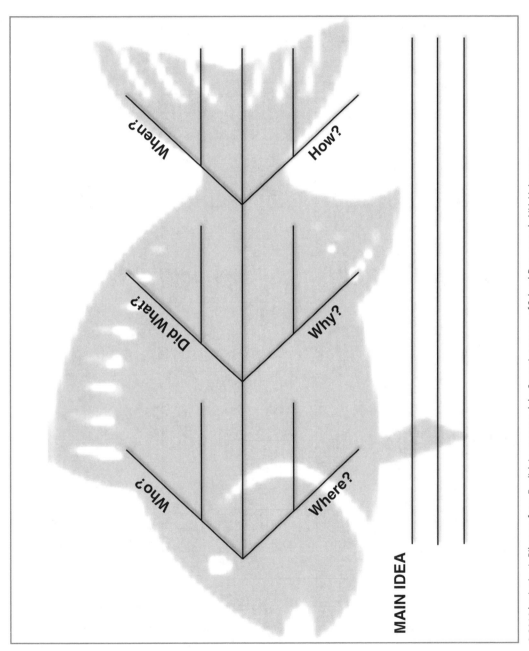

When?

How?

Did What?

Why?

Who?

Where?

MAIN IDEA

APPENDIX D Cause-Effect Relationships

Signal Words	Cause	Effect

APPENDIX E Making Inferences:
Reading Between the Lines

Question #	Page	"Iffy" Words	Textual Clues	Answer to the Question

APPENDIX F Using Context Clues

Word	Page Number	Column Number	Paragraph Number	Clues	Meaning

APPENDIX G AIM Secondary Reading Inventory: Attitude, Interest, Motivation

Name: _____ **Date:** _____

To the student: Please be as complete as possible and don't worry about spelling!

◎ *Write an answer on the line after each question.*

What is your favorite...

movie? _____   TV show? _____

music? _____   video game? _____

subject at school? _____   memory? _____

thing to do when not at school? _____

◎ *Put a <u>check</u> by any of the following that you do regularly. Next, answer the question by each of the things you checked.*

Play a sport _____ If so, which one(s)? _____

Belong to a club at school, church, or other group _____ If so, what kind of club or group? _____

Play an instrument _____ If so, which one? _____

Play in a band _____ Sing in a group _____

Have a job after school _____ If so, what kind of job? _____

◎ *Put a <u>check</u> by any of the places below you have seen. Then, write a 1, 2, and 3 by your first, second, and third favorite places:*

beach _____   mountains _____   on a boat _____

museum _____   zoo _____   summer camp _____

long trip _____   airplane _____   music concert _____

bookstore _____   library _____   restaurant _____

theatre (with actors doing a play or a musical) _____
theme park (like Disneyland or Six Flags) _____
Other _____

◎ *Tell how often you use any of the following. Use the code below. If you don't know what one of them is, leave it blank.*

N = Never;   S = Sometimes;   O = Often

Twitter _____   Email _____   Texting _____   Computer games _____
Word processing (computer writing program) _____
Google, Yahoo!, or another way to search on the Internet _____
Blogs _____   Other technology (please list) _____

◎ *Write an answer on the line after each question.*

What is your favorite book? _____
Why do you like it? _____
Do your parents like to read? _____
If they do, what kinds of things do they read? _____
Do you ever talk about books at home? _____
Do you ever talk about things you've read with your friends? _____
Besides reading for school, do you ever read something because you want to? _____
If yes, what do you choose? (This can include anything, like comics, magazines, graphic novels, romance novels, etc.) _____
Do you have a computer at home that you get to use? _____

◎ *Tell how often you…*

Use a computer:	Often	Sometimes	Never
Go to the library:	Often	Sometimes	Never
Go to a bookstore:	Often	Sometimes	Never
Read by your own choice:	Often	Sometimes	Never

What do you like the best (circle one):   Writing   Reading   Talking
Listening   Drawing   Tell why: _____

_____

_____

How important do you think being able to read is?   Very Important
Sort of Important   Not Very Important
Tell why: _____
Tell what kind of reader you think you are:

              Excellent   Good   OK   Poor

◎ *Put a check by all of the following that are true for you.*

What do you do when you are reading something that is hard to
understand?
Reread _____ Skip the hard part _____ Ask for help _____
Look for clues in what I just read _____ Use the dictionary _____
Use a highlighter (color marker) _____ Take notes _____
Use "sticky notes" to mark ideas or questions _____
Connect what I'm reading to something I already know _____
If you ask for help, who do you ask?
Teacher _____ Friend _____ Relative _____

APPENDIX H Flexible Reading

Scanning: Quickly locating target information

Skimming: Reading main ideas located in topic sentences (typically
                 placed first or second in the paragraph)

Reading: Reading all of the material at a natural or normal pace

Study-reading: Reading material in-depth, usually utilizing a note-taking
                 approach, study guide, or graphic organizer

If your purpose is to: **You would:**

1. Cuddle up with a book just for enjoyment   _____

2. Get the most important statistics from the latest
   football game in order to discuss them with your friends _____

3. Find the main ideas in an article that explain the
   importance of the ozone layer   _____

4. Memorize information for a unit test in history about
   the Mayan civilization (which you know very little about) _____

5. Consult an Internet article written about the effects of
   smoking in order to convince your younger brother/sister
   not to smoke   _____

6. Surf the National Geographic website to find a selection
   about the activity of pirates on the Barbary Coast in order
   to write a summary   _____

7. Use the remote to find the TV guide menu to see what
   time your favorite show has been scheduled in order to
   plan homework around it   _____

© 2010 by Janice L. Pilgreen from *English Learners and the Secret Language of School*. Portsmouth, NH: Heinemann.

8. Get an overview of the main points that you will be reading about in your biology text this evening   _____

9. Use Google to locate a local florist to order flowers for your girlfriend/boyfriend whom you just insulted   _____

10. Review for a test (and you *have* read the material once already)   _____

11. Cram for a test (and you *have not* read the material once already)   _____

12. Answer "easy" (detail) questions at the end of your U.S. Government chapter   _____

13. Answer "hard" (inference) questions at the end of your Health and Guidance chapter   _____

14. Use the Internet Sport Chalet catalogue to order running shoes for your friend's birthday   _____

15. Learn all about a courtroom case that was tried in your city in order to role-play it with other students in your government class   _____

16. Consult the address book in your cell phone to find your dad's office number in order to request an emergency loan   _____

17. Select five articles or other text pieces to use for your term paper on foreign policy   _____

18. Use the five articles you selected in order to write your term paper on foreign policy   _____

19. Use the subtitles from a text chapter to create an assigned advance organizer for class   _____

20. Pay attention to every word Dr. Phil has written you on Twitter about how to handle inappropriate text messages   _____

Possible Answer Key for Flexible Reading (Answers may vary.)

1. read
2. scan
3. skim
4. study-read
5. read or skim, depending upon your background knowledge
6. scan and then read or skim, depending upon your background knowledge
7. scan
8. skim
9. scan
10. skim, read again, or study-read, depending upon your background knowledge
11. skim (to get the main points; no time for anything else!)
12. scan (if you do not recall the answers)
13. read and use textual clues
14. scan
15. read or study-read, depending upon your background knowledge
16. scan
17. scan (for subject-relevant titles) and then skim the articles to validate their appropriateness for the paper
18. read
19. scan
20. read

APPENDIX I Types of Questions

Main Ideas

The main idea of this section is _____.

What is another possible title for this article?

A good title for this passage is _____.

The third paragraph is mainly about _____.

The first paragraph provides information about _____.

This section has to do mainly with _____.

The second paragraph of this article contains information about

_____.

This section of the newspaper is mostly about _____.

Details

Who   _____?

What   _____?

When   _____?

Where   _____?

Which   _____?

Why   _____?

How   _____?

How long   _____?

How much   _____?

How many   _____?

Sequence

Which of these steps will be done first?

What happened right after _____?

During _____, what happened?

The boxes below show some important ideas in this article. Which of the
   following events belongs in the empty box?

The boxes show some things that happened in the story. Which of these
   belongs in box 2?

The last thing that _____ (person) did was _____.

The second event that occurred was _____.

In the beginning of this story, _____ happened.

Before you can do X, you must _____.

At the very end of the procedure, you should _____.

Inferences

Which detail is the best clue to the time when the story takes place?

This notice would most likely appeal to students who _____.

There is enough information in this article to show that _____.

You can tell _____ because _____.

The writer assumes that _____ already knows

_____.

The author believes that people _____.

From _____ the reader can infer that _____.

The last line of the story implies that _____.

Approximately how many _____?

According to the graph, what seems to be the best _____ for

_____?

One reason you might want to _____ would be to

_____.

The character may now _____.

The next thing that will probably happen is that _____.

Cause-Effect

Because of _____, X happened.

So that the boy could _____, he did X.

_____ caused _____ to happen.

As a consequence of X, _____ occurred.

In order to _____, people can _____.

X happened, so _____ happened.

Due to _____, X happened.

The effect of someone doing X was _____.

_____ made it possible to _____.

Since the character _____, he was able to _____.

_____ was created by X doing _____.

Context Clues

In which sentence does X mean the same thing as the sentence above?

In this selection, the word X means _____.

X is most like _____ in this passage.

In this article, the phrase "_____" means _____.

The word X in this story probably means _____.

We can tell from the paragraph that X is most likely a type of

_____.

Advance Organizer (for use with text that has subtitles)

Gives reader the big picture and sets purpose for reading

Helps identify content for schema (background knowledge) building

Supports reader in the questioning process

Shows relevance of subtitles to content

Scanning (for use with any type of text)

Provides method for reader to identify target information

Leads to finding of target information quickly

Emphasizes process of *not* "reading" at usual pace

Focuses on details

Skimming (for use with connected text that has clear topic sentences)

Initially gives reader the big picture of textual (subject-matter) content

Offers a summary or review with subsequent use

Helps reader find main ideas located in topic sentences

Helps reader de-emphasize supporting details in paragraphs

Anticipation Guide (for use with any type of connected text)

Provides sense of big picture

Offers an avenue for "investing" the reader in the topic

Stimulates interest and sets purposes for reading

Activates reader's schema

Predict the Text (best used with narrative, or storylike, text)

Gives reader an opportunity to make meaning before reading

Focuses on selected vocabulary words/concepts that are important

Sets a purpose for reading—to validate predictions (stories) made before reading

Is interactive and fun!

Cloze (for use with any type of text)

Targets a category of information or content vocabulary

Focuses the reading on details

If used as part of an initial response to the text, helps set a purpose for reading

Highlights details for comprehension and long-term memory

Herringbone (for use with any type of connected text "chunks")

Helps reader put "detail" information into one main idea statement

Provides a graphic structure as support

Highlights comprehensive (not general) main ideas

Becomes easier with practice!

Triple Read (for use with connected text that has clear topic sentences)

Allows practice in finding topic sentences

Shows reader how topic sentences are supported by details

Emphasizes how several topic sentences may be combined

Leads to outlining and summary writing

Timelines and Sentence Strips (for use with connected text where order of events is not completely stated chronologically)

Highlights chronological order of events

Shows that events can be written in nonchronological order

Focuses attention on sequence key words

Helps reader to keep order of events in mind to aid comprehension

Detective Search (for use with any type of connected text including graphic novels)

Helps reader identify *clues* to make inferences

Useful for bringing reader "back to the text"

Relies upon some schema, as well as textual support

Can be used with narrative or expository pieces

Cause-Effect Procedure (for use with text that includes cause-effect key words)

Emphasizes the concept of cause-effect, not just sequence

Provides key words to indicate possible cause-effect relationships

Helps reader to see that cause-effect descriptions have no prescribed order

Utilizes a graphic organizer for support

Context Clue Strategies (for use with text that includes context clue signals)

Provides support for unknown definitions during reading

Can lead to uninterrupted reading and during-reading learning of vocabulary

Offers an alternative to using the dictionary or asking for help during reading

Can be used at all reading levels with success, providing clues are present

REFERENCES

Abedi, J. 2004. "The No Child Left Behind Act and English Language Learners: Assessment and Accountability Issues." *Educational Researcher* 3 (1): 4–14.

Abedi, J., C. Lord, C. Hofstetter, and E. Baker. 2000. "Impact of Accommodation Strategies on English Language Learners' Test Performance." *Educational Measurement: Issues and Practices* 19 (3): 16–26.

Afflerbach, P. 2007. *Understanding and Using Reading Assessment*. Newark, DE: International Reading Association.

Airasian, P. 1996. *Assessment in the Classroom*. New York: McGraw-Hill, Inc.

Allen, K. Z., M. K. Bachman, K. M. Berry, R. H. Fronk, D. R. Harden, K. Kaska, J. R. Kyle, W. G. Lamb, J. S. Leventhal, P. E. Malin, T. Nolinke, A. Palaez, and R. J. Sager. 2007. *California Earth Science*. Austin, TX: Holt, Rinehart, and Winston.

Alvermann, D. E., and P. R. Boothby. 1986. "Children's Transfer of Graphic Organizer Instruction." *Reading Psychology* 7 (2): 87–100.

Alvermann, D. E., and S. F. Phelps. 2005. *Content Reading and Literacy: Succeeding in Today's Diverse Classrooms*. Boston: Pearson Education, Inc.

Alvermann, D. E., S. F. Phelps, and V. G. Ridgeway. 2007. *Content Reading and Literacy: Succeeding in Today's Diverse Classrooms*. Boston: Pearson Education, Inc.

Alvermann, D. E., and S. Van Arnam. 1984, April. "Effects of Spontaneous and Induced Lookbacks on Self-Perceived High and Low Ability Comprehenders." Paper presented at the Annual Meeting of the American Education Research Association, New Orleans, LA. (ERIC Document Reproduction Service No. ED246384.)

Anderson, R. C. 1984. "Role of the Reader's Scheme in Comprehension, Learning, and Memory." In *Learning to Read in American Schools*, edited by C. R. Anderson, J. Osborn, and J. R. Tierny, 243–58. Hillsdale, NJ: Lawrence Erlbaum.

Appleby, J., A. Brinkley, and J. M. McPherson. 2000. *The American Journey: Building a Nation*. New York: McGraw Hill.

Armbruster, B. B., and A. G. Wilkinson. 1991. "Reading to Learn: Silent Reading, Oral Reading, and Learning from Text." *The Reading Teacher* 45 (2): 154–55.

Ausubel, D. 1963. "The Use of Advance Organizers in the Learning and Retention of Meaningful Verbal Material." *Journal of Educational Psychology* 51: 267–72.

Ayers, E. L., J. F. De la Teja, D. G. White, and R. Shulzinger. 2007. *American Anthem: Modern American History*. Austin, TX: Holt McDougal.

Ayers, R., and A. Crawford, eds. 2004. *Great Books for High School Kids: A Teacher's Guide to Books That Can Change Teens' Lives.* Boston: Beacon Press.

Barrentine, S. J. 1999. "Introduction." In *Reading Assessment: Principles and Practices for Elementary Teachers*, edited by S. J. Barrentine, 1–7. Newark, DE: International Reading Association.

Bean, T. W. 2002. "Making Reading Relevant for Adolescents." *Educational Leadership* 60 (3): 34–37.

Brozo, W. G. 2002. *To Be a Boy, to Be a Reader: Engaging Teen and Preteen Boys in Active Literacy.* Newark, DE: International Reading Association.

Buehl, D. 2007. "A Professional Development Framework for Embedding Comprehension Instruction into Content Classrooms." In *Adolescent Literacy Instruction: Policies and Promising Practices*, edited by G. Moorman and J. Lewis, 192–211. Newark, DE: International Reading Association.

Bunting, E. 1988. *A Sudden Silence.* New York: Ballantine Books.

Burke, J. 2004. *School Smarts: The Four C's of Academic Success.* Portsmouth, NH: Heinemann.

Burstein, S. M., and R. Shek. 2006. *World History: Medieval to Early Modern Times.* Austin, TX: Holt, Rinehart, and Winston.

Calkins, L. M. 2001. *The Art of Teaching Reading.* New York: Addison Wesley Educational Publishers, Inc.

Calkins, L., K. Montgomery, and D. Santman. 1998. *A Teacher's Guide to Standardized Reading Tests: Knowledge Is Power.* Portsmouth, NH: Heinemann.

Carnine, D., C. E. Cortes, K. R. Curtis, and A. T. Robinson. 2006. *World History: Ancient Civilizations.* Evanston, IL: McDougal Littell.

———. 2006. *World History: Medieval and Early Modern Times.* Evanston, IL: McDougal Littell.

Cary, S. 2000. *Working with Second Language Learners: Answers to Teachers' Top Ten Questions.* Portsmouth, NH: Heinemann.

Caverly, D., T. Mandeville, and S. Nicholson. 1995. "PLAN: A Study-Reading Strategy for Informational Text." *Journal of Adolescent and Adult Literacy* (39) 3: 190–99.

Cayton, A., E. I. Perry, L. Reed, and A. M. Winkler. 2003. *America: Pathways to the Present.* Upper Saddle River, NJ: Prentice Hall.

Cizek, G. J. 2005. "High-Stakes Testing: Contexts, Characteristics, Critiques, and Consequences." In *Defending Standardized Testing*, edited by R. P. Phelps, 23–54. Mahwah, NJ: Lawrence Erlbaum Associates.

Cobb, C. 2005. "Effective Instruction Begins with Purposeful Assessments." In *Reading Assessment: Principles and Practices for Elementary Teachers*, edited by S. J. Barrentine and S. Stokes, 20–22. Newark, DE: International Reading Association.

Collier, V. P. 1987. "Age and Rate of Acquisition of Second Language for Academic Purposes." *TESOL Quarterly* 21: 617–41.

Collins, M. D., and E. H. Cheek, eds. 1999. *Assessing and Guiding Reading Instruction.* New York: McGraw Hill Companies, Inc.

Combs, D. 2004. "A Framework for Scaffolding Content Area Reading Strategies." *Middle School Journal* 36 (2): 13–20.

Constantino, R. 1998. "I Did Not Know You Could Get Such Things There! Secondary ESL Students' Understanding, Use and Beliefs Concerning the School and Public

Library." In *Literacy, Access, and Libraries Among the Language Minority Population*, edited by R. Constantino, 53–67. Lanham, MD: Scarecrow Press.

Cook, S., and K. Babigian. 2000. *Secondary Reading Assessment Inventory*. Upper Saddle River, NJ: Globe-Fearon, Inc.

Cummins, J. 1980. "The Construct of Language Proficiency in Bilingual Education." In *Georgetown University Roundtable on Languages and Linguistics*, edited by J. E. Alatis, 76–93. Washington, DC: Georgetown University Press.

Cummins, J., and S. Schecter. 2003. "School-Based Language Policy in Culturally Diverse Contexts." In *Multilingual Education in Practice: Using Diversity as a Resource*, edited by S. Schecter and J. Cummins, 1–16. Portsmouth, NH: Heinemann.

Daniels, H., and S. Zemelman. 2004. *Subjects Matter: Every Teacher's Guide to Content-Area Reading*. Portsmouth, NH: Heinemann.

Davidson, W. J., P. Castillo, and M. B. Stoff. 2005. *The American Nation*. Boston: Pearson Education, Inc.

Deshler, D., A. S. Palincsar, G. Biancarolsa, and M. Nair. 2007. *Informed Choices for Struggling Adolescent Readers: A Research-Based Guide to Instructional Programs and Practices*. Newark, DE: International Reading Association.

Dewitz, P., E. M. Carr, and J. P. Patberg. 1987. "Effects of Inference Training on Comprehension and Comprehension Monitoring." *Reading Research Quarterly* 22: 99–121.

Droop, M., and L. Verhoevan. 2003. "Language Proficiency and Reading Ability in First- and Second-Language Learners." *Reading Research Quarterly* 38 (1): 78–103.

Elley, W. 1992. *How in the World Do Students Read?* Newark, DE: International Reading Association.

Finders, M. J., and S. Hynds. 2007. *Language Arts and Literacy in the Middle Grades: Planning, Teaching, and Assessing Learning*. Upper Saddle River, NJ: Pearson Education, Inc.

Fisher, D., and N. Frey. 2007. "A Tale of Two Middle Schools: What Works and What Doesn't." *Journal of Adolescent and Adult Literacy Skills* 51 (3): 204–11.

———. 2008. *Improving Adolescent Literacy: Content Area Strategies at Work*. Upper Saddle River, NJ: Pearson Education, Inc.

Fjeldstad, M. 2006. *The Thoughtful Reader*. Boston: Thomson Wadsworth.

Freeman, D. E., and Y. S. Freeman. 2004. *Essential Linguistics: What You Need to Know to Teach Reading, ESL, Spelling, Phonics, and Grammar*. Portsmouth, NH: Heinemann.

Freeman, Y. S., and D. E. Freeman. 2009. *Academic Language for English Language Learners and Struggling Readers: How to Help Students Succeed Across Content Areas*. Portsmouth, NH: Heinemann.

Galda, L., and M. Graves. 2007. *Reading and Responding in the Middle Grades: Approaches for All Classrooms*. Boston: Pearson Education, Inc.

Gambrell, L. B., and V. R. Gillis. 2007. "Assessing Children's Motivation for Reading and Writing." In *Classroom Literacy Assessment: Making Sense of What Students Know and Do*, edited by J. R. Paratore and R. L. McCormack, 50–61. New York: The Guilford Press.

Gambrell, L. B., B. M. Palmer, R. M. Codling, and S. A. Mazzoni. 1996. "Assessing Motivation to Read." *The Reading Teacher* 49 (7): 518–33.

Garcia, G. E., G. McKoon, and D. August. 2008. "Language and Literacy Assessment." In *Developing Reading and Writing in Second-Language Learners*, edited by D. August and T. Shanahan, 251–74. New York: Routledge and International Reading Association.

Gee, J. P. 2004. "Language in the Science Classroom: Academic Social Languages as the Heart of School-Based Literacy." In *Crossing Borders in Literacy and Science Instruction*, edited by E. W. Saul, 13–32. Newark, DE: International Reading Association.

Goodman, K. S. 1994. "Reading, Writing, and Written Texts: A Transactional Sociopsycholinguistic View." In *Theoretical Models and Processes of Reading*, edited by R. B. Ruddell, M. R. Ruddell, and H. Singer, 1093–1182. Newark, DE: International Reading Association.

Graves, M. 2006. *The Vocabulary Book: Learning and Instruction*. New York: Teachers College Press.

Graves, M. F., C. Juel, and B. B. Graves. 2007. *Teaching Reading in the 21st Century*. Boston: Pearson Education, Inc.

Gunning, T. G. 2008. *Creating Literacy Instruction for All Students*. Boston: Pearson Education, Inc.

Guthrie, J. T., ed. 2008. *Engaging Adolescents in Reading*. Thousand Oaks, CA: Corwin Press.

Hadaway, N. L., and T. A. Young. 2006. "Changing Classrooms: Transforming Instruction." In *Supporting the Literacy Development of English Learners: Increasing Success in All Classrooms*, edited by T. A. Young and N. L. Hadaway, 6–21. Newark, DE: International Reading Association.

Hahn, D., L. Flynn, and S. Reuben, eds. 2008. *The Ultimate Teen Book Guide (More Than 700 Great Books)*. New York: Walker and Company.

Harper, H., and T. Bean. 2007. "Literacy Education in Democratic Life: The Promise of Adolescent Literacy." In *Adolescent Literacy Instruction: Policies and Promising Practices*, edited by G. Moorman and J. Lewis, 319–35. Newark, DE: International Reading Association.

Harris, T. L., and R. E. Hodges, eds. 1995. *The Literacy Dictionary: The Vocabulary of Reading and Writing*. Newark, DE: International Reading Association.

Harvey, S., and A. Goudvis. 2000. *Strategies That Work: Teaching Comprehension to Enhance Understanding*. York, ME: Stenhouse Publishers.

Helgeson, M. 1993. "Read and Run." In *New Ways in Teaching Reading*, edited by R. R. Day, 131–32. Alexandria, VA: Teachers of English to Speakers of Other Languages.

Hughes-Hassell, S., and P. Podge. 2007. "The Leisure Reading Habits of Urban Adolescents." *Journal of Adult and Adolescent Literacy* 51 (1): 22–23.

Irvin, J., D. R. Buehl, and R. M. Klemp. 2007. *Reading and the High School Student: Strategies to Enhance Literacy*. Boston: Pearson Education, Inc.

Israel, S. E. 2007. *Using Metacognitive Assessments to Create Individualized Reading Instruction*. Newark, DE: International Reading Association.

Jenner, J., L. C. Jones, M. Losowski, B. B. Simons, T. Wellnitz, and M. Wysession. 2008. *Focus on California Earth Science*. Upper Saddle River, NJ: Prentice Hall.

Karlsen, B., and E. F. Gardner. 1995. *Stanford Diagnostic Reading Test, Fourth Edition.* San Antonio, TX: Harcourt, Inc.

Kohn, A. 2000. *The Case Against Standardized Testing: Raising the Scores, Ruining the Schools.* Portsmouth, NH: Heinemann.

Krashen, S. D. 1985. *The Input Hypothesis: Issues and Implications.* London: Longman.

———. 2004. *The Power of Reading: Insights from the Research.* Westport, CT: Libraries Unlimited.

Lassieur, A. 2006. *Clara Barton: Angel of the Battlefield.* Mankato, Minnesota: Capstone Press.

Leonhardt, M. 1993. *Parents Who Love Reading, Kids Who Don't: How It Happens and What You Can Do About It.* New York: Crown Publishers, Inc.

———. 1996. *Keeping Kids Reading: How to Raise Avid Readers in the Video Age.* New York: Crown Publishers, Inc.

Leslie, L., and J. Caldwell. 2005. *Qualitative Reading Inventory-4.* Boston: Pearson Education, Inc.

Lewis, J. 2007. "Academic Literacy: Principles and Learning Opportunities for Adolescent Readers." In *Adolescent Literacy Instruction: Policies and Promising Practices,* edited by G. Moorman and J. Lewis, 143–66. Newark, DE: International Reading Association.

MacGinitie, W. H., R. K. MacGinitie, K. Maria, and L. G. Dreyer. 2000. *Gates-MacGinitie Reading Tests.* Itaska, IL: Riverside Publishing Company.

Manning-Dowd, A. 1985. *The Effectiveness of SSR: A Review of the Research.* Information Analysis (Report No. CS008 607). (ERIC Document Reproduction Service No. ED 276 970.)

Manzo, A. V. 1969. "The ReQuest procedure." *Journal of Reading* 13: 123–26.

Marshall, E. K., and L. Mongello. 2003. *Literature and Language Arts.* Austin, TX: Holt.

Marzano, R. J. 2004. *Building Background Knowledge for Academic Achievement: Research on What Works in Schools.* Alexandria, VA: Association for Supervision and Research Development.

———. 2007. *The Art and Science of Teaching: A Comprehensive Framework for Effective Instruction.* Alexandria, VA: Association for Supervision and Curriculum Development.

McCabe, P. 2003. "Enhancing Self-Efficacy for High Stakes Reading Tests." *The Reading Teacher* 57(1): 12–20.

McCracken, R. 1971. "Initiating Sustained Silent Reading." *Journal of Reading* 14 (8): 521–24, 582–83.

McEwan, E. K. 2007. *40 Ways to Support Struggling Readers in Content Classrooms, Grades 6–12.* Thousand Oaks, CA: Corwin Press, Inc.

McGinley, W. J., and P. R. Denner. 1987. "Story Impressions: A Prereading/Writing Activity." *Journal of Reading* 31: 248–53.

McKenna, M. C., and D. J. Kear. 1990. "Measuring Attitude Toward Reading: A New Tool for Teachers." *The Reading Teacher* 43 (9): 626–39.

McKenna, M. C., and R. D. Robinson. 1997. *Teaching Through Text: A Content Literacy Approach to Content Area Reading.* White Plains, NY: Longman Publishers USA.

McKenna, M. C., and S. A. Stahl. 2003. *Assessing for Reading Instruction*. New York: The Guilford Press.

McQuillan, J. 1998. *The Literacy Crisis: False Claims, Real Solutions*. Portsmouth, NH: Heinemann.

Miller, M. D., R. L. Linn, and N. E. Gronlund. 2009. *Measurement and Assessment in Teaching*. Upper Saddle River, NJ: Pearson Education, Inc.

Minskoff, E. 2005. *Teaching Reading to Struggling Learners*. Baltimore: Paul H. Brookes Publishing Co.

National Reading Panel. 2000. *Teaching Children to Read: An Evidence-Based Assessment of the Scientific Research Literature on Reading and Its Implications for Reading Instruction: Report of the Subgroups*. (NIH Publication No. 00-4754.) Washington, DC: National Institute of Child Health and Human Development.

Northwest Evaluation Association. 2009. *Triangulation of Data*. www.nwea.support/article/528.

Newkirk, T. 2002. *Misreading Masculinity: Boys, Literacy, and Popular Culture*. Portsmouth, NH: Heinemann.

Oliver, M. 1970. "High Intensity Practice: The Right to Enjoy Reading." *Education* 91 (1): 69–71.

Opitz, M. F., and T. V. Rasinski. 1998. *Goodbye, Round Robin: 25 Effective Oral Reading Strategies*. Portsmouth, NH: Heinemann.

Pearl, N. 2007. *Book Crush for Kids and Teens: Recommended Reading for Every Mood, Moment, and Interest*. Seattle: Sasquatch Books.

Pearson, P. D. 1993. "Teaching and Learning Reading: A Research Perspective." *Language Arts* 70: 502–11.

Peregoy, S., and O. Boyle. 2008. *Reading, Writing, and Learning in ESL: A Resource Book for Teaching K–12 English Learners*. Boston: Pearson Education, Inc.

Pilgreen, J. 2000. *The SSR Handbook: How to Organize and Manage a Sustained Silent Reading Program*. Portsmouth, NH: Heinemann.

———. 2006. "Supporting English Learners: Developing Academic Language in the Content Area Classroom." In *Supporting the Literacy Development of English Learners: Increasing Success in All Classrooms*, edited by T. A. Young and N. L. Hadaway, 41–60. Newark, DE: International Reading Association.

———. 2007. "Teaching the Language of School to Secondary English Learners." In *Adolescent Literacy Instruction: Policies and Promising Practices*, edited by G. Moorman and J. Lewis, 238–62. Newark, DE: International Reading Association.

Raphael, T. 1982. "Teaching Question-Answer Relationships." *The Reading Teacher* 39: 516–20.

Reutzel, D. R., and P. M. Hollingsworth. 1988. "Highlighting Key Vocabulary: A Generative-Reciprocal Procedure for Teaching Selected Inference Types." *Reading Research Quarterly* 23: 358–78.

Richardson, J. 2000. *Read It Aloud! Using Literature in the Secondary Content Classroom*. Newark, DE: International Reading Association.

Richardson, J., R. F. Morgan, and C. Fleener. 2006. *Reading to Learn in the Content Areas*. Belmont, CA: Thomson Wadsworth.

Robinson, F. P. 1946. *Effective Study*. New York: Harper and Brothers.

Roe, B. D., and P. C. Burns. 2007. *Informal Reading Inventory*. Boston: Houghton Mifflin Co.

Roe, B. D., B. D. Stoodt, and P. C. Burns. 2006. *Secondary School Literacy Instruction: The Content Areas*. Belmont, CA: Wadsworth Publishing Company.

Rosenblatt, L. 1969. "Towards a Transactional Theory of Reading." *Journal of Reading Behavior* 1 (1): 31–51.

Rumelhart, D. E. 1982. "Schemata: The Building Blocks of Cognition." In *Comprehension and Teaching: Research Reviews*, edited by J. Guthrie, 3–26. Newark, DE: International Reading Association.

Rupley, W. H., and V. L. Willson. 1997. "The Relationship of Reading Comprehension to Components of Word Recognition: Support for Developmental Shifts." *Journal of Research and Development in Education* 30: 255–60.

Russikoff, K., and J. Pilgreen. 1994. "Shaking the Tree of 'Forbidden Fruit': A Study of Light Reading." *Reading Improvement* 31 (2): 122–23.

Scieszka, J., ed. 2005. *Guys Write for Guys Read*. New York: Penguin Group.

Sejnost, R. L., and S. Thiese. 2006. *Reading and Writing Across Content Areas*. Thousand Oaks, CA: Corwin Press.

Shanahan, T. 1982, March. "Specific Learning Outcomes Attributable to Study Procedures." Paper presented at the annual meeting of the American Educational Research Association, New York. (ERIC Document Reproduction Service No. ED220536.)

Shanker, J. L., and E. E. Ekwall. 2000. *Ekwall/Shanker Reading Inventory*. Boston: Allyn and Bacon.

Silvey, A. 2006. *500 Great Books for Teens*. Boston: Houghton Mifflin Company.

Smith, F. 1988. *Understanding Reading*. Hillsdale, NJ: Lawrence Erlbaum Associates, Inc.

Smith, M., and J. Wilheim. 2002. *"Reading Don't Fix No Chevys": Literacy in the Lives of Young Men*. Portsmouth, NH: Heinemann.

Sprague, M. M., and K. K. Keeling. 2007. *Discovering Their Voices: Engaging Adolescent Girls with Young Adult Literature*. Newark, DE: International Reading Association.

Taylor, W. L. 1953. " 'Cloze Procedure': A New Tool for Measuring Readability." *Journalism Quarterly* 30: 415–33.

Thompson, G., M. Madhuri, and D. Taylor. 2008. "How the Accelerated Reader Program Can Become Counterproductive for High School Students." *Journal of Adolescent and Adult Literacy* 51 (7): 550–60.

Tierney, R. J., J. E. Readence, and E. K. Dishner. 1990. *Reading Strategies and Practices: A Compendium*. Boston: Allyn and Bacon.

Todd, R. W. 2001. *Life Science*. Austin: Holt.

———. 2001. *Physical Science*. Austin: Holt.

Trelease, J. 2001. *The Read-Aloud Handbook*. New York: Penguin Books.

Vacca, R. T., and J. A. Vacca. 2007. *Content Area Reading: Literacy and Learning Across the Curriculum*. Boston: Allyn and Bacon.

Valencia, S., and M. Riddle Buly. 2004. "Behind Test Scores: What Struggling Readers Really Need." *The Reading Teacher* 57 (6): 520–31.

Vardell, S., N. L. Hadaway, and T. A. Young. 2006. "Matching Books and Readers: Selecting Literature for English Learners." *The Reading Teacher* 59 (8): 734–41.

Vasudevan, L. M. 2007. "Looking for Angels: Knowing Adolescents by Engaging with Their Multimodal Literacy Practices." *Journal of Adult and Adolescent Literacy* 50 (4): 252–56.

Vygotsky, L. 1978. *Mind in Society: The Development of Higher Psychological Processes.* Cambridge, MA: Harvard University Press.

Walker, B. 2008. *Diagnostic Teaching of Reading: Techniques for Instruction and Assessment.* Upper Saddle River, NJ: Pearson Education, Inc.

Wheelock, W., N. Silvaroli, and C. J. Campbell. 2009. *Classroom Reading Inventory.* New York: McGraw-Hill Companies, Inc.

Wilhelm, J. D., T. N. Baker, and J. Dube. 2001. *Strategic Reading: Guiding Students to Lifelong Literacy, 6–12.* Portsmouth, NH: Boynton/Cook Publishers.

Wood, K. 1986. "The Effect of Interspersing Questions in Text: Evidence for 'Slicing the Task.'" *Reading Research and Instruction* 25: 295–307.

INDEX